We Have Been
Invaded by the
21st Century

We Have Been Invaded by the 21st Century

DAVID McREYNOLDS

Introduction by Paul Goodman

PRAEGER PUBLISHERS
New York · Washington · London

Grateful acknowledgment is made for permission to reprint the following articles:
Life in Jail; *Prague: Viewing a Disaster*; *Two Faces of Dixie*; *The Bomb in the Brooks Brothers Suit*; *The Hipster General Strike*; *Vietnam Is Our Hungary*; *Open Letter to RFK: What Is Loyalty?*; *A Letter to the Men of My Generation*; *Philosophy and Tactics: Answering an Answer*; *Let the Punishment Fit the Crime*; *Baldwin Versus the White Negro*; *Notes on Another Death—And Our Shadowed Future*; *CIA and US: The Face You See May Be Your Own*; *A Prophetic Minority*; copyright *The Village Voice*; Copyrighted by the *Village Voice, Inc.*, 1959, 1961, 1962, 1963, 1964, 1966, 1967, 1968.
Saigon: A City's Agony (November, 1966); *The Majority Generation* (September, 1965); *New York Letter (Are We Ready for Space)* (February, 1966); *Automation: One More Headache for the American Negro* (March, 1965); copyrighted *Saturday Night*.
Notes for a More Coherent Article (November 15, 1969); *A.J.* (February, 1967); copyrighted *WIN Magazine*.
England: Home Truths from an Alien (August 18, 1967); copyrighted *Peace News* in London.
Notes from Japan (November, 1966); *In Defense of Butter* (May, 1962); copyrighted *Liberation*.

PRAEGER PUBLISHERS
111 Fourth Avenue, New York, N.Y. 10003, U.S.A.
5, Cromwell Place, London S.W.7, England

Published in the United States of America in 1970
by Praeger Publishers, Inc.

© 1970 by Praeger Publishers, Inc.

Library of Congress Catalog Card Number: 77–106892

Printed in the United States of America

TO PETER

Contents

David McReynolds visiting Orlovsky-Ginsberg household over a decade ago invited inhabitants to circumambulate Manhattan with pacifist friends to exorcise fear of Atomic Bomb from public consciousness. I was too proud of my solitary inspiration to walk with him then, but I came to walk in his prophetic community many times sadly since.

ALLEN GINSBERG
January 27, 1970

Introduction
by Paul Goodman

My heart sinks when the phone rings for me to sponsor a demonstration or a protest ad, because I may be asked to sign a half-truth, and be picky about it, and make my friends angry. But if it's Dave McReynolds calling, O.K. His indignation will be genuine as well as tactical. He won't be fanatical or wear blinders; he won't be fighting the Cold War in reverse; and he certainly won't lie. He never was tainted with the phoniness of the "Old Left," and he recognizes it when it turns up in the "New Left." He and I agree that, for a minority to build a dissenting movement (and, as an anarchist, I am not interested in any other politics), truth is the best politics. Why should a complacent majority join us, unless we touch their better selves?

Typically, in the recent hot campaign for Mayor of New York, Dave was appalled when Lindsay's lieutenants, for a petty advantage of position on the ballot, got the Socialist Workers and Socialist Labor parties stricken off; and, though he himself probably voted for Lindsay, he organized the campaign to censure him. (Nat Hentoff joined us in this one, though he had just put out the Mayor's campaign biography.) A more important case: Dave is outraged at the dragnet jailing of the Panthers; but he also remembers that all other nation-states, including those with the Panthers' Marxist ideology, have, at least, equivalent numbers of political prisoners; so, he dutifully publishes as many names as he can get in the newsletter of the War Resisters League. But of course we have to concentrate our efforts on our own horrors, which we can conceivably do something about.

Another thing is that Dave's ads and leaflets are clearly written, in vigorous English, without spiteful demands and bloody epithets, so that I would be willing to sign them without reading them—but I read them, because it would set a bad precedent not to. Indeed, I almost welcome those troublesome phone calls from Dave Mc-Reynolds, because I too much like to mind my own business, and he drags me back to the public business.

When Dave was running for Congress in 1968, he spoke for the abolition of the marijuana penalties. This was troublesome for him and cost him votes, but it was not out of line, considering the largely youthful constituency he hoped for (vainly) as the Peace and Freedom candidate; and, in the long run, it was not unpolitical, because this issue is bound to become a major one, like the abolition of Prohibition in the twenties, and somebody has got to begin by losing. But, much more significantly, Dave spoke out against the penal system altogether, just because it demonstrably does great evil and almost no good and, even though he, like anybody else, had no alternative to offer. Politically, this was from outer space, and I guess he was the only candidate in the country, radical or otherwise, who mentioned it. The Panthers want to put blacks in black jails, and other militants want to put their opponents in revolutionary jails. But, in honor, the issue is unavoidable, because the prisons and insane asylums essentially and crucially characterize our bad societies as much as war, exploitation, and regimenting schooling, and the older radicals—long before the "Old Left"—used to point this out.

In my opinion, Dave is not a philosophical person; he is not a profound political scientist; but his need to be consistent and conscientious and to act on as deep a level as he knows gives him a peculiar dignity. It makes him potentially a statesmen, whereas most of the others are just politicians.

His pacifism is admirable in the same way. Some lucky folk

are just animally pacifists, affectionate, considerate, and fearless, and that's that. I think Igal Roodenko, the present head of the War Resisters League, is like this. Others—A. J. Muste was our great example—seem to have a religious conviction of a future beloved community when the lion will lie down with the lamb, and this gives them courage. Others, for example myself, just think organized violence is a stupid way of settling conflicts; violence is natural, though sad, but it is intolerably boring to live in a world of war, and we refuse to discuss it. Dave has none of these advantages. His disposition seems to be choleric and under tight control; he does not seem to me to rest in any peace of faith; he is not driven by common sense, and, indeed, his Marxism seems to call for organized violence on the right occasion. But he knows that, for various reasons, the pacifist position is correct, and he wills it and stubbornly insists on being consistent to it. It is an act of character.

My conjecture is that there is an unusual split in his personality and he manages to hold the parts together. On the one hand, he is a thoroughly political animal: He takes the structure of institutions, power, and public opinion with a seriousness that puzzles me, as an artist and anarchist. (He is probably right.) On the other hand, he is, like everybody else, a suffering and desiring creature. But, unlike other politicos, he refuses to subordinate the embarrassing fact of his humanity to his societal role, not to speak of trying to annihilate it. He has to face his friends, not chosen politically, for what he does and says politically, and this must be a tough proposition. He cannot condone political policies or brutality that he would not perform in the saner environment of everyday life.

The split, and Dave's virtuous solution to it, appears poignantly in the piece on homosexuality written for *WIN,* the most amiable of the movement magazines, and republished in this book. As a contributor to *WIN*'s symposium, I was bemused by Dave's struggle about taking part—after all, he is not an adolescent confronting Mama and Papa. But the way he finally handled it, the self-irony, the odd episodes he conjured up, the stylistic vigor with which he wallowed around, made his contribution real to most readers, certainly much realer than my matter-of-factness. *WIN* had many canceled subscriptions because of the symposium, but I'm sure it was not because of Dave's piece, which could only win respect.

The theme of social science is the tension between social role and the underlying human being. Dave lives in this tension; he takes it seriously, so people take him seriously.

In any normal society, Dave, at forty, would be at least an Under-Secretary or the chief of a big Agency and bound for promotion. I don't mean this as a snide remark. I'm just saying. He is intelligent, accurate, and energetic. He is responsible and dutiful, but not pedantic. He is sociable, bibulous, and kindly, and gives attention to individual cases—he is his own ombudsman, just the type of politician that people can both respect and have affection for. When the occasion is authentic, he can be a splendid speaker. I am almost never moved by radical speeches—the low quality of oratory at recent peace rallies, for instance, has been scandalous and significant; it is because the speakers are narrow fanatics or half-liars. But I have been deeply moved by Dave McReynolds talking to collegians about draft resistance. He takes them seriously, with their hang-ups, which also includes taking them as better than they "are."

He is patriotic. He knows what has been and is good in America, and he is proud of it, and he knows what is bad and won't stand for it. And, as I have said, he is a political animal who seeks the democratic will very earnestly. What I judge to be his sociological and psychological shallowness is probably a political advantage, for he can stick with gut issues, he sees a little better than the average, and he does care to lead.

I don't mean at all that Dave is a square or an organization man. Rather, he is an extreme oddball who respects the conventional, and that is the oddest thing about him. This explains his success in the marginal world of pacifist organizations, where he is constrained to move. But it is the same in American life as a whole: Our society is homogenized and conformist, but there *is* room for excellent eccentrics, in the loony bin and in the top echelons.

Unfortunately, we do not have a normal society; nor do we have the right kind of politicians, like Dave, in high places. (I suppose many of us could tick off at least a couple of dozen acquaintances who are better qualified for high office than anybody in national or local government.) And, obviously, the superabundant vitality of people like Dave cannot be constrained in the lovely but sandlot politics of the Socialist Party and the War Resisters League.

There have been two main outlets for their political energy. One is the proliferating populist protest demonstrations, sit-ins, acts of civil disobedience, and pro tempore political campaigns, in which Dave has done more than his share of organizing and getting into trouble. The pieces in this book are the history of the sixties. "It is wonderful to see 3,000 people in front of the U.N., as I saw on August 6," said Dave in 1960. How far we have come! It has been a lousy ball game, but the only ball game in town.

The other outlet for those too honest and talented for Establishment politics has been the kind of participatory journalism collected here. Dave said, concerning an action in North Carolina, "I found myself, quite without meaning to, participating instead of observing"—and he completed the arc by working the article up in the peculiar style of commitment writing that has become the characteristic genre of our period. Its older classics were, I guess, Orwell, Macdonald, Agee. It is halfway between literature and politics, more "committed" than partisan, more existentialist than analytic or programmatic, too honest to be propaganda, too personal and passional to be mere reportage, too journalistic to have much theoretical exploration or poetic depth. Such writing is itself a political act, but as part of movement politics rather than party politics or conspiratorial Leninist politics. It has called into being (and been called into being by) an amazing proliferation of media for it—underground papers, movement magazines, and rock records—and finally taken over big sections of conventional magazines, broadcasting, and book publishing.

For a movement, such writing is a matrix of thought, attitude, shared experience, and style of speech, and it is essential that it be high level. Dave is good at it and keeps the level high, sometimes almost noble, far better than the kids who lack, precisely, character. (Frankly, more of the young were interesting persons before they all began to do their thing.) It is a pity that the underground papers do not continually use Dave. His heart gravitates in their direction; he is properly mad for the temporarily correct music. His head is more sober, and he knows something, but they ought to be able to put up with that.

There is plenty of lack of wisdom in the writing of Dave McReynolds. As I read through his pieces, I jotted down half a dozen examples. Naturally, I judge from my own biases, except that I am right.

Speaking of the New Left in August, 1965, he said, "These young people are decent and humanistic. . . . I have no doubt that, if Russia invaded Rumania tomorrow, the same group of students would be sitting in at the Soviet Embassy." This was a bad guess. They left the Czechoslovaks flat.

He also overvalues the physical courage of the radical young. Every jock will get his head broken in a football game; young marines are astoundingly brave; early-teen-agers dive thirty feet from a pier into the polluted Hudson. They are all beautiful, but not much follows from it.

Ten years ago, he predicted that the Pentagon and the Military-Industrial Complex would emerge into politics as the extreme Right. But it was, rather, as Kennedy liberalism that the military emerged at its most virulent.

In June, 1967, he predicted the imminent invasion of North Vietnam. He erred here because he tends to neglect big world politics as the essential background, for example, the need for the Russians and Americans to come to terms in a new Congress of Vienna. A. J. Muste never lost the woods for the trees in this way.

Discussing urbanism, he falls completely for the usual liberal-radical clichés. (What is usually called radicalism—for instance, Marxism—is extreme liberalism without civil liberties.) "Some of the Negroes trapped in urban ghettos could be drawn off into integrated and attractive suburban housing, if the cost were subsidized. Middle-class whites could be drawn back into the city, if crime were not so rampant and the quality of education were improved." He has no feeling for the fundamental unworkability of present world-wide urbanization. Talking to him about education, I found, to my surprise, that he had never questioned the premises of mass schooling.

He buys the Le Corbusier stereotype of planning: "Perhaps, the future city will consist entirely of a cultural center surrounded by suburban housing, shopping centers, and automated factories, linked to the hub by swift transportation." This is the schizophrenia that has destroyed city and country both.

He rightly refuses personal guilt for racism, and he rightly accepts responsibility for its consequences. But he seems also willing to accept the blacks' "hatred," and he agrees not to try to talk to them. But hatred is stupefying and self-corrosive for anybody who hates; one cannot leave it at that.

He thinks there is virtue in "massive doses of heavy industrial capital to the underdeveloped nations." But this method of foreign aid compounds their disaster. He never seems to have thought of the cultural and social meaning of various kinds of technology. In general, in speaking of technology, he betrays the kind of innocent ignorance that is possible only for latter-day Marxists or the Center for the Study of Democratic Institutions, in Santa Barbara.

He wants to suspend the moon shot in order to help winos on the Bowery, as if we knew what to do for winos in a big city, whereas we do know how to get to the moon; or as if it were not better to entertain 500 million viewers rather than to harass a hundred old gentlemen, which is what it would come to.

I could extend this list of small and crashingly great misconceptions, as I see them. Indeed, when one considers his acute intelligence, his broad experience, and his stature as a human being, it is astounding how ill informed and cliché-ridden Dave is, just like a statesman in Washington or a schoolboy in SDS. Nevertheless, there is a fundamental difference. It is that Dave is morally mature; he has a will to consistency and moral courage and scrupulous honesty; and, therefore, he can really learn something when he really needs to know it.

But perhaps the chief advantage that Dave has is the following. He is in between, not between the "Old Left" and the "New Left"—both of which, in my opinion, are uninteresting groups— but between an older generation of people who used to know something and a younger generation of people who know something very different that is also very important. For the young are in Modern Times and speak the language like native sons, whereas we older people hardly speak the language at all, even when we have something to say. Without losing respect for the older, Dave can also listen to the younger. I do not envy him the role.

P.G.

Author's Note: Paul Goodman's introduction is all that a radical introduction should be—controversial and of no commercial value. It will help to keep me poor, honest, and striving to become. My editor was unhappy because Paul's introduction, if neatly excerpted, could serve as a hostile review. I am disturbed for a different reason: I suspect Paul has caught me as I am, limitations and all. I feel like the student I was in college, always receiving a "C" at the end of the term. The final grade, in this case, will have to be given by the reader. Assuming he believes in grades. (Where else but in the radical movement does an author answer his introduction?)

D.McR.

Introducer's Note: Dear Dave, You will find that hostile reviews are no disadvantage. It is only the inches that count.

P.G.

I
We Have Been Invaded by the 21st Century

"We can't fight alone against the monster"

We Have Been Invaded by the 21st Century

The essays in this book range from the intensely personal to the broadly political, and no single theme can give them coherence. They are brought together here because they are a reflection of our times. Yet I am not satisfied to let it go at that—each of the essays touching an aspect of reality, with few of them making the links that responsible politics demands.

I have sought, therefore, in this first essay, to set forth some of the reasons for concern about the invasion to which our culture has been subjected, an invasion that has already littered the streets with walking dead and wounded. I am uneasy in the role of essayist. In every other case in the book, I've written because of a specific grievance, out of a particular anger, for immediate publication. I wrote because the fury was upon me. This essay, a quiet effort to state some of my guiding concerns, is enormously more difficult.

Time as Location: The pace of change in our society has been so swift that it tells more about me to say that I am from 1929 than to say I am from Los Angeles. McCarthy (Joseph, not Eugene) and Wallace (Henry, not George) are not merely history to me, nor is World War II. Those are areas of time that I visited.

3

Pearl Harbor on the radio that Sunday morning, December 7, 1941. My parents worrying about my aunt and uncle who lived in Hawaii. The long sober drive the family took that day, my mother telling me not to ask daddy why he was so quiet. My father going off to the air force, eventually to India, China, Japan. Rationing of sugar, meat, gasoline, funny little red plastic tokens for food, and stamp books, and steel pennies, price control and the black market. The black-out in Los Angeles, the rumors of Japanese planes sighted. The deportation of all Japanese from our city to concentration camps, where my grandparents used to go regularly to visit my grandfather's Japanese secretary. The long trip we kids took with my mother by wartime trains to Phoenix, where the night air was warm as a blanket and grapefruit lay on the ground in the park, to visit my father before he went overseas. V-Mail—funny little letters, photographed and reduced in size so that the planes could carry more. The headlines: 300 BOMBERS BLAST BREMEN; 1,000 BOMBERS MAKE HAMBURGER OF HAMBURG. The memory of my high school teacher breaking down suddenly, weeping uncontrollably in front of the class, as the news came in that President Roosevelt was dead. The atomic bomb, and news of it reaching me at a Baptist Camp in the California mountains.

Humans are curious creatures with a habit of accepting things so easily that we absorb the present as if it were also the past. We avoid the trauma of discontinuity. It is obvious, of course, that things were not always as they are now, but we act as if that were the case, and, losing sight of the past, we find it hard to measure how swift is our advance toward the final crisis. Let me suggest the speed with which events now move, by looking at four different time periods.

Less than 500 years ago, the earth was flat, monsters lived in the deeps at its far edge, the sun moved around the earth. The New World, with its many wonders—tomatoes, turkeys, potatoes, corn, chilis, chocolate, tobacco, syphilis—had yet to be discovered. Trade with the Orient ran overland, and Venice, now sinking into the seas, was the center of Western civilization.

In the year 1770, our second time segment—just two hundred years in the past—the United States did not yet exist. The North American continent was only thinly settled on the East and West coasts. Nowhere in the world were there trains, steamboats, or telegraphs. Electricity, untamed, leaped at the earth from clouds or surprised us when we stroked a cat. Doctors operated without anesthetic. A very small minority of mankind lived in cities, with the rest scattered in villages and hamlets or in nomadic tribes. Two hundred years ago.

Let's take, as the next time period, the year 1946, after the atomic bomb has been exploded and the "modern age" has truly begun, penicillin and all. Since 1770, we had developed steamboats, trains, cars, aircraft, telegraph, radio, telephone, and, even, television—although, because there were no TV stations, there was no impetus toward building or buying TV sets, and it would be several years before Milton Berle and Kukla, Fran, and Ollie would be in everyone's living room. Mohandas Gandhi was alive and struggling for India's freedom. Indonesia did not exist. The state of Israel did not exist. Nasser did not control Egypt. Stalin was alive. Almost no one in the West had heard of Mao, for Chiang Kai-shek ruled China—or pretended he did. Alaska and Hawaii were federal territories. Yugoslavia was loyal to Moscow, and Czechoslovakia was totally free of any foreign control. LSD had been discovered a few years earlier in Switzerland, but Americans knew nothing of it. The old 78 RPM records were giving way, and the fight was on between RCA Victor and Columbia as to whether the new "long-playing, unbreakable discs" would be 45 or 33 RPM. FM radio was experimental and expensive. We listened to AM and laughed at Henry Morgan, Fred Allen, and Fibber McGee and Molly; we shivered at *Inner Sanctum* and *The Shadow*, never realizing that a unique form of drama was about to die, having only barely come of age. One of the few things that did not change from 1946 to the present was Vietnam—then called Indochina and consisting, also, of Laos and Cambodia—which, under the leadership of Ho Chi Minh, was entering its struggle against Western rule.

Today, everyone is aware of air pollution and the threat it poses to all of us. It is a new threat. In the early 1940's, there was no air pollution, even in Los Angeles, where "smog" first got its name and became the thing for which L.A. is perhaps most famous. From the front porch of our home at 92nd Street and Dalton Avenue, which was on a low hill in the southwest part of town, with vacant lots and bean fields at our backs, where lupin and poppies and wild wheat and mustard grew in early spring— from there, looking off toward the center of town, we could, except on rainy days, see City Hall and, beyond it, the mountains that ring the city. When, early in the war, Java and Sumatra fell to the Japanese, our supply of natural rubber was cut off, and plants were set up in Los Angeles to manufacture synthetic rubber. Our eyes began to sting and itch, and we blamed this on the chemicals from the rubber factories—whether rightly or not, I don't know. It was not until late in the 1940's that smog came visibly among us like a thin cloud, a mist that did not burn off by noon, and it was then, with the vacant lots behind our house built up and the bean fields transformed into housing developments, that one looked toward the center of the city and saw nothing but haze.

A final segment of time, the last ten years: 1960, the end of the Eisenhower years and the inauguration of John F. Kennedy. We entered the 1960's with the Soviet triumph of Sputnik I only three years behind us. Before the decade was out, men would walk on the moon. In 1945, we, alone, had the atomic bomb. By 1970, five nations had developed hydrogen bombs. Soviet missiles were accurate to within a half mile of their target.

Israel, nonexistent in 1946, fought its third successful war before the 1960's were out, and Indonesia proved its full sovereignty by slaughtering a half million communists (without a murmur of moral concern from anyone in Washington). Biafra was born and died, and perhaps two million Biafrans starved to death late in the decade in the greatest single human tragedy since the extermination of Europe's Jews during World War II. When the decade opened, Fidel Castro had just come to power, and his country was about to suffer an abortive invasion. Algeria was experimenting with its freedom. Hungary was trying to forget the Soviet invasion of 1956, and, by the end of the decade, the Russian invasion of Czechoslovakia confirmed the absolute and unequivocal failure of the Kremlin to win the loyalty of Eastern Europe.

In 1946, there were no jets in commercial service. By the end of the 1960's, all prop planes were being phased out by commercial lines, and the nation was about to see the new "super jets," able to carry nearly 500 passengers. Between 1960 and 1970, AM radio gave way to FM, FM gave way to FM-stereo, and proud owners of the latest stereo equipment were beginning to learn, as the decade closed, that their equipment would soon be outmoded by "four-track stereo," carried over four speakers. A new fight, similar to the ancient one among 33, 45, and 78 RPM records was being fought again among tapes, discs, tape cartridges, and tape cassettes. In 1960, no one had color TV; by the end of the decade, it seemed most people had it.

Lungs, kidneys, and hearts had been transplanted from one human being into another. Perhaps too late in the game, we had become aware of environmental dangers. Years after Rachel Carson had warned of an impending silent spring, DDT was being taken off the market, and food additives were being checked. The pollution of our water had kept pace with the pollution of our air, and, gradually, very gradually, we began to understand that our whole life was lived out in a thin envelope of air and water, an envelope so thin that even jet planes flew above it and needed pressurized cabins.

These were not, however, the important events of the 1960's. It would pay us to look at some of the upheavals that occurred within our own society in that decade, events far less pleasant than the moon landing, but more urgent, more determining of our future. Four-track stereo is fun, but psychedelic drugs are more important. Heart transplants get headlines, but the ghetto is in rebellion.

The focus, here, is on America alone, yet some of these problems afflict other societies. Prague and Warsaw have hippies. Moscow has rebellious poets confined to mental institutions. England, France, Germany, Japan—no advanced state is exempt. Even "developing" nations such as Laos find themselves engulfed with hippies not of their own making.

As we pass through time zones, the shift in society is interesting, but it is this most recent time zone about which we all know. Let's put this in closer focus.

Black America: Because so much of the book is given over to an examination of racism, I won't do more, here, than note the extraordinary shift among the "Negro vanguard" that occurred in this ten years. We entered the decade with every liberal and radical—black and white alike—absolutely committed to integration. Among whites, even conservatives supported integration—if reluctantly—and the segregationists were politically isolated. Among blacks, only the Black Muslims opposed integration. By the time the decade ended, whites—liberals, radicals, and conservatives alike—were stunned and trying to reorient themselves in a situation where every organization seemed to have a black caucus and the demand was no longer for integration but was "Black Power" or "Power to the Community." Integration—to which I am personally committed beyond equivocation—is now out of date, and, on that question, I find myself counted as a conservative. (I believe the ghetto should have home rule and power over its schools and police, as long as ghettos exist. But—a more basic point—I don't believe that ghettos, enclaves, restricted neighborhoods, and so forth should be our goals. In the long run, separatism is a sickness, warping parents and children alike, white and black.)

The other observation about black America is that it began the 1960's following Martin Luther King, Jr., and ended the decade disillusioned with the nonviolence he preached. When King was murdered, the black ghetto in the nation's capital observed his death with a rebellion so massive that tanks rumbled through the streets while whole blocks went up in flames. By the end of the decade, there was hardly an American city that had escaped the kind of serious rebellion that first broke out in Watts, Los Angeles, in 1965.

Students: Historically, students were a luxury, something only the upper middle class could afford. The university was the special preserve of fraternities and sororities, dances, and wealth, and swallowing gold fish. College students were always rowdy but never threatening. They were jailed overnight for drunken driving and released the next day by judges who fondly remembered their own fraternity days. The only riots we had in the 1950's were the "panty raids."

I feel, with special intensity, the contrast between the 1950's, when I was in college, and the 1960's, when the student revolt erupted, because I was one of the handful of students who was a radical in the early 1950's, at the height of McCarthyism. I was then at UCLA, which I entered in 1947 and from which I departed, B.A. in hand, in 1953.

When I arrived on campus, UCLA was considered one of the most radical universities in the nation, one of the last strongholds of the powerful student Left of the 1930's. Our songs were those of the Spanish Civil War and the trade-union movement, events and movements that seemed ancient and romantic history, but that, in fact, were often closer to us in time than the civil rights struggle of the late 1950's is to students today.

On campus, there were somewhere between fifty and a hundred members of the Communist Party, perhaps ten members of the Socialist Party, and two or three members of the Socialist Workers Party. Grouped around the CP were several hundred students who could be mobilized for action. The Socialists had perhaps fifty persons, at most, in their "fringe." The Trotskyists, because they were socially inept, had no fringe. When one speaks of the CP being able, back in the early 1950's, to rally several hundred student followers, one thinks, of course, of the Columbia SDS, weak in itself, but able to mobilize hundreds of students for the seizure of buildings. But, alas, the most the CP could expect of its fringe was a vote in the student elections or, perhaps, a signature on a petition. The Communists, "dreaded agents of Moscow, enemies of the Constitution, infiltrators extraordinary," proved in the end to be nothing but "violent resolutionists." As Attorney General Mitchell has since observed, how marvelous it would be if we could have back our loyal, subversive, Moscow-guided Communists. The group to which I belonged was the Socialist Party, which I joined in 1951 when Vern Davidson approached me and said "We've had a discussion in the Party about how to raise money, and we will do it by getting more members. We have decided you will join. You owe me a dollar." Eventually, I filled the place held first by Don Thomas and then by Vern—the role of non-Communist radical leader on campus. And, in those days, the SP *was* radical; we deplored Norman Thomas as being far too moderate; and our leaders all eventually got indicted for refusing induction. Don Thomas won his case, Vern went to prison, and, by a stroke of luck and a technical error on the part of the government, my own indictment was dismissed.

By the time I graduated, McCarthyism had won at UCLA.

I am still ashamed for my school because the faculty, liberals that they were, ran for cover when the loyalty oaths came. A broad student front, including fraternity men, had offered to call a student strike, but the faculty sold out. (At Berkeley, upon whose record the honor of the University of California rested in those days, the faculty fought the oath and a number of faculty members were fired.) Don Thomas had graduated. Vern Davidson was headed for prison to begin serving a three-year sentence. I was about to graduate, and, looking around in desperation, I could find no one to take my place as "the campus radical." Always, we had had around us a group of ten to fifteen solid kids, and, now, the number was so few that it was pointless to call a meeting. (The SP was not alone in its troubles. The CP, which had always been several times larger than us, disintegrated and vanished under the impact of McCarthyism. An important record of that period is Clancy Sigal's *Going Away,* a book of particular interest to those of us who knew Clancy at UCLA.) Yet, even at the height of the McCarthy period, we never went underground or stopped demonstrating. I can recall the forlorn little peace demonstration the Youth Section of the Fellowship of Reconciliation put on very early in the 1950's, when we learned of the government decision to proceed with the development of the hydrogen bomb—not more than a dozen of us walked through the heart of downtown Los Angeles to protest. Today, hundreds of thousands march.

Two memories come to me. One will make no sense at all to anyone except those who were young radicals in the 1950's. Late one night, a small group of us met at 132½ Ashland Avenue in Ocean Park (a termite-ridden little beach shack I would later inherit from Margaret Phair) to discuss whether or not to flee the country. The meeting was supposed to start at 11 P.M., but, because a suspected FBI agent was present, we waited until after midnight, when he had gone. Stan was learning to fly a plane and making arrangements to buy it. We had gathered to debate whether to leave the United States for Mexico or Costa Rica, flying down in groups of two and three. As I remember it, Vern, Margaret, and I argued that, if war came, there was no protection anywhere and, therefore, no point in going south, and, if we believed in revolution, it was a mistake to think people would ever listen to radicals who had left the country when the pressure was on—we had to be part of the apocalypse, if it came, and hope to survive it and play some role in the period following it. The discussion was serious, and two of our people did leave for Mexico, despite our collective decision to stay. For us, there were the personal joys and delights and frustrations of being young, exploring the world, falling in and out of love. But, *politically,* we felt no hope at all. None of us expected to be alive in 1960, let alone 1970, for war, we knew, would come before then. We were more alienated than today's youth, because, aside from the two or three dozen of us at UCLA and down by the beach, there was no "subculture" with which we could identify.

The other memory is from the same period, when I came across a huge crowd moving across the campus. I asked a friend of mine, a fraternity man who was part of the mob, what was going on. He explained, patiently, knowing I was totally ignorant of sports, that, after years of defeats, UCLA had won the annual football game against our arch-rival, USC, and the mob was headed for Westwood Boulevard, there to sit down and block traffic in celebration. I said that, because this was the closest I would probably ever get to seeing the masses moving in the streets, if he didn't greatly mind and despite my lack of enthusiasm about sports, I would just join the mob. Which I did, marching down to Westwood Boulevard, there to squat in the street, blocking traffic, feeling, for a moment, part of something larger than the tiny cell-group of radicals. Only two or three years later, the revolution broke out in Montgomery, Alabama. How irrelevant this seems today. The laugh was on us after all, those of us who had rejected capitalism and refused to accept Stalinism, who knew we were too few in number to make any difference in the scales, our only hope being that we might preserve intact some human values—particularly the concept of freedom—to pass along when the time came, and who, to this end, had decided not to flee the threat of prison. When the time came, it turned out the values were intact without our help. Students were decent without being educated by us, and they revolted in their own effective ways without the benefit of our political experience. Only others of the Old Left will know how poignant was our defeat, will understand how joyous and sad we were, as we discovered our values could survive without us, proving their worth even as it proved us expendable and forced us to begin again, learning from the childern we had thought to teach.

What has happened in the past ten years is that students have become a motor force for history, the importance of which the older and more orthodox Marxists do not grasp at all. Marx taught us that the proletariat would be *the* motor force that would move history, and, in Europe, he was right. In the United States, the workers not only failed to carry out a revolution, they didn't *want* a revolution, and they even failed to build a reform-oriented labor party, as in England and the Scandinavian countries.

Today, we have, in the United States, no single "motor force" but several different forces, and one of these is the student community. No more panty raids, but the shock of Weathermen moving through downtown Chicago, smashing windows. The Weathermen, a tiny fraction of the population though they are, politically isolated and foolish as they may be, yet suggest to us how the terms of conflict have been changed, how great the distance between generations is.

Mores: I might use the word "customs," but it does not carry the weight of "mores." *Webster's Unabridged* (1960) defines the word as: "Folkways that are considered conducive to the welfare of society and so, through general observance, develop the force of law, often becoming part of the legal code." Styles and fashions change swiftly. But mores change only very slowly over an extended period. Yet, in the ten years from 1960 to 1970, the mores of America were smashed. The petulant speeches of Spiro Agnew reflect the hysteria of the Nixon Administration, rather than a "return to sanity and good manners." To understand the terrain on which we stand, listen to Bob Dylan, one of the first to explore and map the area.

In 1960, we didn't have a drug problem—for the heroin addicts were centered in New York City. No one chewed peyote, smoked pot, or vanished into another dimension with LSD. Yet, in 1969, at the end of the decade, 400,000 youth gathered in Woodstock to listen to rock and take dope openly. So totally was the law smashed that policemen on the scene abandoned any notion of enforcing it. Nixon, who had entered office promising to deal with the drug scene, turned around 180 degrees and said he would modify existing drug laws and lower the penalty for smoking pot.

It is not clear why we have a drug problem today. The drugs —except for such manufactured ones as LSD—have been with us for a long time. American Indians were using hallucinatory mushrooms and cactus when the Spanish arrived. The Old World knew of hallucinogens. In the literary circles of nineteenth-century Paris and London, both opium and marijuana were used and were common enough so that Sir Arthur Conan Doyle didn't cause any stir when his creation Sherlock Holmes shot himself up with a fictional needle. What happened in the 1960's was that drugs became a part of American culture, of interest to the teeny bopper standing on St. Mark's Place and to the Madison Avenue executive. Whatever it was, drugs were "in," and the moral and legal prohibitions on their use collapsed.

Sex was suddenly with us openly. *Hair* and *Oh! Calcutta!* and *I Am Curious (Yellow)* brought nudity and sexuality to the stage and screen and out of the back room of the local American Legion Hall.

The "pill" and penicillin made sexual relations less risky. In areas previously taboo for discussion, such as homosexuality, there was an extraordinary openness.

Our music changed so radically that it became a new kind of music. When I was in junior high school, the big debate was over whether a skinny young guy named "Frankie" Sinatra could sing better than Bing Crosby, the established crooner. The girls went to the Sinatra concerts, screamed, fainted, and made Sinatra a part of the 1940's. And the songs? Ah, let me see, there was a song about letting it snow because of the fire being delightful to sit by, a song about an old lamplighter, a song about how it might as well be spring, and a very daring song about rum and Coke (which promptly got banned). And some marvelous World War II songs about the Dover cliffs, Paris *cafés,* apple trees, and so forth. They were good songs, and they will be around a long time, but they are hardly important music.

Musically, the 1950's were a desert, offering us Elvis Presley, a pale imitation of decent rhythm and blues. But, suddenly, in the 1960's, something happened, launching us on what may be the greatest period of popular music in centuries. White music became dark; Bessie Smith would have understood Janis Joplin.

The Beatles, the Stones, Dylan—the music we heard was filled

with social comment, protest, resistance, drugs. The singers themselves led, personally, in the revolution: John Lennon and his
wife Yoko took out full-page ads on behalf of peace; Joan Baez,
the most "together" of the lot, went off to jail for trying to close
down a draft center, and her husband, David Harris, is presently
in prison for resisting conscription.

In the 1920's, 1930's, 1940's, and 1950's, music was for danc-
ing. Today, the dances that are done can't be taught by Arthur
Murray, and much of the music is for concerts. *Groups of young
people perform music for groups of other young people.* Above
all, the music is great: The lyrics say something; the tunes are
complex and genuine.

If we look at humor, we find the same shift. Every Christmas,
Bob Hope, a political illiterate but a nice guy all the same, gives up
his Christmas to go off with his troupe and buck up the morale of
our men in uniform. In the meantime, Dick Gregory, younger and
black, gets arrested for defending the Indians; Mort Sahl can't
get on TV because he doesn't accept the Warren Report; and
Lenny Bruce was hounded by the law to the point that he took a
fatal overdose of drugs. (Lord Buckley, where are you now that
we need you?)

And clothing: Women's styles change, the hemline going up and
down, but when, in the last century, did the hemline come as
high as during the mini period? Men's clothing changes, slowly
but steadily, from gray to black to gray. But now the American
male may walk the streets looking like a peacock and not be
arrested. Ten years ago, there was an eccentric little man in the
Village who wore striking costumes that he had designed himself.
As I recall, he also wore a single earring, but my memory isn't
clear on that. He had an odd way of walking—anyone who has
been a Villager will know who I am talking about. In the 1950's,
we all turned our heads to watch him as he walked by, looking
like a court jester on the loose, his clothing a tasteful but blazing
array of different-colored diamond-patterned fabrics. The other
day, I saw the same fellow walking down the street and realized
that, while his outfit was as bizzare as ever, the attire of the kids
walking in front of and behind him was even more flashing.

When, in the last century, has men's clothing permitted so much display of color? And when was the last century in which men could wear beads? And when—in any century—did we have a drift to "unisex" clothing?

Men may laugh at the women's liberation movement, calling them lesbians or "dogs" that no one wants to make it with anyway. But, if their wives and girl friends and lovers were to speak frankly, men would realize that women in our society have a powerful collection of resentments based on the social discrimination between men and women. Women behaved themselves in past decades. What had happened, late in the 1960's, when they began to picket the Miss America contest?

An item that is hard to classify—it isn't exactly a violation of the mores, but it isn't clear where else it goes—is the underground press. In 1955, *The Village Voice* began, the first and only paper of its kind in the nation; it was headed—it seemed—straight for oblivion. Now every city of any size, including Washington, D.C., Atlanta, Dallas, and New Orleans, has at least one "underground paper," and the *Voice* is successful and, even, staid. These papers, with their ads for rock records, their weird "personals," notices of gay movies, and so on, are more than commercial ventures. They are a kind of tribal voice for new communities that have sprung up just at the moment when the media were supposed to be centralizing.

Plato warned us that, when the mode of music changes, the walls of the city shake. Our music, our comedians, our dress, our sexual habits, and our choice of drugs—pot instead of alcohol— have *all* changed, and all within the past ten years. One more thing has happened in the past that Americans have not given sufficient thought to. The world's conception of America has changed, and our own conception of our nation has changed. The American myth is dead.

Those under thirty may not realize the extent to which America, from the time of its inception, fascinated and radicalized the rest of the world. Students see America through the dark glass of war and racism. But, in 1776, our Declaration of Independence and, later, our Bill of Rights helped shape the politics of Latin

America, Asia, and Europe. We were, then, as much a "revolutionary fact" as Cuba is today to Latin America. We were an open society, without rigid classes, and with mobility between classes (always excepting the black American, who was part of a *caste* system from the beginning, never a part of a class structure). We were noninterventionist regarding other nations (simply because we were too weak to do anything else—the doctrine of nonintervention being invariably the doctrine of shrewd but weak powers).

To a Europe rigidly bound by classes, the United States was a door into Utopia. Even into the twentieth century, American history influenced African and Asian radicals. The constitution of North Vietnam was patterned after the American Declaration of Independence. I know that America was not so benevolent as it seemed to others. I know that Tom Jefferson kept slaves, that we slaughtered tens of thousands in the Philippines, that we meddled in Cuba, and "invented" the nation of Panama. One could go on. The point here is not what the facts were, but what the myth was. And the American myth had an extraordinary power that every nation envied. Only one other nation in recent history has drawn so deeply on the loyalty and faith of men and women distant from her borders, and that is the Soviet Union. Stalin, Hungary, and, finally, Czechoslovakia did for the the Soviet Union what racism, assassination, and Vietnam did for us.

Europe watched Southern cops club down women and then found, in the mid-1960's, that the liberal North was no better, as tanks cruised the streets of the nation's capital and troops moved into Detroit. Racism was no longer a hidden issue, something everyone knew was there and about which we all felt badly. Suddenly, racism was Molotov cocktails, machine guns, snipers, broken windows, and kids running with radios, shoes, TV sets. And black bodies, lying in pools of blood, in Watts, Detroit, Newark, Washington.

More important, I think, were the assassinations. I do not think most Americans realize that our "level of violence" has always been unusually high. If we lump together murder and suicide and count that as the "violence index" we find the United

States to be a world leader. There is a strange quirk of murder in America's head, like some spider in the darkness, and that quirk broke through in the 1960's. Medgar Evers, John F. Kennedy, Malcolm X, Martin Luther King, Jr., Robert Kennedy. And, in an eerie finish to the decade, the murder of Joseph Yablonski, on New Year's Eve, ushered the 1970's in with blood.

No other democratic society has a record of political murder that can equal ours in the 1960's. If no one else was killed, if all our wars ended, and if racism vanished—if all this happened tomorrow—it would be twenty years before the world would trust us again. But our murders are not done; they breed on one another.

Vietnam is the third factor that destroyed world confidence in us. Youth in America feel this is a war of unique evil. They feel this because they are ignorant of history, having disdained its study. German slaughter of the Jews exceeded by many times our murder of Vietnamese. Soviet Russia, it is generally agreed, killed millions of her own people during the Stalinist period. England watched without any great concern while hundreds of thousands of Irish perished in the famines that hit Ireland in 1848. And even in the 1960's, the death toll in Biafra exceeded that in Vietnam.

(The famines are real to me because of my great-aunt Mary Corkey, now dead, whom I recall as a fragile, hunchbacked, ancient woman, living out her life as a servant in Los Angeles, her mind so filled with the poetry she learned as a child that, even when blindness finally came, she could "read" pages from the record of her mind, in her thick brogue. She was one of those who had to flee Ireland during the famine, to take some pressure off the family. Her sisters remained behind, and they, too, are now buried—the last living link I had with Europe.)

The problem is not that Vietnam is unique, but that, in the eyes of the world, America is no longer unique. We are able to be as brutal as the Soviets, as murderous as the Nazis, as complacent as the British. We are just another empire, murdering, oppressing, imprisoning.

But, if our image has changed for the world, it has also changed for ourselves, and the 1960's were the decade when unquestioning patriotism died. In the bars of Middle America, one can see this sign: "If your heart is not in America, get your ass out." Or sometimes the sign above the bar, in slowly fading red, white, and blue, says, "America—Love It or Leave It." The response of our youth is to say, "America—Fix It or Forget It."

There is something very American about both the disillusionment of our youth and the hostility of the hard-core, old-fashioned, 100 per cent Americans. The Anglo-style patriot will tell us to go back where we came from, if we aren't happy here. That kind of remark is left over from the days when Americans were immigrants, born elsewhere, but living here by choice, and it made some sense to suggest that malcontents should go home. (A lot of malcontents did go home, as a matter of fact.) But where could we go today?

America is not the freest, best, most wonderful nation in the world. It is simply our country, as much a part of us as the color of our skin.

If there is any special decency to America, it is demonstrated by the disloyalty of our youth. The German youth under Hitler obeyed orders to the end, killing Jews, Communists, and civilians, with the pride of our own Special Forces. Every country can find men for the Green Berets, but Hitler found a nation of Green Berets, unquestioningly loyal and patriotic. Our youth, confronted by a murderous war, resisted. By their very disloyalty to the state, our youth demonstrated, unwittingly and against their will, the force of a national tradition that included slavery, but also Thoreau; Teddy Roosevelt, but also Eugene Victor Debs.

The values of the youth, the very values that are used to bludgeon the Establishment, are values that came out of this rich, complex, contradictory culture of America. It is—and Middle America does not understand this—an evolving culture. Once, after a protest meeting where I had denounced our Vietnam policy as a betrayal of every decent value America had stood for, a friend said that, while he fully agreed that the Vietnam war was treason against the best in our past, the kids were opposed to the war because it violated their concept of what America *ought to be,* that it represented to them a kind of *treason against the future.* He was correct, of course. The youth of today are stuck with this country. They don't have to love it any more than blacks have to love blackness or whites have to love whiteness. Being American is a condition of our existence, and, rather than waste our time praising the nation, we should put our energies into transforming it.

The Invasion: The world has changed with increasing speed. Two hundred years ago, we could travel only as fast as our horses could run. Today, we walk on the moon. Five hundred years ago, the American continents were still undiscovered. Now, we are mapping the solar system.

Perhaps 2 million years ago, the human race became a biological fact, having evolved at last from the dust and the sea: life, drawn by cosmic tides to move from water to land, to creep, to crawl, and, at last, to stand, cunning, fearful, and loving. Perhaps fifty thousand years ago, we entered upon a period of savage splendor, with tools and pottery and a fear of the gods. Not more than seven thousand years ago, civilization began along the Indus Valley, the Nile, the Yellow River of China (and, inexplicably, in the high Andes of Peru and the mountain-rimmed region of Mexico). Man is not new, but his civilization is. It is recent and fragile. The discovery of the wheel and the taming of fire were much more important to us than the first landing on the moon.

Then, when we had not yet integrated "civilization" into our psyche, along came the Industrial Revolution, followed, in the last fifty years, by the Technological Revolution and, now, by the Cybernetics Revolution. These things are "invasions" from our future, and whatever the future may be—whether it be a planet laid to waste by nuclear war, devastated slowly by shifts in the ecology, or blossoming forth with abundance for all—that future will be determined by our technology.

In the recent past, man lived with the forces of nature, both as a constant companion and an occasional enemy. Today, it is not nature that impinges on our lives, dictating our behavior, but, rather, it is our own machines. They are, at present, as much a threat to us as any raging storm, because we have invented them without knowing how to control them. The future has invaded us.

Tick off, in your own mind, the major problems we face. They do not include fires, floods, hurricanes, tidal waves, or earthquakes. Within limits, we have learned how to deal with these. It is air pollution that burdens our lungs and water pollution that makes it risky to swim in our rivers.

Chemical miracles, such as DDT, now haunt us. We build freeways to speed the flow of traffic and find that this only encourages more people to drive more cars, requiring more freeways to speed the flow of traffic, and freeways become a blight creeping across our major cities.

We found the chemicals that will control pain, but, now, we see heroin, a plague as cold as ice, as deadly as poisoned snow, drifting through the slums. We exist in a world infiltrated by nuclear bombs, missiles, germ- and chemical-warfare devices. The science-fiction writers in the 1930's saw a future that glistened with little air-cars flitting through vast clean cities, a world where man, having dealt with his physical problems, could at last explore his own meaning. But we don't have that: Our hospitals are overcrowded; the noise level of city life is hard to tolerate; our transportation is worse now than twenty years ago; we are all coughing from cigarettes or smog and depressed to learn that some of the food additives we've been using may be giving us cancer. More people live to an old age and find themselves without friends or employment or social meaning, driven into the ghettos of the aged, where, rejected by a society of the young, they can find no meaning in remaining alive. We have Telstar for instant communication, but little of value has been thus communicated.

We are losing control to the machines, the computers, the electronic brains. We shape our society—and our own lives—around the needs of the machinery, rather than shaping the machinery around the human needs of our lives. We are becoming mechanized rather than finding ways to humanize and gentle the technology.

New York in the 1960's was a frightening example of battles lost to the invading forces. In November, 1965, our power failed. I was leaving the WRL office for a TV show in midtown when the lights flickered, dimmed, and went out. Using my cigarette lighter, I walked down ten flights and caught a bus, assuming, all the while, that the failure extended only into lower Manhattan. But the bus, roaring up Second Avenue that night, oblivious of the fact the signals were no longer working, carried us into the darkness of midtown Manhattan. There was a strange, frightening beauty to the canyons of central Manhattan, darkened streets caught between black towers, only skylight for a guide. My own mind was sick with tension, because I had burned my draft card on November 5th and, the next morning, Roger LaPorte of the Catholic Worker had immolated himself at the United Nations and lay dying in the hospital. Tom Cornell and I both felt that LaPorte, aware of the tremendous public antagonism directed toward the five of us who had burned our cards, was trying to "draw the violence to himself" by the act of immolation. When the power failed, three days after LaPorte had incurred the burns that proved fatal, I could only think of the New Testament with its statement that, as Jesus was crucified, "from the sixth hour there was darkness over all the land." (The power failure came about 5:30 P.M., and LaPorte did, in fact, die during the time of darkness.)

I got to the TV studio, still assuming the power failure was local and temporary, and asked one of the men how serious the failure was. "All the way from New Jersey to Canada," he replied. I walked home from Times Square, stopping for drinks at some little bar on Third Avenue. When I got home, I found Peter and Ernesto there. We all lit candles and drank, and I relaxed, and then, much later, Peter and I wandered downstairs in the darkness and out onto the streets, filled with people curious at the disaster. We walked from the Bowery and Fourth Street up to Sixth Avenue and Eighth Street and, there, peered in the window of Bigelow's

Pharmacy, realizing we were looking into another century—for Bigelow's had never dismantled their gas lamps from the last century and, with the failure of electricity, they lit the old lamps, leaving their store in a warm glow.

A couple of years later, we had a subway strike, and we all walked to work, or cadged rides from strangers: the weather, bitter cold and very January: a city under siege. When the subways started again, we had a garbage strike, and grateful we were it came in winter, for the garbage, piled high on every street, would have made Manhattan smell like the Orient, if the strike had come in July. By the end of the decade, our phones phased out and became a problem and a joke. The efficiency of the New York Telephone Company hardly matched that of some obscure, newly emerged African or Asian state. And, all the while, the crime rate went up. To Middle America, the phrase "law and order" may mask anti-Negro attitudes. In Manhattan, it just means we are all afraid, with statistically verified reason, of being mugged, as we walk the streets. The city was becoming feudalized, as New Yorkers moved into those buildings that offered the best protection. We imprisoned ourselves with bars across our windows, double locks on every door.

The 1960's also saw a major water shortage, which could not be alleviated by drawing on the Hudson River because of its pollution. Joking signs like "Save Water—Shower With A Friend" went on sale in head shops, while serious signs like "Don't Flush After Every Use" went up in the subway rest rooms. The lawns in Queens and Brooklyn dried and went brown. City fountains were turned off. We held our breath, prayed for rain, and survived.

All of these troubles hit us within five years, reminding us how vulnerable the great cities are.

The invasion we endure has not left us joyous, healthy, cheerful, but, instead, frightened, gasping, and cautious. Technology has not liberated us but, rather, has constricted us. The imperatives of American power have taken our youth off to war, killing them even as they kill Vietnamese. We do not live in peace but in terror. Nuclear energy has not ended hard labor but only left us fearful of radiation.

We approach this invasion in a state of shock, with little guiding sense of our power to deal with this crisis. We submit to madness, not so much because submission is inevitable, but rather because we feel it to be inevitable. Our history, up to the Age of Rationalism, was always a civilization looking either backward or to heaven. Both the Renaissance and the Reformation are terms implying that the best days were in the past and that one might live them again, reorganizing society to match an earlier ideal. But the past remained our guide. To the Europe of the Middle Ages, it was heaven that vibrated with reality and Jesus who stood in the trembling cloud above us, watching every movement, monitoring the final details workmen lavished on their gargolyes, stone beasts that, once set in place, would be seen by God alone.

Sometime between the beginning of the eighteenth century and the end of the nineteenth, God died, though theology could not arrange a formal burial until the 1960's. God died as rationalism arose, celebrated as a goddess by the French Revolution, beloved by our own American revolutionary leaders Jefferson and Paine. Science was seductive. The world could be known; all mysteries finally would be answered. For the first time in history, man looked forward, rather than back, and looked to this planet, and not to heaven. H. G. Wells was a spokesman for this age of endless optimism, as was Jules Verne (whose account of the moon flight, 100 years before such a flight took place, is unnervingly accurate, even to locating the rocket site in Florida and calculating the speed needed to break out of earth orbit).

Before his death, Wells noted uneasily that "something queer" had come into the world. In 1914, World War I broke across the length of a Europe that thought it would never see such wars again. It was the most cruel and pointless of recent wars, destroying not only millions of people, but also those illusions of rationality and progress that had replaced God as a reason for life.

Socialists had missed their chance to break the back of history in 1914. If the German and French socialists had refused to vote war credits and, instead, had led general strikes, the war would have ground to a halt. But the socialists voted for death. Only the Italian party, the Bolsheviks, and, interestingly, the American party voted against support of the war. (What a bitter irony that the American Socialist Party would have the courage to face down their government, refusing support to the most popular war in our history, while what is left of that party today, a party once led by Debs and Thomas, has given tacit support to the invasion of Vietnam, the most criminal war in our history.)

The convulsions of Europe in 1914 became the convulsions of the planet in 1939, as we entered World War II, edging unhappily into the territory of mass murder. The madness of the trenches became normality with the slaughters by Stalin and Hitler, the creation of our own CIA, and our own national experiment in genocide—Vietnam. (Actually, our *second* national experiment along that line—since, somewhat unwittingly, and over a longer period of time, we had come close to annihilating the American Indians.)

I have read three particularly shrewd visions of our future. The earliest is Aldous Huxley's *Brave New World,* issued in 1932. *1984,* by George Orwell, and *The Twenty-Fifth Hour,* by C. Virgil Gheorghiu, were both published in 1949.

Huxley suggests the role drugs will play, and Orwell carries the totalitarian state to its logical conclusion. But, in some ways, I think Gheorghiu was closest to our reality. In his world, set in his own time and place, the Europe of World War II with its concentration camps, it is already too late. The twenty-fifth hour is the hour after midnight, the point beyond hope. The machines have won. Not the new, quietly humming, blinking machines of the future, but the older machines, which clank, and the vast machines into which men turn themselves when they organize bureaucracies. Johann, the hero, is trapped, in turn, by the Nazis, the Communists, and the Allies, becoming only a cipher in the system, a notation on a file. He is Everyman, lacking any faith that he might succeed in dismantling the machine (he even assumes the machine must be right), hoping only for his file to be misplaced, for a fuse to burn out, knowing his survival depends on error, some friction of the parts. This is the enemy—a technology uncontrolled.

If there is an invasion, there are victims, collaborators, resisters. And this collection of essays is very much about these groups. The sketch about the Bowery derelicts, much of the material on the American Negro, and some of the comments on the youth refer to the victims. Four blocks from where I live, at St. Marks Place and Second Avenue, one can find some of the casualties: the speed freaks, the acid heads who flipped out, the hollow men with headpieces stuffed with dry air and morning coughs. Half a block west from my apartment, are the Bowery derelicts, bearing their vomit like some memory of battle.

Then there are the agents, the men of the CIA, correctly dressed, their bowel movements in order, their ties straight, their sexual lives neatly combed, with only a pipe to betray some vanished youthful stab at integrity. They have sold us out and wonder why we hate them. The men from the FBI who occasionally came into my office, half-apologetic, half-confident, broken little pieces of men, who will, when they leave the service of Hoover, wander off to become the Police Chief or the Men's Dean of Students or a special assistant to Ronald Reagan. They are like Soviet apparatchiks transplanted to a free land, spying on us, listening to our phone calls, monitoring our living thoughts, and jealous because we, for all our faults, are alive and free, and they, for all their virtues, are owned body and soul by the machinery of our times—by the invader. The betrayers of the dream of America, the most obvious collaborators with the invader, will be found in the Pentagon, where generals, lit up with brass and medals, rush about pushing us further and further into the technological madness of ABM and MIRV.

But, if there are victims and collaborators, there is also a resistance to this invasion. It is generally young, though not invariably so. Its ranks range from the late A. J. Muste and Norman Thomas to Allen Ginsberg to the kid down the block, lighting up a stick of marijuana and hiding from the military police. All the best people these days are in the Underground. The Underground reaches from Madison Avenue to the Pentagon. We have friends on the police force of every city, and, in the days to come, the FBI will leak information to our side, because even the FBI must have some men left in it somewhere. The outcome of the struggle is not clear. I place no bets. We struggle, because, if we fail to struggle, we will have failed totally, and we would know it.

It is an uneasy and, even, desperate moment in history, and, for those of us past thirty, I think it is good to close this essay by quoting from a song written by John Kay, a refugee from Soviet-dominated East Germany, and performed by Steppenwolf, one of the better rock groups:

> America where are you now
> Don't you care about your sons and daughters
> Don't you know we need you now
> We can't fight alone against the monster

None of us can fight alone against the monster. It is real enough and deadly enough, dressed in the words of Agnew and wearing the mask of Mitchell, twitching to the invisible controls of a computer, so that we must break down generation gaps and racial gaps and a lot of old ideological gaps and join the fighting that will determine whether the future will overwhelm us or whether we can establish it as a liberated zone.

II
Where Were You When It Happened?

"But every last mother's son and daughter among us, rich or poor, wise or foolish, has the inalienable right to be jailed for his beliefs."

Life in Jail

Less than a month has passed since my release from Hart Island jail, where I spent twenty-five days for my part in the April 28 Civil Defense Protest. Yet, already, the experience seems far behind me, and I am writing these notes on my stay there for one reason only—to acquaint the reader with some idea of what jail is like, so that the experience will not seem strange and alien. Most of the 2,000 who joined the April 28 protest refused to take shelter and, therefore, broke the law. Many of them will join the protest next year—which means that my own recent past may well be their future.

There is this to be said for jail: It is the most democratic of all weapons available to those who would change society. Not everyone can write clearly, speak forcefully, or contribute heavily. But every last mother's son and daughter among us, rich or poor, wise or foolish, has the inalienable right to be jailed for his beliefs. It is not the happiest weapon we might choose, but it is one of the few remaining to us, and, so, let us cherish it.

Let me first speak for the ten of us who were sent to Hart Island and thank all who wrote us; it was impossible to answer every note, but those letters were extremely good for our morale, and we are enormously grateful. We are also grateful to the people of Grove Press, who sent books to all of us, out of their own pockets and the goodness of their heart.

The jail experience began dramatically enough with 2,000 or more of us crammed into City Hall Park on the afternoon of April 28 to protest the Civil Defense drill. More than 50 were arrested there (a total of over 160 were arrested in 4 states).

The trials were scattered over two weeks, and, by the time of my own trial, on May 16, it was clear I would be lucky to get twenty-five days. Nine men had already been sent to Hart Island. One boy, Allan Hoffman, had already received a sixty-day term on Rikers Island. (He is momentarily out on appeal, after serving three weeks of his time, but the appeal seems likely to fail, and, if it does, he will have to return to prison and finish his full term.)

Despite the realization that a harder term would be handed out than I had expected, the sustaining sense of drama carried over to the trial itself. But then, suddenly, sentence was passed, and the drama ended. I found myself in the basement of the Manhattan Arrest Court in a solitary cell, facing twenty-five days in jail because I would not pay my $50 fine. I had some money, toothpaste and toothbrush, cigarettes, and a paperback on Lao-tze. (Books are forbidden, but, sometimes, they will let you take in a religious book.)

After about an hour, I was taken out with other prisoners; we were handcuffed in pairs and loaded into a paddy wagon for the trip to the Bronx jail, where we stayed overnight. (I shared a cell with Burton Pugach, of lye-case fame.) The next morning, all watches, wallets, money—everything but toothpaste, toothbrush, and cigarettes—were taken from us, and we were given receipts. (The money you bring in is transferred to your account with the prison commissary at Hart Island.) We were then handcuffed and packed into a bus for the long ride to the ferry that would take us over to Hart Island.

Immediately upon arrival at Hart Island, you are "processed." This takes several hours; it is the most unpleasant part of the whole experience; and, when it is over, you have exchanged your identity for a number. First, your clothes are taken from you. Those that are soiled with urine and vomit and infested with lice are thrown away. Good clothes are held until your release. Because half of those processed with me were alcoholics (known as "skids" to the prisoners), there was an appalling stench as men took off their clothes and shoes, exposing ulcerated bodies and —literally—rotting feet. You are deloused, fingerprinted, showered, given a medical examination (consisting of the question: "You feel all right? Okay, go ahead"), and finally given clean clothes. You are never asked what size you wear—you get whatever is on top of the pile of shirts and pants (except for shoes, which are given out by size). The clothes are clean, but often ragged. Clean clothes are issued once a week. By the time the men had showered and were dressed, the smell had abated a bit, and we were served tin bowls of soup for our lunch.

After the processing was finally over, we were marched to Dorm 10—the admissions dorm, where men are held for a day or two until assigned to regular jobs. The trip over to Dorm 10 gave me my first real look at the island. Hart Island is a very small bit of land just off the east coast of the Bronx. It has a fascinating history, having, at various times, served as a Confederate cemetery, a mental hospital, and, currently, a prison workhouse. Small as it is, the island houses Potter's Field and, also, a Nike base. I was amused that ten of us who were jailed for resisting war preparations should have to share even our prison quarters with the military.

The weather on the island is cool—or was while I was there. I am told it is bitter cold in winter, which I believe, as the island is constantly swept by a river breeze. The shores of the Bronx, on one side, and Long Island, on the other, seem terribly close. On a weekend, the river is alive with sailboats, and, every once in a while, an excursion boat makes its way majestically past the island. There are no special walls to enclose the prison buildings—the swift current of the river does that—and, from a short distance, the complex of buildings resembles a drab Midwestern college. It is only on a closer approach, when you see the heavy wire grill over the windows, that you realize it is not a college.

The first day in Dorm 10 was my introduction to prison life. The men are not locked into cells but share a large dorm—about 100 to 150 men to each dorm. The dorm itself, of course, is locked, and a hack—prison slang for guard—is always on duty. The lights go out at 9 P.M. After the lights are off, there is a buzz of talk and dirty stories, which finally dwindles away, to be replaced by a strange symphony of farts, night coughs, and snoring. Since sleep was the only time in the whole day when you were alone, I looked forward to it and had no difficulty in almost immediately entering a private oblivion. The men are wakened at 5 A.M. Toilets are grouped together, and, unless you have the immediate knack of relieving yourself while seated on cold porcelain in the presence of other men, you will be constipated.

Prison food is not bad; the inhabitants of all the dorms eat together in a central mess hall. After three days, I could eat the food, and, after five days, I was looking forward to the meals. One of our men, John Ingersoll, is a vegetarian and had to trade his meat around to get extra vegetables, and another, Gregor Rowland, complained about the lack of fresh fruit. It is true we did not have any fresh fruit, but, since I don't like fresh fruit, I don't think I have a right to object. I asked Phil Havey, who is with the Catholic Worker, how the prison food compared to the meals at Chrystie Street. He said the prison food was better and there was more of it than he got at the Catholic Worker.

After a couple of days in the admissions dorm, you are given a regular job and assigned to a permanent barracks. Work assignments range all the way from being a clerk to digging the graves in Potter's Field. I was assigned to a labor squad and ended up in a dorm with Ralph DiGia and Colin Gonze. Ralph is an old jailbird, with experience from his C.O. days in World War II, so he had already made contacts and was able to get me some cigarettes to replenish my vanishing supply. (It is hard to stop smoking when you want to, but to be forced to stop smoking when you don't want to is hell.)

The "labor" we were doing consisted of breaking up some concrete and hauling it to a truck, which took it out to the sea wall for dumping. It was easy work. The men work only four hours a day on Hart Island, the rest of the time being spent in the dorms reading, writing, sleeping, or else, out on the large playing field, where, in the evenings, for a couple of hours, the men pitch horseshoes, play baseball, or stretch out on the grass to catch the sun. We discovered that some of the prisoners were illiterate, and Colin Gonze persuaded the warden to let us set up a class, which he and I would teach in place of our regular jobs and to which the illiterate prisoners would be assigned. My brief experience as a teacher on Hart Island convinces me that (1) teaching is much harder than using a sledge hammer, (2) reading and writing is a miracle I had never appreciated, and (3) teachers should be treated as public heroes, which, in fact, I now realize they are. Our pupils were southern Negroes, eager to learn, and, in our short stay, we had made some good progress, leaving the class in the hands of two other college graduates doing time.

The worst work assignment was the graveyard, to which three of our men were assigned (Al Bonk, who runs a Mexican shop down on MacDougal Street, Bruce Brown, and Happy Traum). It was unpleasant, not only because digging is hard work, but also because, in digging new graves, the men often ran into old ones. More than once, they struck their shovels into bodies that were still largely intact, except for, perhaps, an arm or a leg, where the flesh had fallen off. One reward of the graveyard shift was the chance of finding gold teeth, which might, with luck, be smuggled out past the hacks.

Each man may write one letter daily—on a single sheet. He may receive any number of letters. Nothing can be sent in by friends, except letters, small photos, stamps, and money (which is deposited to your account at the Commissary). However, books and papers can be sent in direct from the publisher. We were grateful for the *Voice*, which was carefully shared among ɪne ten of us and then passed on to the other prisoners. All mail, both coming and going, is censored. The prison will allow no adverse comment on the prison itself. For example, it would have been impossible for me to write to anyone about the man who dropped dead one afternoon on the playing field (considering the poor health of many of the skids, this death was not surprising and does not reflect on the prison).

My only really unpleasant encounter with prisou authority

came over this question of mail. I had made some comment in a letter to the effect that prison had a corrupting influence on both guards and prisoners. The hack in my dorm who censored the mail reported this to Deputy Warden Cavallo, who called me in immediately. Cavallo is an incredibly fat man. Looking at me from eyes that seemed almost lost in the flesh of his face, he informed me, and I quote him literally: "Youse are a moron." This seemed the only sentence of English he had mastered, because he repeated it fifteen times with varying inflections. Then I was ordered to tear up the offending letter and get out.

Prisoners have Commissary one day a week and can spend up to $10 for tobacco, cigarettes, candy, writing paper, toilet articles, and so forth. It is pathetic to see an old skid spend a nickel for a packet of 250 cigarette papers; he then collects butts and rolls his own cigarettes.

There is a medical clinic open daily, but the level of medical care is poor. When you report to the clinic, the nurse assumes you are malingering—as long as you can get there under your own power. You must report two or three days in a row before you will get anything more than aspirin. You may, in fact, not get treated at all. I, personally, saw one nurse order a man to get out, saying: "You got that cut on the outside, and you can get it treated when you get back outside." Two of the doctors I met seemed decent and qualified. But one other doctor was incompetent and a painful joke to the prisoners who had to have blood tests taken—he could never find a vein without jabbing five or six times. One junkie got so mad at him he finally said: "God damn it, man, give me that thing," and jabbed the needle at once into the vein for which the doctor had been industriously digging with so little success.

There was one near tragedy, for which the medical staff was not really to blame. A prisoner, through his own carelessness, backed a tractor over the sea wall and was trapped underneath it, crushed against the rocks. The tractor was too heavy to be moved immediately, and the doctor sent to the prison hospital for morphine; the man pinned under the tractor was screaming in pain. It turned out the hospital didn't have any morphine, because they were afraid the addicts would steal it. The doctor was furious, but nothing could be done—the man continued to scream in unabated agony. Fortunately, he did not die, was finally extricated, and, I understand, was transferred the next day to Bellevue.

There was little physical brutality. On one or two occasions, I saw men struck by the hacks, but they were not struck hard; the hacks do not carry guns, so they have reason for caution in how hard they hit. The worst punishment was to be sent to the "Bing," which meant being locked in a cell and forced to stand all day without talking or cigarettes or anything to read. But men confined to the Bing got regular food. The attitude of the hacks was generally unpleasant, but probably no more so than a drill sergeant in basic training. And there were a few hacks who were decent in their treatment of the men.

The most interesting hack was an old fellow named Captain Walsh, who was known as "Donkey Walsh" to the prisoners. He was an unpleasant man, but he was so very old and infirm and had been a hack for so many years that he was treated by the prisoners as an institutional joke, like the dull razor blades or the breakfast "coffee." What made him interesting was his uniform, which was the most ragged, filthy outfit I have ever seen on any official. One might say he was Hart Island's answer to skid row.

People have asked whether we were treated differently from the other prisoners. The answer is no. As far as the hacks were concerned, they didn't know why we were there, unless they looked at our I.D. cards and saw the offense. Prison clothes are a great equalizer. The warden, however, did keep a sharp eye out to prevent any difficulties from arising, as he knew we had some backing from the metropolitan press.

What did the other prisoners think of us? Some of them were deeply shocked to learn we had deliberately broken a law. They asked us what would happen if everyone went around breaking laws—and didn't we have any respect for law and order? I admit I was a little surprised to find so high a degree of social responsibility among them. Other prisoners felt we were morally right but pretty stupid to get jailed on a moral question. There was unanimous agreement that those of us who had been given a choice of paying a $50 fine or serving twenty-five days were insane to have chosen the twenty-five days. There were moments when we agreed.

By and large, the prisoners are a good lot and give you much less trouble than the hacks. I was interested to find the "Scofflaw King" in my dorm. He is a respectable Village resident, with whom I had once had a violent political argument. I don't think he was surprised to see me in jail, and he probably felt it was where I belonged. But I know he was astonished that I should see *him* there. The bulk (over two-thirds) of the men are Negroes from Harlem, held on policy and numbers charges, and, for them, jail is an occupational hazard. Some of the men are junkies. Some are in for nonsupport, some in for traffic fines, and perhaps a fourth of the men are jailed for "being drunk in a public place."

Regarding sex in prison, I am sorry I have nothing sensational to report. There isn't much sexual life on Hart Island, since the terms are short—ten, thirty, or ninety days, mostly. There was a good deal of homosexual activity in the dorm that housed the youngest prisoners—who had been segregated, I suppose, to keep them from the harmful influence of older men—but there was no evidence of homosexuality I could see in any of the dorms I was in. Three of our men were in the young prisoners' dorm, and it is from them that I learned of the situation there, as all of them had been propositioned more than once. They were surprised to find that the homosexuals in the dorm seemed to be the most masculine and normal-looking of the lot, but, then, life is full of such surprises.

From what I have said, it should be obvious Hart Island is not a bad place—probably no worse than basic training in the armed services and perhaps not as bad. The food is okay, the work is light, and there is ample time for playing cards. It is like a boys' camp with impolite counselors. Looking at it another way, Hart Island is a perfect example of Communism—everything is taken care of, including your freedom.

There is one aspect of jail that I have not mentioned and that, more than anything else, made our stay unpleasant. Time does not move. Readers who are considering taking marijuana to see if it alters the time sense don't have to bother with drugs—just try jail. Or try drugs, and you may go to jail anyway and can compare the two. The first twenty-four hours I was in jail, I sustained myself by thinking over my courtroom speech to the judge. It was, I thought, a pretty good speech. At least, the audience applauded, and the judge ejected some of my friends from the court. But, after twenty-four hours, I was less impressed with how nobly historic it was to be jailed and more impressed—or to be accurate, depressed—to learn that, on a twenty-five-day term, you do not get any good-behavior time off, which meant I would serve the full twenty-five days and not twenty. After the first week, in which there are all kinds of new experiences to get used to, time simply stops. It does not slow down, or pause, or hesitate. It just stops. All of us were normally active and busy people. Suddenly, we found ourselves doing nothing, cut off from the whole stream of events, unable even to know what time of day it was (for some reason, it is a prison rule to allow no clocks anywhere on the island within sight of the men, and the hacks will not tell you what time of day it is). It is this aspect—this timelessness of the experience—that I found horrible. In subjective terms, all of us spent much longer than twenty-five days on Hart Island. But, once you are released, the time you spend in jail seems to collapse, to shrink in upon itself and dim away, so that, now looking back, it seems as if I had spent only a few days there instead of nearly four weeks.

(1961)

The Bowery: A Ghetto Without a Constituency

On November 2, the Saturday before the election, I led a "voters meet your district" walking tour of the Bowery. Quarter-page ads announcing that tour ran in the *Voice,* the *Chelsea-Clinton News,* the *West Side News,* and the *New York Free Press.* Three people—aside from my campaign committee—turned up at 2 P.M. that Saturday to walk down the Bowery, and that depressed me because it was clear that, as always, the Bowery is a ghetto without a moral constituency, and because I know that the Bowery has no resources for its own redemption.

Because there had been so few of us standing on the corner of Fourth Street and the Bowery on that hazy Saturday, I was overjoyed to open the November 7 issue of the *Voice* and find Steve Lerner's article and the photos by Jay Good. God bless the *Voice* for its occasional reminder that the worst ghetto in the nation sits here in Lower Manhattan. If I add some comments to those of Steve Lerner, it is to fill in the record—and it is also because I don't think the city will really look at the Bowery until it gets slammed with that vomit more than once a year.

Jay Good's pictures were great, but they had the defect of having been taken by a photographer who knew what he was doing. I would rather fill four pages of the *Voice* with nothing but shots of men who have passed out. There is no drama to such a picture—certainly not to more than one such picture—but I think

38

it might shock some people if they knew that, during the warmer months, you can pass ten or twenty men lying against buildings in each block between Houston and Spring streets. When the weather turns colder, the men scramble against buildings or crawl into doorways or apartment buildings in hopes of escaping the cold. More than once, I've opened my fourth-floor door and found a bum passed out in the hall—weary cockroaches hiding in the cracks of the city.

The Bowery's real problem is that it has no "attractive power." It isn't, for the most part, black, and so it doesn't mobilize middle-class guilt feelings. It isn't young or pretty or sexy. It has no votes. Worst of all, the work done on the Bowery is usually wasted—the man who reforms today will be in the gutter tomorrow. The Bowery is poor, but it is poor with that kind of poverty for which Americans have such hellish contempt. The men here would be failures in almost any society (including a socialist society). They are the slag of our industrial and technological system, but they were broken less by accidents of the economy than by flaws internal to themselves. And so we have contempt for them. They deserve what happens to them. America is Puritan at heart, and we have no room for compassion for cowards or failures—precisely those who most need compassion.

Who is down here? About 75 per cent of the men are derelicts but not drunks. They are loners who have lost their families or left them—for the most part, older men, spending out their final years in the rooming houses and flop houses that run from Fourth Street to Chinatown. Twenty-five per cent of the men are drunks, and, somewhere in their brains, suicide moves. They come here to die. I've been drunk enough to pass out but never so drunk as to challenge cars for the right of way in the middle of the block. These men stagger out directly into traffic and usually avoid being hit. Sometimes, they don't avoid it, and so get a free ride home—to the morgue, the destination they had sought since they came down here. (An ex-police-captain who had become an alcoholic once told a photographer friend of mine that he had, simply, come to the Bowery because he wanted to die.)

It used to be easy for me to excuse my lack of compassion for these men by arguing that they had really destroyed so many brain cells from drinking that they were subhuman. An easy conclusion to come to, God knows. Faces caked with dirt, heads scabbed over, eyes glazed, as they sit watching you pass by. My own visit to Hart Island, the men's workhouse, changed my mind. I found, in those brief twenty-five days of jail, that men who entered jail looking as if alcohol had dissolved the God within them and crushed out the last spark of the human, would—after three or four days of food and sleep and medical care and showers— begin to work their way back to humanity. I felt their loneliness more there, in jail, than when I pass them on the street. There was never mail for them during mail call. They had not a penny to buy tobacco and used to grub butts and borrow cigarette papers to salvage enough tobacco to make their own stale cigarettes. They are hated in jail by men who have no one else to look down on. And there, shaking a little but sober, they weave fantastic lies to explain why they are in jail, to lift themselves out of the category of derelict, so that they might at least be accepted by the criminals around them. They became human beings to me, and I wish, very much, they had not gone through that transformation. Where it had before been easy to pass the bodies in the street, it has since been very hard.

Partly because I am a hesitant person, not given to spontaneous gestures, and partly because I know I am only helping buy them an earlier death, I almost never give money to those who beg. But, sometimes, a man looks so defeated, so broken, and so terribly *alone*, that to give money is important—a small touch of fellow feeling. Whether one gives or doesn't give, however, the derelict will invariably say, "Thank you, sir," or "God bless you." There is no fight left in them. Years ago, when I hitch-hiked back and forth from Los Angeles to San Francisco, I remember how, if I stood in one place for an hour or so without a ride, I would begin to curse the Cadillacs and Chryslers as they swept by, their solitary drivers in speeding comfort, and how my uplifted thumb shifted to the middle finger waved in impotent fury. But not these men, not the men here, on the Bowery. It is always "Thank you." Once, as I walked home and passed an old man without giving him money (or even pausing to listen to his request), I heard his benediction trail after me . . . "God bless you, sir." I stopped, came back, and gave him a dime, and then, as I walked on, I could hear him muttering in wonder, "He said 'no,' and he came back! He said 'no,' and he came back! He said 'no,' and he came back!"

On Second Avenue near Fifth Street, there is an old toad of a woman, monstrous, fat, unpleasant, ugly inside. She used to sit on a box in front of a delicatessen there, like a gargoyle. Sometimes, she helped out behind the counter. One night, while I was getting cigarettes, an old derelict came in. He was sober, and he actually wanted to buy coffee and a roll. The old toad screamed at him to get out. He held the change in his hands and said, "But, ma'am, I've got money, I just want coffee and a roll—see, ma'am, here's the money," and she screamed again for him to get out, and he, proud that he was sober, proud that he had money in his hand, proud that he wanted coffee and a roll, backed through the door, still treating the woman as if she were royalty, very gently holding out his hand and repeating, "But, ma'am, the money is here, I only want coffee and a roll." The fight was gone from him, and only dignity was left.

If anyone wants to become a saint (which, despite its relatively low pay, is a job with great prestige value and a probable claim to history's attention), the path is easy and wide and waiting. Dorothy Day pointed the way. You lift up the derelict who is freezing to death on the street, not minding the shit-caked pants, the damp of urine, the raw vomit on his shirt, and you minister to that man. You bathe him, and feed him and put him to bed, and comfort yourself with the fact he has lived one night longer, but knowing that, a week or two later, you will find him again lying on the sidewalk. You learn to live with the bedbugs and lice such men bring into your house of charity. If you can do this, day after day, and still believe in mankind, you are a saint.

I can't do this. I can only observe the Bowery and wish there were more saints so that I wouldn't have to see men lying on the sidewalk. Sainthood is a silent agony made up of vomit and poverty and failure, and I am not cut out for it. So I send, once or more a year, a very small contribution to the Catholic Worker, knowing there are people at that address who have what it takes to do what I cannot (or will not) do.

If I told my friends in Scandinavia that I walked down the street yesterday and saw a man fallen upon the sidewalk and that I did not stop to see if the man were ill or drunk or dead, they would recognize me as a moral monster, for they would be applying the standards of civilization to Manhattan. Even in Los Angeles, I never saw this kind of thing when I was growing up, and the hardest thing about this city was learning to pass by the bodies. But what else do we do? If we give money to all who ask, we will have none at all and will have to take up begging on our own. If I stopped and examined each man I see along the Bowery, checked his pulse, called an ambulance, the police, or the morgue, then I would never get to work at all. So, in order for me to function, I become dehumanized.

There are projects on the Bowery—one operating out of the Men's Shelter on Third Street, right around the corner from where I live, where teams of three (plain-clothes cop, former alcoholic, and social worker) go out and ask men on the Bowery if they would like a five-day rest with medical care, food, a clean bed. No coercion. About 75 per cent say yes. But they are back on the Bowery again in a week or a month. Part of our problem is to recognize that we may not be able to save or cure these men, but that we can at least try to show compassion toward them, provide nurses to get them into clean beds and off the streets.

Most alcoholics in this country (and there are more than 5 million) are hidden by their families and friends. Most of us have family or friends to shield us. Thanksgiving and Christmas now, the cold bright season, with snow and burning logs and a round of parties and gifts and family and friends. We take them for granted, these relatives and friends of ours, screaming at them, bickering with them, occasionally realizing we love them.

If I get sick at a party this season, I know someone will tidy up, get me in bed, and make coffee in the morning. They may not like doing it, but they will.

But down here in the Bowery, you have no family and no friends. God help you if you pass out, because none of us will help. The Bowery not only measures the given number of failures visible to the naked eye, but it measures also the failure of the whole of society, for societies are judged by how they treat the weakest in their midst, not by how graciously they deal with the most powerful.

Jesus once spoke of the day of judgment, saying:

> Then shall the King say to those on his right, "Come, you whom my Father has blessed, come into your inheritance in the realm prepared for you from the foundation of the world. For I was hungry and you fed me, I was thirsty and you gave me drink, I was a stranger and you entertained me, I was naked and you clothed me, I was ill and you looked after me, I was in prison and you visited me." Then the just will answer, "Lord, when did we see you hungry and feed you? Or thirsty and give you drink? When did we see a stranger and entertain you?" The King will answer them, "I tell you truly, insofar as you did it to one of these my brothers, even to the least of them, you did it to me."

This is a hard teaching, and, because most Christians don't accept it, perhaps those of us who are not Christians should not be haunted by it. But the line, "insofar as you did it to one of these my brothers, even to the least of them, you did it to me," is a reminder that Christ, who entered the world in a stable, is also the man over whose body I step on my way to work.

(1968)

England: Home Truths from an Alien

As was reported in the July 28 *Peace News,* I was detained for nearly eight hours on the morning of July 23 at Gatwick Airport, when I sought to enter England to attend a meeting of the War Resisters International. I actually was issued a deportation order and was on the verge of being forcibly ejected from Gatwick Airport, when the timely intervention of Fenner Brockway stayed the hand of the Home Office, and I was allowed to enter.

In two respects, the affair was healthy, but it also raised some disturbing questions. It was healthy for an American to be reminded that we have not yet actually annexed Great Britain, and that, while Harold Wilson has long since abandoned the notion of conducting an independent foreign policy, he does at least retain the right to exclude from British territory those Americans of his choice. Secretly, the heart of every Englishman must glory that Her Majesty's Immigration Service still dares to seize the documents of an American citizen, search his person, treat him with rudeness, and issue him a notice of deportation.

And the affair was also healthy for my own ego. I am not a very famous or dramatic peace leader. Certainly, I am far less known and less influential than Dave Dellinger or Professor Staughton Lynd or Dr. Benjamin Spock. I had to come to Gatwick Airport to find how truly important—and perhaps even dangerous

—I must be. For the Lynds and Dellingers and Spocks are free to come and go. Ralph Schoenman enters and departs without difficulty. Even Stokely Carmichael was at least allowed to enter before being hustled out. But I am issued with a deportation order. My papers are considered important enough to seize and copy. If only the Home Office had backed up the stupid little bureaucratic error made by the officials at Gatwick, I could have had the glory of flying back to America and saying that I, almost alone of American radicals, had been denied entry into England! And, even though I was, at last, permitted to enter, there is no American radical who cannot help but envy me that unexpected, inexplicable, but irrefutable proof of my importance—Aliens Order, 1953, Home Office Form 1B 31.

Out of my little experience, which now seems merely amusing, but which, at the time, left me feeling like a refugee trapped at a frontier station in Eastern Europe in the early 1950's, I would pass on some brief advice to other travelers who might have reason to expect trouble.

1. If you are not so lucky as to enter the country in the company of Devi Prasad, who can get in touch with Peggy Duff, who can ring Lord Brockway, who, in turn, can phone the Home Office, then carry with you the phone number of the National Council for Civil Liberties. During the day, ring EUS—2544. At night, ring 01-340—9322.

2. If you have important or private or incriminating documents and letters with you that you would prefer not to have photocopied by the authorities or even examined by them, mail them into England ahead of you.

3. Why, in the name of God, the immigration authorities thought I was carrying a stash of pot with me I do not know. But the search was careful, and I would advise against trying to smuggle things like marijuana into the country.

4. Immigration officials vary in their attitudes. They can be charming or nasty. The British have, over the course of centuries, developed a special class of civil servants who just barely made it through public school and are not terribly bright, but are just bright enough to realize they are never going to be more than

night clerks at immigration offices. Such were the officials I encountered at 3 A.M. on July 23 at Gatwick. (I here parenthetically commend the gracious and friendly treatment I received at the hands of the working-class employees of BEA who were in charge of keeping track of me—I was trying to sleep on a bench, so it wasn't hard—while the immigration officials pored over my papers.)

5. Be careful what you doodle. When I got my papers back, some hours after they had been seized, I found, among them, a couple of "war doodles." When I'm at peace conferences I take out my aggressions by drawing imaginary islands complete with forts, and towns, and roads, and an attacking fleet offshore. Such a doodle, when examined by the kind of immigration officials who are likely to be stuck with night duty, can be seen as an aerial map of British harbor defenses, sketched with the aid of an infrared flashlight from 10,000 feet, while zooming over England on an SAS night flight. So, make sure your doodles are innocent.

There remain some really significant questions. My own case is important precisely because I myself am not. The Carmichael case is outrageous, but the Home Office can argue that some of his statements in England violated certain laws; thus, for many, the issue will be blurred. This cannot be said in my case, which is nearly ideal. I am a radical but only a very moderate one. I have never belonged to any Communist of Trotskyist organization; I have never been convicted of a felony. I have never been arrested for using drugs. I have never been divorced (or married); I have no bastard children; I have never spoken ill of the Queen. My only serious offense was urging, in public, that people vote for LBJ back in 1964. But I have long since repented that offense and urged his impeachment. I doubt if the Home Office would be interested, but I have also never (1) served in the armed forces of any nation, (2) worked in a war plant, or (3) given public support to the war in Vietnam.

Despite this exemplary record, I have been held up at the immigration desk every time I have tried to enter England since 1966. On three occasions in 1966, I was detained for periods ranging from ten minutes to half an hour. On one occasion, documents were taken from my brief case for examination but not held long enough—I think—to be copied. There were certain nominal protests made to the Home Office at that time through friends in the Labour Party, and I assumed the trouble was over. Certainly, I was unprepared to be handed a deportation notice when I flew into Gatwick on July 23.

The first question is how in the world my name ever got in the special book the immigration officials check before admitting one to the country. It could not have been put there because of the War Resisters International's work on supporting deserters from the U.S. Army, because my name was in that book and I was detained before the WRI had passed a resolution on this matter, let alone taken any concrete action. It is possible that my name is in the "book" at the request of U.S. authorities, but I find that difficult to believe, not only because more prominent Americans have not suffered these delays, but because, after my first run-in with British Immigration, I found no difficulty at all in entering Canada, Japan, South Vietnam, West Germany, Switzerland, Italy, France, Norway, Sweden, and Denmark.

No, I think, for once, I would exempt the United States from the blame. I think this is simply a Kafka-like snafu on the part of the Home Office. But, once one's name is in the book, it seems that it stays there.

The second question is why the British have the "book" at all. One can travel freely in Scandinavia without having one's name listed in a special book of dangerous foreigners. If Scandinavians don't need such a book, why do the British? The third question is: What happens to the traveler who, in his innocence, lands at a British airport but has no friends to come to his defense when he has a run-in with Immigration? How many such people get deported? Are there others, dozens or hundreds of people, who, lacking contacts, have been deported quietly, not knowing how to protest or to whom they might appeal?

Finally, I must assume that there is some connection between Wilson's support of Johnson in Vietnam and the attempt to prevent me from entering England. The only logical reason for trying to ban me from England would be my attitude toward the war in

Vietnam and my profound contempt for Harold Wilson—and my willingness to urge the British to spend less time attacking Johnson (for whom they can't vote, in any case) and more time attacking Wilson (against whom they can vote). I was the person who, last year, drafted the statement and solicited the signers for a special appeal by American Socialists (including Norman Thomas and Erich Fromm) to the British Labour Party to break with U.S. policy on Vietnam. When I spoke in Trafalgar Square in 1966, the burden of my remarks was to urge increasing pressure on the Labour Party and not just on Washington.

If I am admitted again to England, I will again, if the occasion arises, denounce the leadership of Harold Wilson because of his involvement with the slaughter in Vietnam. Does the effort to deport me mean that the Labour Government has carried its support of LBJ this far? Is it now to be said that someone whose political position is democratic and nonviolent will be deported, if he utters a word against British complicity in the Vietnam war? British visitors here are free to criticize LBJ. Are American visitors in England to be denied the right to comment on Wilson?

These questions can be answered by the Home Office. I would think an effort should be made to get some response from Roy Jenkins on them. The hell of it is that I like England. I know I am a difficult visitor, complaining about the warm beer and the lack of ice cubes in my whisky, but the fact is I do like England and the English and, if I find myself permanently banned, it will not only be devilishly inconvenient—since a number of important meetings take place there—but it will be, for me, a real personal loss. But the greatest loss would be England's. Not because it would be denied such wit and wisdom as I might try to smuggle in, but because an England that issues deportation notices in this way would be a new and not very pleasant England. Paradoxically, I guess I would say that if England were a place where I could not go, then it would also be a place where I would not want to go.

(1967)

Prague: Viewing a Disaster

What follows is a simple, eyewitness account of two days in Prague under Soviet occupation. This is a report, not an analysis or a commentary. It is because I know that every "Cold Warrior" welcomes the events in Prague that I must note simply that, bad as the invasion was, it does not compare to U.S. actions in Vietnam, where a million or more have died. Prague and Saigon are linked, symbols of the contempt great powers have for the right of smaller nations to self-determination. Let all those who so correctly demand complete and total U.S. withdrawal from Vietnam apply that same standard to the Czech situation.

I had gone to Europe to attend two working conferences, one in Vienna (War Resisters International) and the other in Ljubljana, Yugoslavia (International Confederation for Disarmament and Peace). Between the conferences was a space of four days, and I chose to spend that time in Prague as vacation. I arrived there on Saturday evening, August 17. I was due to leave early Wednesday morning, August 21.

Other American radicals in Prague spent their time to good advantage, seeing student leaders, liberal writers, political figures. I simply wandered, having fallen under the charm of the city, the most beautiful I've seen in Europe. I stood in Church on Sunday morning, listening to the chants and smelling the incense. I

49

visited the old Jewish cemetery, the most tragic graveyard I've ever seen, filled with thousands of tombstones leaning on one another for comfort in their eternal sorrow. Graveyards are places where the living come, the sons and daughters and the grandchildren, to honor their ancestors. Graveyards fascinate me, for they are not a symbol of an end, but proof of beginnings— here we stand, observing the gravestones, and there lie the ancestors from which we have sprung. Between the living and the dead, these is a silent communion. But, in the Jewish cemetery, carefully enclosed by high old walls, there was the chilling knowledge that only death was there, for those who should have come to lay flowers had perished in the death camps. The ancestors lay beneath the stone tablets, and only tourists visited, strangers to the family. I wept twice in Prague, and the first time was when I spent an hour wandering through this silent field of graves.

I roamed through the National Museum, drank beer in small *cafés,* and walked out on the Charles Bridge to take pictures of the chalk drawings done by the long-haired young rebels—slogans in English against the war in Vietnam and slogans in German against Ulbricht. I walked down the broad main street, Vaclavske Namesti, watched students in Wenceslas Square, and stood listening to debates in the "Hyde Park" of Prague, a little square off Na Prikope.

And, in this way, I spent my time. I had some contacts through Allen Ginsberg, but they were never home when I phoned. By Tuesday night, my last scheduled night in Prague, I felt sharp pangs of guilt that I had not been more "responsible" and "political" in looking people up. I wandered Prague late into the night, until it was a city asleep and moving toward dawn. (At 11:00 P.M., invasion forces crossed the frontier.) I got to bed at 2:30 A.M. (At that hour, Russian aircraft had landed at Prague airport.) I slept fitfully, waking once at 5:30 A.M. to the roar of jets. I slept again until 6:30 A.M., when I had to get up to catch my early flight to Yugoslavia. I went down for coffee and sensed a crisis in the air— *Rude Pravo,* the Communist Party daily, had appeared printed on only one side of the sheet and with large headlines. At one point, the Czechs in the room stood by the window, and I joined them to watch tanks roll by in the streets below. Still groggy with sleep, I took it for granted they were Czech tanks. (Who else would have tanks in Prague?) I finished my coffee, packed, and, then, a thin edge of anxiety working through my mind, went down to the main lobby to make sure the airport was not affected by whatever crisis had brought Czech tanks into Prague at 8:00 A.M. There, at the front desk I found this note:

> *American Embassy advises (5.50 A.M.) American citizens to stay where they are. Listen to the Voice of America at 1200 KC (if you were foresighted enough to bring a radio). Stay off streets.*

It was now just after 8:00 A.M., Wednesday, August 21.

I went out in front of our hotel, the Hotel Flora, on Vinohradska Street, about twelve blocks from the center of town. I watched tanks and troop carriers roll by. Czechs stood weeping openly on the streets, gathered in small, quiet groups. And now, for the second time in Prague, I wept. I had profoundly identified with the Czechoslovak experiment in "Communist democracy." The Russians had done more than invade Czechoslovakia—they had sent their damn tanks crashing into our skulls; they had invaded the hopes of socialists all over the world.

There was an unreal quality to the invasion. The troops were all in trucks or tanks, not on foot. The sidewalks belonged to us, and we stood silent and unmoving. The streets belonged to the tanks. Tanks are ugly things. They were filled with young Russians, men who had been told they were going on maneuvers and found out they were invaders of another socialist country. They were frightened. The troop carriers had machine guns mounted on the front and men with automatic rifles watching the windows and roofs of the buildings they passed. In the distance, one could hear the harmless, toyish sound of automatic weapons being fired —a kind of "pop-pop-pop." People moved along the streets, lining up at food stores, which were virtually the only stores open.

The streetcars were not running, and few cars were on the streets. I had shot my last frame of film Tuesday evening and had to hike several blocks to find a drugstore open where I could buy some film. I came back, then, having seen Russian troop carriers lining the road all the way toward town, as if they were in a traffic jam. I shot some tanks with a telephoto lens from my hotel window.

Perhaps it was because we were motionless on the sidewalks, while the Russians sped by in trucks and tanks, that the invasion was like a dream. The tanks were motorized images with which the population was not interacting, only observing. It was not yet noon, but the resistance was beginning, as a car moved down the street throwing out mimeographed copies of *Rude Pravo*. Then it was noon, and the first organized resistance began. A young man pulled his bicycle into the street and blocked traffic—which consisted, actually, of a single Czech truck, which pulled over to one side. Horns began to blare for a two-minute general strike. At that moment, with the kid in the street and the horns blaring, a Soviet troop carrier came speeding down the street. The kid held his ground, perhaps paralyzed with fear or courage, but it would have made no difference to the troop carrier, which wasn't even slowing down. At the final moment, as most of us nervously pulled away from the corner, fearful of gunfire or of seeing the boy run down, an older man moved out from the crowd, put his arm gently around the boy, and guided him to one side of the street. The troop carrier shot by without ever having paused.

A student walked past our hotel, moving away from the center of town, holding a large Czech flag.

Radio Prague went off the air early, and Radio Pilsen began broadcasting. It used German, Russian, Hungarian, Bulgarian, and Polish, as well as Czech. It was beaming its appeal to the invading Warsaw Pact troops, explaining that there was no basis for the invasion, Socialism was safe, the invasion, illegal. It was also urging the population not to provoke an incident, but simply not to cooperate. Radio Pilsen went off the air while I slept in the afternoon, but other stations then came on and the Russians, having forgotten to bring tracking equipment with them, could do nothing.

The dream quality came back at dinner, for the Flora is a first-class hotel with an excellent restaurant presided over by an imperious headwaiter. We all went to our tables, ordered cocktails or wines and our dinners, as if nothing had happened. People chatted in the muted luxury of the Flora; they ate and drank quietly. Outside, somewhere, Czechs were organizing. Some were dying. Some were already dead.

All night long, there was the buzzing of motor bikes back and forth through the city. The students were organizing. The underground papers were now being printed, having found presses. About 9:30 P.M., I took another walk toward the center of town and found out why the line of Russian troop carriers had been backed up earlier in the day.

The Czechs had built up a barricade about ten blocks from the hotel and two blocks from the National Museum, trying to stop the tanks from getting to the radio station. When I got there, I saw a fantastic tangle of burned-out streetcars, buses, trucks, and debris—including at least one Soviet truck, half blown-up and hurled into a side street. This was where the firing has been coming from in the morning, and some had been killed—no precise figures. (Note—In fairness to the Russians, I will say that they generally fired into the air and no estimate of the dead exceeded thirty for the first day, about par for an American riot.) Hundreds of people were milling around the barricade, while the Russians were staying discreetly in their trucks, a block away. It is reported that at least one Russian tank was set on fire during the morning at this barricade area.

The milling of so many people made me nervous, and I went back to the hotel. It was about 11:00 P.M. when, looking out my window, I saw fireworks coming from the area where I had just been. Beautiful orange rockets going up in the air. I didn't understand why fireworks should be going off and went to the window for a closer look. Suddenly, the crowd in the street below me broke and ran as if a heavy summer shower had hit them. I leaned farther out to see why they were running for shelter, when I heard a "flick" against the building near my window and realized that the fireworks were tracer bullets and that they were falling in our area.

Suddenly, my window, large enough in any case, seemed to fill the whole wall, offering the entire room as a target. I scrambled for the side of my bed, where I stayed for perhaps two minutes, until I realized that, even though the firing was getting closer (the gentle, almost lazy "pop-pop-pop" had shifted to a harsher "tat-tat-tat"), with tracer bullets you could see which way the fire was going. I edged back to the window and, standing at one side, watched the tracers climb into the sky. I had never realized before that bullets had a finite speed, that you could see the graceful blazes of orange climb slowly, like Roman candles, and, like Roman candles, wink out.

Thus, Wednesday came to an end. The Czech army had put up no resistance, on the direct orders of the party. The only real fighting anywhere near us had occurred around the makeshift barricade ten blocks away. But it was already clear that non-violent resistance was taking place. When I woke up Thursday, it was clear at once to me that the Russians had made three mistakes. First, they had waited eight months too long. The Czechs, once the most docile of Communist populations, had enjoyed eight months of genuine press- and radio-freedom. Freedom, like tyranny, can become a habit. Second, the Russians had assumed they would have some support from within the country, and, as it turned out, they had almost none at all. Third, they let the first twenty-four hours pass without any decisive action.

The Russians may well have assumed, having seized the radio- and TV-stations, the airport and the train station, and, having surrounded the National Assembly, arrested Dubcek, and sealed off every large area that might have been used for demonstrations, that they had "won." Certainly, their actions had been decisive, total, and overwhelming. They had encountered no effective or organized resistance. They had occupied the city. But it became obvious they didn't know what to do with a population that "refused to recognize them." They had failed to shoot the occasional flag-carrying student on that first day. They had not counted on the underground radio and TV.

They had not, it seems, thought about the problems of suppressing illegal papers, and, Thursday, one could see that manifestoes and leaflets and papers were everywhere in evidence. Posters had gone up on all buildings. Trams had "SVOBODA—DUBCEK" chalked on their sides. Trucks and cars had posters draped over their fronts. Signs in Russian were everywhere, telling the troops to leave, as well as signs in Czech urging no support for collaboration and no cooperation with the traitors Moscow was seeking to install as a provisional government. The national flag began to appear in apartment windows. Half the people on the streets were wearing bits of ribbon showing the national colors. Police cars (Czech police) carried large Czech flags. A special appeal to the occupying army had been printed up. The Czechs were also churning out short leaflets in French, English, and German to make sure the tourists understood the situation. Their radio was still on the air, and this gave citizens hope. People grouped themselves around little portable radios. People appeared on the streets with petitions, and other people stopped and signed the petitions.

An ambulance corps had been organized, and civilian cars flying Red Cross flags shot up and down the streets. The people were beginning to give a loud whistle whenever the tanks clanked past (this being something in the nature of a hiss). The Russians had taken Prague, but they had not managed to capture its people.

I went for a long walk Thursday afternoon, at one point walking directly under the gun of a Soviet tank, to get down to the National Museum and see if—as was rumored—it had been burned out. (It hadn't been, although along with a number of apartment buildings that I saw, its façade had been heavily raked with machine-gun fire, breaking most of the windows.) What I did see (and found incredible) was that each Russian tank or troop carrier was surrounded by groups of Czechs. Whatever spontaneous spitting or rock throwing that may have occurred early Wednesday was gone—the crowds were arguing, pleading, explaining. I remember one tank on which a student was perched reading some manifesto to the two Russians sitting in the tank. If the image the West has of the Hungarian uprising in 1956 was a youth throwing stones at a tank, the image from Prague was of dialogue and verbal confrontation.

(I learned that on Wednesday night all the bars had been closed to prevent anyone from getting drunk and charging at the tanks. The radio broadcast steady appeals for calm—for neither provocation nor cooperation.)

I walked into Wenceslas Square and found the main street leading into it filled with thousands upon thousands of persons. As I watched, two truckloads of Czech students drove up waving flags and headed straight for a Soviet tank, which, somewhat to my surprise, yielded the right of way.

My time in Prague was drawing to an end. I walked back to the hotel, realizing that I understood at last what a student had meant when I asked him, early in my stay, what would happen if the Russians invaded. He said, "For us, they will not be here." Shortly after 5:00 P.M. the American Embassy notified us of a special train leaving for Vienna. We got taxis and boarded the train.

(1968)

Saigon: A City's Agony

To pretend I entered Saigon as an unbiased observer would be dishonest, and to claim that, in forty-eight hours, I could uncover a wealth of information would be fatuous. I went to observe, however briefly, and I pass on here the sort of impressions that one might, if one were to stay longer, take so much for granted as to overlook them.

With me was Peggy Duff, general secretary of the British Campaign for Nuclear Disarmament, a remarkable woman and a great comfort to someone as timid as myself when venturing into unfamiliar and possibly hostile territory.

We had gone into Saigon to see and talk with the Buddhists, and, in this, we were successful. We spent one afternoon talking with Thich Thien Hoa, deputy leader of the militant Buddhists, at the An Quang pagoda—a crowded complex of two-story buildings alive with monks and Vietnamese boy scouts and proudly flying the Buddhist flag. Thich Thien Hoa apologized for his delay in getting an interpreter for our meeting: The government had cut his phone lines that morning. He arranged a meeting for us with Thich Tri Quang, the charismatic and brilliantly political monk who leads the Buddhist "struggle movement" that nearly brought down Ky early this year.

Thich Tri Quang had been fasting for seventy days when we

met him, and he was staying at a clinic in the downtown area. He was under guard: A secret-police agent patrolled the sidewalk in front of the clinic; a smiling young soldier, two policemen, and a second secret-police agent guarded the third-floor room where Thich Tri Quang actually lived.

Thich Tri Quang was in the clinic partly for his health, partly because the government was hesitant to imprison him, and partly because the Buddhists felt he was less likely to be assassinated in a clinic. He had been living on a solution of 5 per cent dextrose—a litre a day—and vitamin pills. I have learned, since leaving Saigon, that he has broken his fast. We met with him for an hour and a half, and, although he was terribly thin, he was in good spirits and seemed to gain energy and to become more animated as our visit wore on.

He was concerned that we convey to the world what he felt were the facts on the election that was about to take place. In his view—and I agree fully from what little I saw—the elections were a farce intended for American public opinion. It's pointless at this late date to comment in detail, but I note the following points about this highly touted "free election": Only those who agreed with the policy of the Ky government were allowed to run; the government ran its own slate of 150 candidates, known—even in Saigon—as "the Military Slate"; Ky's men had full and absolute charge of the entire election process—setting up the polling places, counting the ballots, and so forth; the government, while claiming control of virtually the whole country, was unable even to deliver voting cards to one third of the population of voting age; the assembly, which has now been elected, has power only to write a constitution, after which it will be dissolved; Ky may amend the constitution as he sees fit. In addition to his immediate concern about the election—which all the major Vietnamese political groups were boycotting—Thich Tri Quang was deeply concerned about the fate of some 5,000 Buddhists who were still in prison despite Ky's promise to release them. And he was concerned—as were all the Buddhists with whom we spoke—about the need for some move toward peace. He did not urge the immediate withdrawal of U.S. troops—a point on which we differed sharply in our discussion—but he did appeal to the Americans to scale down the fighting and put more emphasis on social reform. He said several times that the terrible error of the Americans was that they were "manufacturing Communists" among the peasantry. (That, too, is confirmed by events: There are now more South Vietnamese serving with the Viet Cong than when the American escalation began, and desertions from the Saigon forces are up 30 per cent this year over last year—when something over 100,000 government troops deserted.)

We were encouraged to learn that, at some levels, Buddhists and Catholics are now working together. We had asked someone else—a leading journalist in Saigon—whether the military suppression of the Buddhist uprising earlier in the year had crushed them. "No," he replied. "The people are stunned and, therefore, silent. Never before has a government used force against the Buddhists, but Ky's victory will prove very costly, for we all are Buddhists in Vietnam. Buddhism is in our veins, and you can get rid of it only by draining our blood. I think Ky's 'victory' is only the calm before the storm." Saigon was once called the Paris of the Orient. Today it's falling to pieces, burdened by a population of over two million, many of them refugees from the American bombing of the VC.

I pass on these impressions for what they are—results of a swift and inadequate glance at one of the great tragedies of our century. Vietnam is more complex than it may appear from New York (or Toronto), but the agony is also more real when seen directly: the agony of the American soldiers wandering the crowded streets of Saigon, lonely and desperate for something better than whores and liquor; the agony of the Vietnamese themselves, who are now mere spectators at a struggle being waged on the orders of Washington and Peking.

(1966)

Author's Note: The closing sentence here cannot be excused. It may make for balanced prose but it is political slander. By 1966

I should have known—surely did know—that the Vietnamese were struggling to rid Vietnam of all foreign interventions and not because of any orders from any foreign capital. I suspect my old anti-Communism was at work here, carefully balancing one side against the other, when no such balance, in this case, is possible.

(1970)

Two Faces of Dixie

Having come almost to the end of a five-week speaking tour in the South—covering Virginia, Florida, Louisiana, and North Carolina—I find my own attitudes toward the South undergoing a sharp modification. It is increasingly difficult for me to accept what might be called the "Herblock cartoon" view of the South. I realize that Northern attitudes toward Dixie are, in many ways, as warped as the attitudes of the South toward the North.

If some traditional liberals think the following paragraphs constitute some kind of apologia for the South, they are entirely wrong. Having spent one night in jail here already as the penalty for attending a Negro mass meeting, having sat in court while my friend Pat Cusick and three others were tried for "trespass," having talked with young people dressed in blue coveralls—the new symbol of freedom—and, having heard their reports and knowing, even as I write these words, that there is almost certain to be—before this article can reach the *Voice*—a renewal of mass action here in Chapel Hill, North Carolina, and in Danville, Virginia, the last thing I want to imply in these brief comments is any support for the mental illness we know as Southern racism.

But honesty demands we understand that the South is more complex and more troubled in its own heart than we, in the North, assume it to be and that it is by no means united in its attitude

61

toward the Negro. I think I have some understanding now of what James Baldwin meant when he wrote that conditions in the South are not really worse than in the North (which, obviously, was not written as an apologia for the South, but as an attack on the North).

The South has lived with a conscious lie ever since its colonial beginning—the lie that slavery could, in some way, be justified. There was resistance to slavery from the beginning, and that resistance was once stronger in the South than in the North. We forget (or were never taught) that the antislavery movement was essentially Southern in its origin, that the underground railroad was founded here in the South. It is true that, for a variety of reasons, the South rationalized slavery (as it was later to rationalize the semislave status of the post-Civil War Negro) and that, ultimately, the South would wage a war to defend an institution its finest minds knew was wrong. But I think there is much truth in the statement that, in its own deepest mind, the South has never been free from guilt over the question of the slave and over its treatment of the Negro following abolition. And, from the hidden guilt, a guilt that has stained Southern history, has flowed the hatred, the fear, and the violence.

It is also true—and this, too, we are not really taught in our Northern schools—that the period of reconstruction was a period of horror, which continued for decades and which left the South so stricken with poverty that the region as a whole did not emerge from the disaster until World War I, and that many pockets of the South are still today afflicted with a poverty that has its roots in events now a century old. I talked with an elderly man here, a Quaker who is deeply committed to civil rights, and he spoke quietly of how five of his mother's eight children died before they reached the age of twenty—of malnutrition. The North, in short, executed upon the South a policy so vengeful and destructive that both whites and Negroes suffered unspeakable agonies for decades.

It was inevitable that, under these conditions, the Negro would be used as a scapegoat, for he was seen as a constant reminder not only of the South's own guilt in relation to him, but also of the treatment imposed by the North upon the whole South. The North cannot escape some real share of the burden for the pattern of racism, for the creation of conditions in which so many whites were brought so low that they felt compelled to keep the Negro lower still in order to maintain some illusion of dignity.

Despite these conditions and a depression that struck, at the end of the nineteenth century, with more force (in the South) than the depression of 1929, the South did make a truly heroic effort to change its own pattern. The Populist movement, which I had always thought of as essentially Midwestern, was, in fact, basically Southern. Its strongest base was in Georgia, Oklahoma, Louisiana—in distinctly Southern states. And, while the Populist movement eventually foundered on the rock of racism, the true story is that the dirt-poor farmers, the "crackers" and "rednecks" of Georgia and elsewhere, made a conscious effort to build an alliance with the Negroes and, together, attempted to break the political power of the so-called aristocracy. In one campaign in Georgia, a Negro Populist leader was threatened with lynching and fled for protection to Tom Watson, the Populist leader (who, tragically, turned to racism in his closing years). Watson sent out a call, and within twenty-four hours (no telephone, mind you) 2,000 Georgia "crackers" had rallied to Watson's farm to defend the Negro against lynching.

If the Populist movement failed, as it did, it is, nevertheless, true that, at its high point, it forged a genuine link between poor white and poor Negro, and it is also true that the same Northern forces that today categorize the South in such bitter terms for lacking any real sense of liberalism were, then, terrified of the Populists and rejoiced in their downfall.

Now, once more, the South is breaking open—only this time it is the poor Negro, not the poor white, who is leading the way and calling for the overthrow of the power structure. The North has applauded this movement without realizing several things.

One of the major things the North has not realized is that the South is not alone in having a "Negro problem." The second thing the North has not seen is that a fair number of native Southern whites have joined the movement, have accepted Negro leadership, and can be found living in Negro communities in order to have some protection from the police, and that a bond of brotherhood has been forged by beatings and by jail between these Southerners, black and white. The third thing the North has not seen at all—or, more accurately, has seen but has not understood —is that it is the South that has taken the first serious step toward the historic resolution of this national problem of Negro-white relations.

That is to say, the present movement is not the result of Northern agitation, and, while often dependent on financial help from Northern liberals, it was not launched from the North. The Negroes and the whites involved in the movement are products of the South, of that "other side of Dixie" the North has chosen not to see. And there is, I think, a simple reason why the North has been blind, why we have chosen to think of the South as simply a region in the grip of terror, brutalized by poor white trash. And the reason is that we suffer from a social pathology of our own, which is our sense of moral purity. Baldwin has argued that this nation needs the Negro—needs him on the bottom of the social pile, as a permanent proletariat, as an eternal safeguard against our own (white) failure, as security that there will always be someone at least one step below us. That is, in an insecure society, one man's superiority is proved by another's inferiority.

There is much to Baldwin's argument—but it needs to be carried a step further. The North needs the South as proof of Northern virtue. If, in the year 1863, I argue that the free Negro in New York is half-starving and lacking in education, effectively segregated from the opportunities of the society, I will be answered by the liberal of 1863 with a speech about slavery in the South, a condition that is obviously so much worse that, by comparison, the North is the very essence of virtue. If, in 1963, I argue that Harlem is no better and, perhaps, worse than it was twenty years ago, that Negroes are demoralized and unemployed and subject to police brutality, the Northern liberal will, again, "answer" with a speech about the Birmingham bombing. I will deliberately ignore, if I am a Northerner, any of the positive aspects of the South, lest my image of the South become confused and I be thrown back upon an examination of myself, my own society, and my own relationship with the Negro.

The South is, of course, a very special and very terrible kind of hell—for Negroes and whites alike. It is a land that is both aware of its guilt and insistent upon denying that guilt. When the Negro leadership says it seeks the liberation of both black and white and when King speaks of his "dream" of a new South, we tend, in the North, to write these statements off as sentimentality. Yet the North does not understand that white and Negro in the South are tied together, not only by so obvious a thing as blood relationships, but also by the historic experience of living together in close relationship, of having suffered for a century, in an effort to reconstruct some kind of society out of the ruins of the Civil War. If there is hatred, fear, guilt involved in Negro-white relationships here, there is also a strong element of love—confused love, misplaced love, paternalistic love, but still a sense of love and compassion, which is the other face of Dixie from the one we persist in seeing. It is absolutely true that very few Southerners want to grant the Negro his rights. But it is also true that very few Southerners approve, in any sense, of actions such as the bombing of the church in Birmingham.

In seeing the tragedy of Medgar Evers's murder, we do not see also the tragedy of Beckwith, a man destroyed. Far more accurate than Herblock's cartoons is Bob Dylan's song concerning the murderer of Evers, in which he repeats, again and again, the refrain "But he's only a pawn in their game." It is true, God knows, that the violence of the South is wielded by the poor—by the sick and tragic poor. It is true that laws are needed—now!—to insure the field workers of SNCC against being shot down or beaten to the ground by men pledged to enforce the law. It is true—I have seen it myself again and again—that the civil rights workers here, even in such safe areas as Chapel Hill, live semiunderground lives, use code on the phone, travel into rural areas with fear, and work in rural districts always stalked by anonymous threats and, often, by real gunfire.

But it is also true that these forces survive, that, while any murder is one too many, there are far fewer murders than one would expect of a revolution as genuine as this, and it is true that the overwhelming bulk of this leadership is drawn from the South.

If I were a Southerner, a white Southerner, I think I should feel an odd mingling of shame and pride in this year 1963. I should feel shame that I had been silent so long, that a black man finally had to lead me, had to suffer to free me from my silence, and that, in so many cases, the real values of the South, the inherent decency of the Southerner, had been stained with blood and violence, and with men like Faubus, Wallace, and Barnett. I would not be ashamed because the North was watching—but ashamed as a Southerner, because these men have violated my own deepest values. But with that shame and sorrow would go a strange kind of pride. The Negroes who chant in the streets are a product of the South, not the North. The whites who march with them are also products of the same South that produced Beckwith. I would feel enormous pride that, after a century of both North and South avoiding this problem, it was the South that began to move toward the solution. And, whether the leadership is Negro or white, it is still Southern, and I would still be proud.

As a Northerner, I can have no such mixed feelings, for I have no reason for pride and every reason for shame. After a century of our moral preaching, it is the South that moved, and I am left holding my sermon in one hand and the reality of racism in my other hand. I know that the North, in large part, created the economic conditions that fed racism and created Beckwith. I know that, in the South, the Negro is feared in the abstract but often loved as an individual, whereas, in the North, the Negro is loved only in the abstract; we do not, in fact, know the Negro as an individual. I know that, although the South has said to the Negro, "You can come close but don't rise high," the North has said, "You can rise high but don't come close."

The great difference between North and South is that the South has always known it has a problem, whereas we have always denied that we have one. The sinner who knows his sin can be saved, but what can God do to touch the heart of the righteous sinner? How humiliating it shall be if, as I suspect will be the case, the South resolves this problem first and establishes racial justice, and, then at last, the North will have no scapegoat, no one to point to, no region to distract its attention or justify its smugness. If it is true that the South most desperately needs the mercy and grace of God at this point of change, it is also true that, if there is a God, and if that God is moving anywhere in our land today, then his grace and mercy is touching the South, fulfilling the prophecy that those who were last shall be first, those who were humble shall be exalted.

(1963)

Notes from Japan

I grew up in Los Angeles during World War II, and Japan was far more in our minds out there than Germany; Tojo, more feared than Hitler; the Orient, far closer to us, psychologically, than Europe. So, when my plane took off from San Francisco on August 5, my impressions of Japan were a blend of childhood fears, a sympathetic curiosity about Buddhism, an amateur interest in Japanese art, some background reading, and a keen appreciation of Japanese skills in such matters as turning out high-grade cameras and tape recorders.

"My Japan" was, in short, a mélange of old memories, secondhand impressions, and indistinct blurs of an odd people seen now and then in movies. Japan, rooted in the Orient, raw fish, brown rice, paper lanterns and cherry blossoms and Mount Fuji and kamikaze pilots. Mysterious, distant, beautiful, treacherous. Land of the Shogun and the Emperor, island kingdom with a young, second-hand culture imported from China, humiliated into international affairs by the threat of Admiral Perry's cannons. Land of grotesque, roof-heavy temples, flaring out over distorted, raging, wooden faces of idols. Japan, with its koto music and kimono-clad geishas pouring tea in an elaborate, endless, meaningless ceremony, and its odd gravel yards with a giant's fistful of boulders strewn at random to make a "rock garden." The delicate prints, stylized and frozen. A graceful, fragile china-doll people. Inscrutable. Untrustworthy. In Los Angeles, they made good gardeners but it was rumored that, by night, they signaled to Jap submarines just off shore, so we sent them all to concentration camps so they couldn't hurt us. Japan and the wordless horror of August 6, and 9, 1945.

Where does one begin reporting the reality of Japan against the impressions one had before arriving? Europe I had seen, two and three times, and, foreign as Europe is, its foreignness is mine, and its very quaintness sets off echoes within myself from a past that is distant but not altogether forgotten—a past that runs in my blood. Even the music of Europe's many languages reduces itself, when the words are inscribed on menus or train stations or street signs, into half-familiar, almost comprehensible symbols. But Japan?

The first shock is to find, on landing in Tokyo, that you have arrived in a city that seems entirely Western, modern, industrialized. The men are not wearing their "native costumes," but are dressed in the latest, most stylish, Western fashion. The women, with very few exceptions, do not move about in the beauty of the kimono, but in Western dress. (There are exceptions—perhaps one woman in every ten does dress in the kimono. These are either older women or young geishas and bar girls.) The Occupation is over, but, in sartorial terms, the Yankees have conquered.

The buildings are interchangeable with new buildings in Los Angeles, Paris, or London—"drab international." It is something of a shock to land in the heart of the Orient and find a city that is so concrete-modern, but, of course, Tokyo would have to look modern if only because it was destroyed twenty years ago. If there is none of the quaint charm of London's narrow streets or the overwhelming sense of antiquity that pervades Rome, it is simply because everything ancient in Tokyo had been burned to the ground by August, 1945.

Tokyo is the largest city in the world and its streets are filled with taxis, trucks, bicycles, and thousands upon thousands of people. The Ginza area is jammed with people every afternoon and evening—the kind of jam one sees only rarely even in New York City: a ceaseless tide of humanity surging back and forth.

For us, the inscrutability (an accurate word with a double meaning—I'll come back to it) of the Japanese is partially hidden by their Western clothes, their modern buildings, and, most of all, their ability to use our language. But, in using our language, they make certain errors that reveal something of the gulf dividing our cultures. I am not a semanticist, but I think it is true that languages help shape the way in which people think or, at the least, reflect the way they think. One gets hints of this from the extraordinary way in which many Japanese speak or write English. The errors of the Frenchman who speaks English, or of a German, are "logical errors"—presenting no real barrier to communication (that is, sentences like: "My car red she is in the garage" or "Now the time to go is" may sound funny, but they make sense). Pronouns and adjectives and verbs are placed a bit differently than in English, but, basically, even with the errors, we can communicate. Not quite so with the Japanese. The way they make errors indicates that their whole grammatical structure is alien. And, probably, therefore, also is their way of thinking about things. Often, the English is cleanly correct, both spoken and written. But sometimes—as with a little instruction sheet that came with a camera gadget I bought in Tokyo—the English is precise, detailed, forceful, even enthusiastic, but utterly and literally incomprehensible. (Happily, I already knew how to use the gadget so it didn't matter.)

Radicals argue that all mankind is part of a single family, and, as a religious concept, that is true. But we cannot reach genuine understandings with people if we overlook the fact that there are often great differences between cultures. We must not be deceived by the Western dress of the Japanese—the Japanese mind is clothed in the culture of Japan. There are subtle tones, mannerisms, shadings, shadows, echoes, and hints that clue one to the differences that need to be explored in order that our understanding might be genuine and not superficial. The Japanese are not a superficial people. To some extent, I am afraid we are. We tend to ignore the subtle hints that indicate the differences and to seize upon the too-obvious similarities and pronounce, on our return, the judgment that the Japanese "are really very Western."

Everyone in Japan wears a wrist watch. Almost everyone I met carried "name cards" to hand out, printed in English on one side, Japanese on the other. Japanese seem always to have a camera with them when traveling. They are a remarkably attractive people, few of them being heavy. The women are beautiful and the men very good-looking. The children are the most beautifully dressed I have ever seen anywhere; they are clean, neat, oddly like dolls. The people as a whole are clean—almost pathologically so. America and Americans are filthy compared to Japanese. The men carry little wash cloths with which to mop their brows, wipe their hands, arms, face, and neck. The water is drinkable. Everyone seems to have three or four innoculation scars on their upper arms—public health is clearly a major concern of the government.

Tokyo is hot during summer. Worse than New York. Worse, it seemed, than Saigon. The heat is damp, but there is no rain. Dust covers the leaves of plants. The sky is blind with smog. The food of Japan is better than I had expected. True, there is raw fish, which tastes exactly like raw fish, except for raw squid, which is marvelous. But there is tempura—fish, shrimp, and vegetables fried in a dry, golden batter that melts in your mouth. And delicate thin beef steaks cooked on cast iron braziers at your table. (Seaweed, when served tempura style, is very good.) There is Japanese beer, very much better than the best beer we produce. And Japanese whisky, better, in my view, than scotch or bourbon and quite different from either. (The Japanese, rather typically, do not tout their whisky as being distinctly "Japanese," but tend to push it as being the equal of excellent scotch.)

The people are polite—a simple word. We don't even know the meaning of it. We don't practice it here, and we rarely encounter it in Europe. It dominates all contacts in Japan. In a political argument, one never rises to say: "Toma-san is quite wrong. I couldn't disagree more. The correct position is. . . ." Instead it would be something like: "Toma-san has stated the case well. Should we not also consider. . . ." In shopping, one finds oneself backing out of a store with one's purchase, bowing in an ungainly way and murmuring the Japanese word for "thank you." It seems natural, because the shopkeeper is bowing to you.

There is also a formality to Japan. In no case, did I feel free to call any Japanese by their first name. Perhaps first names may be used in the home but not in public. It is always "Tsurumi-san" or "Dellinger-san" or "Sugiyama-san." The meaning of "san" escapes me. It is used like our "Mr.," but not quite the same; it has some of the connotations of "sir." But still that isn't it. I would, in this country, be addressed on the following scale of familiarity: Mr. McReynolds, McReynolds, David. In Japan, my impression is that after twenty years I would still, by close friends, be called McReynolds-san and would be addressed the same way by total strangers. It is both formal and gentle.

Tips are not given in Japan. It is true that "service is included" on all bills, but that is true also in Europe, where one must tip anyway. Nowhere in Japan, not once, did I offer anyone a tip (except the very last day, when the taxi driver had three of us and a lot of luggage to get to the airport). After an American occupation, after the destitution of war, after the shock of occupation, still *there is no tipping.*

The taxi drivers are polite to you and rude to other drivers. They are also suicidal. Far, far worse than the taxi drivers of Mexico City, Paris, or Rome. Again—a small insight into the national character. Polite and reserved in personal contacts and exhuberant, fatalistic, and quite dangerous behind the wheel.

There is a beauty to Japan behind the dust of summer's heat and smog. Beauty in small, unexpected places. A single flower. A special sense of order in the midst of the larger chaos.

I said earlier that I arrived in Japan with the impression that Japan had come into the world late, that its culture was somehow no more than a thin overlay of Chinese civilization on a people not far removed from barbarism. May God forgive the Americans for their ignorance—and arrogance. The earliest date given for a European's setting foot in Japan is 1542. But Japanese history does not somehow begin when we "discover" Japan. Japan and its people and its culture had been there for what—by Western standards—is a very long time. The origins of Japan are lost in myth but the first of the unbroken line of Emperors, Jimmu Tenno, probably ruled about the beginning of the Christian era. Very early in history, Japan was unified under the Emperor, and, even during its long feudal period, there was a sense that Japan remain unified around the symbolic figure of the Emperor. Until 1945, Japan had never been occupied, and, except for the ill-fated Mongolian adventure of 1274 and 1281 (in which the Mongols never gained more than the barest foothold before being driven into the sea) Japan has never even been invaded.

Less than a hundred years after the first Europeans made contact with Japan, the Japanese—in 1637—suddenly and almost completely closed Japan off from contact with the world, driving out the Europeans, and enforcing once again Japan's long isolation from the West. (A small settlement was permitted to remain in Nagasaki.) When Admiral Perry sailed into Yedo Bay in 1853 and pried open the door the Tokugawa shogunate had closed in 1637, we were not encountering a gracefully primitive people with a thin facade of Chinese culture. We were encountering a nation with a national history older than that of any of the nations that sought to bring the blessings of Christianity and commerce.

A great deal has been made of the Japanese tendency to imitate, as if this were a mark against them. True, the Japanese have adopted and adapted ideas and methods on a scale so massive and deliberate as to have no historical precedent. They copied from us so swiftly that, less than a century after Perry's first visits, they were able to drive the Western powers out of the Pacific, occupy most of China, and threaten, momentarily, to become *the* Asian power. They have been sufficiently adept at copying to emerge from the desolation of war as one of the great industrial powers of the world. What is remarkable is that, behind this ability to copy and to imitate, the Japanese are not a Western people. They were and are Asians who have sensed that the situation requires them to pick up new techniques in order to survive. The fact that they remain profoundly "Japanese" in the midst of their Western technology surely presents the sociologist with something of a mystery and certainly makes the history of modern Japan not only exceptional, but as fascinating as the history of the earlier periods.

In Kyoto, visiting the great Buddhist temples—which date back a thousand years (earlier than our first "ancient Cathedrals" in Europe) and which are graceful monuments to the religious force of Buddhism—one can see contemporary Japanese in Western dress walk up to the temple entrance, light a piece of incense, bow slightly, and pass inside. Modern and ancient Japan have met, and it is modern "Western" Japan that makes the bow of self-abnegation in that confrontation. It is my guess that Japan and the Japanese are more truly understood by a walk through the temple grounds than through the Ginza. The one seems to be rooted among the trees and mountains, speaking with silence. The other is bright, cheerful, and, one suspects, something of a toy. The Ginza is a lighthearted symbol of modern Japan. The temples on Mount Hei, at peace in their shrouds of drifting mist, *are* Japan.

We had an informal little disobedience project during the conference—sponsored by the Japan Peace for Vietnam Committee (BEHEIREN)—when Ambassador Reischauer was given a going-away party by the Press Club. Street demonstrations at the Press Club are illegal, as is the distribution of leaflets. No one knew quite what would happen because it hadn't been done before. The Americans and those Japanese ready for possible arrest all turned up at exactly the right instant; three Buddhist priests joined us, beating their gongs; and we walked over to the entrance to the Press Club, unfurled our banners, beat our gongs, handed out our leaflets, and waited for the police to arrive. Now, what was being done would be quite routine in New York or San Francisco or Chicago, but it was simply not done in Tokyo. One had mass demonstrations or none at all. Certainly not a little group of thirty people.

As it turned out, nothing at all happened. The police came,

looked confused, retreated to their car. More police came, looked confused, conferred with those in the first car. A couple of police came and shoved on our line to force it back or make it break up, but no one got hurt, and they gave up and went back to their car. The press and diplomatic guests arrived, sneered at us or ignored us. The Ambassador himself came, smiling. The Japanese (who are nothing if not polite) mobbed him enthusiastically, shouting "Reischauer, Reischauer!"—all very friendly. He went in; we went home. The Japanese involved were very excited about all this. Peggy Duff, the General Secretary of the British Campaign for Nuclear Disarmament (who had been one of those pushed a bit by the police) couldn't quite understand what all the excitement was about. We went off—Peggy, Claude Bourdet, Quentin Bassett, Yoshiyuki Tsurumi, myself, and Yamaguchi, my young translator—for a triumphant dinner of tempura and beer and I could see it had been a significant event for the Japanese. From there, we all went off to a marvelous night parade with paper lanterns lit by candles, tramping for miles through downtown Tokyo, hundreds upon hundreds of us, singing the "International" in Japanese and "We Shall Overcome" in English. That I thought was much more exciting, but such great demonstrations are, as I noted, easier for the average Japanese to take part in than individual actions.

I realize that the experience of Japan is not one that I can easily translate. I cannot catch on paper the odd metallic scent of the air when the plane landed at Nagasaki or the tears that leaped to my eyes as the Japanese stood to applaud our group at Nagasaki as we walked in, nor can I convey what it meant to wander through Osaka's outskirts and up to a meeting hall, in the early evening, where Bob Ockene and I were to speak and to hear "We Shall Overcome" pouring forth and sounding as if it were being led by a young American visitor (it was not—it has become a kind of anthem for a section of Japanese radicals).

Some things stand out: the long discussion I had with Dr. Toma, a Japanese Christian—he asked me why I had abandoned Christianity, and I asked him why he had abandoned Buddhism; the constant helpfulness of Kubo, a moviemaker who had been fired for his politics; the energetic and untidy Oda, the driving force and folk hero of BEHEIREN; and, perhaps most of all, the chance to meet and know even briefly Tsurumi, a Professor at Kyoto (who took me, very early one evening, for a walk through the grounds of the old Imperial Palace, in Kyoto, and helped me select some beautiful old prints dating from just before the Meiji restoration).

Not all was sweetness and light. By the fourth day of the Tokyo Conference, I began to realize that, far from having come closer to mutual understanding, I was only becoming aware of how little the Americans and the Japanese had really communicated. Perhaps, if the Conference had lasted ten days or a month, there might have been a meeting of minds. I was at times so irritated and furious at our hosts that I hardly knew what to do. They had a habit of making political decisions that involved the American delegation without consulting the Americans. I was so angry at one point that I walked off the platform at the final and concluding session of the conference. That was rude, and I hope my rudeness can be forgiven. But I cannot say I feel very guilty about it—sometimes rudeness is also a kind of communication, and, even if it only communicates the failure to communicate, that is far better and more helpful in the long run that the illusion of agreement and understanding.

If the Japanese baffle me, I suspect we may be just as inscrutable to them. Beneath their polite manners, there must have been times when they were as irritated with us as some of us were with them. But, if I mention my anger, it is partly in order that my favorable impressions may seem more believable and not read merely as a gesture. I took my last good-bye with tears in my eyes. I do not know if any of the Japanese remember even what I looked like (perhaps all Americans look alike), nor do I have any idea what they felt about me. And, if I refer to "me," rather than to "us," it is because I am a man of the West; it is because I cannot hide how deeply and personally I was moved by the visit to Japan; and it is because my heart opened to Japan and the people I met there and, like any lover, it is important to me how I am thought of. And I shall never know.

(1966)

Two Statements

Those of us who join today in burning our draft cards will be called traitors by some, Communists by others, and "misguided" by almost everyone, including those good friends of ours in the liberal community who agree with our opposition to the war in Vietnam. Yet I hope that some small part of what motivates us may be communicated to our fellow citizens, even in this time of tragedy and of war hysteria.

And what I most want to communicate is that, by burning my draft card, I am trying to live by the values this nation has taught me. I am trying, in the clearest way I can, to act as a responsible American citizen, true to the deepest and best traditions of this nation of which I am so deeply a part.

My act is not directed against the American people but against the present administration. It is the government that is un-American in its actions, and it is the government that would subvert our traditions. As an American citizen, I have no choice but to express my opposition to that government. If I failed to do so, then I should have failed my duty as a citizen.

The present government has openly violated the Charter of the United Nations both in Vietnam and in the Dominican Republic. It has openly, repeatedly, and flagrantly violated the Geneva Accords by its actions in Vietnam. It has openly and ruthlessly violated solemn international treaties with our sister states of Latin America by its military intervention in the Dominican Republic. There is no responsible man today in the American government who would not admit, in private, the truth of these charges, no matter how strongly he might deny them in public. Our only defense is that our national interests were involved. Such a defense carries us back to the law of the jungle, moving us away from a responsible world community.

The present government has repeatedly distorted the facts about Vietnam in its statements to the American people. The present government violates the values of compassion and decency by its barbaric military campaigns against the civilian population in Vietnam.

As a child in church and in public school, I was taught that torture is wrong, that lying is wrong, that wanton violence is wrong. I was taught that aggression is wrong. I was taught that Germans committed a sin by bombing the open city of Rotterdam early in World War II. I believed what I was taught. I believe that I learned values that have merit and by which I seek to live. What can I do now about a government that condones torture, engages in lying, is proud of its violence, and is without any trace of remorse for its aggression? As an American, I must oppose that government, even if it is my own. President Johnson has destroyed solemn treaties. In response, I destroy this visible link with his government—my draft card. And, by this response, I say that the government in Washington, which orders the dropping of napalm on villages in South Vietnam, is now my enemy and the enemy, also, of every American who has not forgotten the religious and moral values he was taught as a child.

Second, I act because the values I was taught are not merely American values, but universal values, valid for all times and places. If I condemn the Communists for their murderous actions in Hungary in 1956—and I did condemn them—can I exempt my own government for its even more wanton actions in Vietnam? If I applaud those German troops who refused to obey the orders of Hitler to fire upon civilians, can I do less than applaud those American pilots who increasingly doubt that it is right to carry out orders to bomb villages which contain only civilians?

The blind and foolish men cry, "My country right or wrong," and mistake that cry for patriotism. But such men do America a great injustice. Patriotism is not measured by blind loyalty to the state, but by determined loyalty to values that transcend even the state. America was not built by conformists—by men of the timid heart, like J. Edgar Hoover, who see treason in dissent and who secretly fear the turbulence of freedom and the workings of democracy. These were not the men who rebelled against English rule. Our freedom was created for us by men with the courage to dissent, to rebel, to act as individuals. Not a single one of our freedoms was won by conformity to the will of the majority or by loyalty to the state. Every freedom we have—religious freedom, political freedom, the freedoms to speak and to write and to assemble—was a freedom won by solitary men or small groups of men who risked their own comfort and, in some cases, their own lives to oppose the majority when they felt the majority was wrong or to oppose the state when they felt the state was wrong.

It is to keep faith with these men who won our freedom that I burn my card. We are not the traitors. The traitors are those who preached peace, who were elected on a platform of peace, and who, then, made war. They are the ones who weaken the democratic process by making a mockery of it. They are the ones who would cruelly waste American and Vietnamese lives solely in order to save face and to avoid admitting their Asian policy was wrong to begin with. In the years to come, long after American troops have been withdrawn from Vietnam and long after the current hysteria has died away, historians will wonder why the American people allowed Johnson to remain in office so long without impeaching him. They will wonder why the senators and congressmen were silent when the President was so clearly wrong, both morally and politically. And, in that day to come, the honor of America in these sad hours will not prove to have been defended by the J. Edgar Hoovers or the William Buckleys in our midst. The honor of America will rest upon those of us who resisted what was evil in order that our own sense of justice could survive and in order that our nation would not be entirely dishonored by silence. It is a sad thing that a man must risk his freedom in order to defend it, and I wish I did not feel the risk was necessary. But, in taking this risk, I do so not as a brave man, which I am not, but as an American who knows that he can only keep faith with his country by keeping faith with himself.

Therefore, we stand firm in our resistance to this government in order to be loyal both to those moral and religious values that transcend all national boundaries and loyal also to this culture, this nation of peoples, this vast land, America.

(1965)

*   *   *

When I was working over ideas for the long introductory essay, Bill Weatherby, of Praeger, suggested I go into some personal detail, some discussion of how an American without a radical family background developed into a radical. What were the causes of that shift; what price have I paid or what penalty have I incurred for taking a radical position? I've heard these questions often enough from others so that, although the very asking of them baffles me, I'll deal with them as directly as possible.

One's life and being are reflections of the world external to oneself. The times, the climates, and events one lives in and the personalities one encounters become the dies that stamp out our uniqueness.

I became a radical because my father is a Republican, and that rebellion, which is generally necessary so that we can become ourselves, had, logically, to be a rebellion "to the Left." If my father had been a Communist, I suppose I might now be writing a column for the *National Review*. I became a radical because of Alvin Ailey, who introduced me to the works of Kenneth Patchen and to an appreciation of modern dance, and who was who he was where he was, on May 25, 1949. I became a radical because of Margaret Feigin, nee Phair, who invited me to that party in Ocean Park (in 1949? in 1950?) and, when I came, timid and trembling, to the door of what I knew would be a wild bohemian, free-loving, radical party whose guests would laugh at me, she came forward at once, took my six-pack of cokes in one hand and said, "David, I'll just put these in the refrigerator so they'll stay cold, but would you mind standing here for a while and welcoming people as they come in? Some of those who are coming are very shy and don't really know anyone"; which evening was my introduction to Bohemia, a state of mind better than any fraternity, more exclusive, with remarkably little in the way of sex or liquor (and, in those days, no pot at all) but that was into poetry, art, writing, plays, and politics, and accepted me as part of its inner ruling circle there in our kingdom by the sea. And a special debt of thanks to 132½ Ashland Avenue for being cheap enough for me to rent. I mourn you now, torn and forgotten, your termites buried beneath tall new buildings. You, in whom Stan and Betty lived, and then Margaret, and then I; you, with your paper-thin walls and calcimine paint; and the landlords, Mr. and Mrs. Bialey, living in the front house while we had the alley view. 132½ Ashland, I salute you, the only house, I'm sure, that ever got put on a black list by the UCLA student government.

And I am a radical because of Vern Davidson, who taught me half of everything I know about practical politics; who was always on an ego trip, pouting if he wasn't the leader, commanding our affection and communal attention as he led our little YPSL (Young People's Socialist League) into the mysteries of Luxemburg, Lenin, Debs, Marx and into that blessed, fraternal, half-Yiddish-speaking local of the Socialist Party in Los Angeles. And I am radical because of Bill and Mae Briggs, Charlie Curtiss, Harry Siitonen, Ernestine Kettler. (Would you mind very much, m'lords and ladies, if I were to say I love you?).

And because of Marsha Berman, whom I first met at a wild New Year's Eve party at 132½ Ashland, in 1951, on a night when everyone was discovering who they were (Marsha still denies all knowledge of her insightful conversation that night). And Harvey Berman, who managed the Stumptown Players up near Russian River, a UCLA group that included Carol Burnett. A carload of us went up—Marsha and Nadina and the Blatt brothers and, I think, Margaret—driving the long hours from Los Angeles, loaded with food from Mrs. Berman that her son shouldn't starve. By the time we got to Russian River, we had eaten most of the cakes and pies and chicken so that, after the show, when Harvey asked us to the cast party, I was the only one who said yes at once, even though we had eaten all the food, because theater people are the masks of God. It was a great party. And Marion Rothman, your voice warm as honey, your laughter so mysterious, pacing my little shack along with the most difficult and complex Edouard de Laurot, the two of you translating some new play by Sartre.

And Nadina Wilson, nee Weiner, and her father, Abe, for introducing me to the works of Henry Miller when, having been bored with the *Tropics,* I was about to give up and, except for him, might never have read *The Smile at the Foot of the Ladder.* And the Rosner sisters, particularly Phyllis and Bobbie, and the Blatt brothers, particularly Jerry and Jonny, and Mrs. Rosner, for her wonderfully acute observation of William Buckley: "That man! He looks like he's got a fly up his nose!" And Sandy, who used to share my 132½ address on weekends for reasons I've forgotten and who was innocent in a helpless way that betrayed her, and she has survived—and peace, Sandy.

To Rex and to Barbara and to their first son, Peter, who, being a teenager, reminds me I am no longer a student. To Ben Jaxon, now, God help me, dead two years, for introducing me to modern jazz and for being one of several doors into that strange little community of delinquents in Pasadena, students who, in an impossible time and in an impossibly stuffy city, dared to be wonderful and radical. To Dug Pomeroy for many things, among which was introducing me to the music of Bessie Smith, who shall live forever. To Glenn Smiley, for allowing me to make mistakes, which is the only way I can learn.

To Rina Garst, nee Winakour, radical from the beginning, part of the scene from the early years into today, and to Jim, whom I barely knew at UCLA and who, after an extra drink, talks politics with the lyric power of Dylan Thomas. To Ben and Ron who have taught me a great deal, perhaps without knowing it;

to Bonny Golightly; to Julia Newman and Betty Berenson and memories of Ocean Park and San Francisco. To Allen Ginsberg who was a folk hero to me before we ever met. To Jack Armstrong, alias the Blue Boy, alias his true name, which we all forgot, who gave me the confidence to be phony. To Bayard Rustin, who made me believe in nonviolence despite my cowardice, and who transmitted a set of values so effectively that, when my teacher swerved from his own path, I did not. Bayard, who taught me everything about politics that Vern had not and who was, more than any single person, the hero in my life.

To A. J. Muste who, morally and intellectually, did more to put my head where it is now than any other single person.

To the Black Cat, the "T.V.," and the Captain's Inn, each for good reason, and to Aggie Dukes, whom I listened to but never really met, who could sing and perform four-dimensional rings around Elvis Presley.

To the New Testament, particularly the first three gospels. To Marx, to Lenin, to Luxemburg, and to Debs very much. To Lincoln Steffens for his *Autobiography*; to *The Grapes of Wrath*, which I read at the right time for me. To the Bhagavad-Gita, the Upanishads, the Dhammapada, and the Tao Teh-ching. To Freud, Jung, Adler, and, particularly, Otto Rank and his last work, *Beyond Psychology*. To Gandhi. To Paul Goodman, for making anarchism seem reasonable; to Igal Roodenko, for making vegetarians seem human.

To *The Memoirs of Hadrian,* which I found on a subway bench late one night, took home, and, thus, became involved in the endlessly fascinating study of history.

To my parents, for having taken the risk of having children and for loving them. To Dad and Grandmother, for serving as strong but gentle elders. To my brother and sister and to the many very close friends I have not named because this is not a dedication but a recounting of influences.

What price have I paid, looking back at forty, for being a radical? None that I can think of. There is little to comfort a man when he dies, but, when that time comes, I will be lucky enough to know that I had a small piece of the action. I do not always act wisely, but I act. Even if all my actions are wrong, they fulfill the imperative need of men to attempt to be meaningful.

No, in terms of paying a price, I am not the man to talk with. Talk with Ralph DiGia or Jim Peck or Igal Roodenko—they are the ones who paid a price, and they are the only ones who can tell you if it was worth it. Talk to the youth as they come out of prison, having suffered jail for refusing to murder, and ask if the price was worth it.

It is perhaps a reflection of Otto Rank's influence on my thinking that I am less concerned with the Freudian question of exploring how one arrived at *this* point in time and space (though I've just spend several hundred words with that game, so that no one would think me evasive) than to discuss how we move from *here* to *there* and which of many possible "theres" we shall opt for. Marx observed that, before him, philosophers sought to explain the world, while he would seek to change it.

Each of us has a life. It is all we really have, and that far too briefly. So long as that life is not lived in such a way as to hurt others, let us rejoice in each other that we have these lives and the living of them, whether as carpenters, teachers, actors, fishermen, and let us live those lives rather than question them too closely. It has been said that the unexamined life is not worth living. However, it is true that the life endlessly examined also ceases to be worth living.

There is, of course, a time when we must ask, "How did you get here?" And that is when we are dealing with dangerous antisocial behavior, such as displayed by heroin pushers, murderers, and men like Robert McNamara or Attorney General John Mitchell. We must find out what went wrong with these individuals so that, hopefully, we can limit the problem of antisocial behavior.

I think, as a radical, that I would like to turn the question "Why Am I a Radical" completely around. Looking at the wars of our time, at the poverty, the racism, the hideous level of anxiety, I would ask, Why aren't you—every single one of you —radicals? It is the only position that makes sense today; it offers us the only hope of survival. The radical has nothing to explain. It is the "silent majority" that must account for itself.

(1970)

III
If There Is an Invasion, There Is Also a Resistance

"I suggest we close ranks with the youth, join them in resisting the invasion and in turning it to our advantage."

The Hipster General Strike

Earlier this year, I read in the papers about a young fellow, originally from Trinidad, who celebrated his high school graduation by organizing a steel band and leading it through the streets somewhere up in the Bronx. After attracting several thousand curious bystanders, he was finally stopped by the police and hauled into court, where he explained that street bands were an old and honored custom in Trinidad. The judge, as I recall, let him off with a sharp admonition against further public joy in the streets of our city.

The incident set me to thinking. I had once heard Allen Ginsburg quote Plato to the effect that "when the mode of music changes, the walls of the city shake." Surely the walls of this city should be shaken. We live in a city where the poor are driven legally from their homes to make way for the apartments of the wealthy; a city where the lives of our youth are so bleak and devoid of purpose that they turn to gang war and brutal murder; a city where a man who has a passion for concrete seems to be an immortal and immovable part of the city administration; a city that serves as home for Madison Avenue and the scandals of TV; a city where a man can lie dying on our streets and no one will stop. A city, in short, from which justice has taken a holiday and compassion is on an indefinite leave of absence.

Those of us who are committed to politics as a method of saving man from himself have done little except lose ground less rapidly to the bulldozers manned by Robert Moses. Even while we were turning the Arch in Washington Square into a monument of a community victory, we saw "progress" advancing all round us, resulting in the destruction of old buildings where at least some of us could afford to live, and the construction of grand new buildings where none of us can afford to live. The story is much the same throughout the city.

While as a square and a socialist (I fear the terms are synonymous), I must continue the struggle by political means, I cannot help contemplating what would happen if "the mode of music" changed—if the beats among us employed some kind of nonpolitical action against City Hall.

I know the beats are alienated from politics, but they have a special interest in the present situation. It is commonly rumored that the coffee shops are gathering places of degenerates, where poetry is peddled openly—even to minors. It is conceivable that, as part of the "morality drive" recently launched by the police, they might close down all the coffee shops in town, thus depriving several dozen poets of what little income they now earn from public readings to the square tourists (who else can afford the coffeehouse price for a cup of coffee?). The folk singers and bongo drummers also have reason for alarm: The cops have been stricter than usual this past summer in dealing with music in Washington Square—even, at one point, arresting that grand fellow who strolls around the park on summer evenings playing what I believe is a mandolin and singing in Italian. And now, finally, the trumped-up and much-trumpeted narcotics raid in the Village makes it clear the beats are scheduled for transformation into public scapegoat number one. Scapegoats, no matter how nonpolitical their natures may be, have an inevitable personal interest in politics.

How could nonpolitical folk such as the beats fight City Hall? May I suggest for consideration the old anarchist concept of the general strike. Why not? If one little steel band can snarl traffic in the Bronx, I am sure the hipsters, acting in concert, could call a tumultuous general strike against City Hall. Having broached the subject, let me be so bold as to discuss it briefly. I realize winter is a poor time for street demonstrations, but, since some preparation would in any case be required, perhaps the idea could germinate through the winter, like some strange seed, bursting into glorious bloom with the first warm day of spring.

I would urge the poets in particular to begin now, to conspire together in various cellars about town, fashioning exciting new visions and drafting incomprehensible manifestoes for the occasion. Artists will, of course, cooperate by making posters and banners inscribed with cabalistic signs and stirring slogans. Let the Zen hipsters use the cold months of snow in dedicated contemplation, so their navel forces will be in perfect readiness for the occasion.

Tempting as it might be to make Rockefeller Center or the Time-Life Building the focal point of the strike, I think the issues will be clearer if action is concentrated on City Hall. In any event, City Hall is logical as being closest to the Village, where, as I understand from the daily press, the beats all live.

Perhaps it would be wise, the night before the General Strike, to have small beat groups scatter through the city, pasting up manifestoes. Then, on the appointed day, events can begin with a motorcycle corps roaring in from the far reaches of the Bronx, from Long Island, from New Jersey, and, by ferry, from Staten Island, scattering leaflets on their way. Harlem, which is born hip, would swing down in a mighty march, augmented by roving bands of boppers from Spanish Harlem, who would have sheathed their weapons in honor of the occasion. I would suggest that a skiffle group start at 59th Street and jazz its way down Madison Avenue, preaching great New Orleans truth into every door and window of that sad, tense street.

Meanwhile, special contingents would be gathering at every coffee shop in the city, each such contingent to be led by a poet and two bongo drummers. Man, in my mind's most inner eye, I dig that sound as it rocks down the great tenement avenues!

These groups then, finally, sustained and inspired by magic horns of jazz, the hip population of our city would march seven times around the City Hall while we stand by the hundreds of thousands to watch. Perhaps—just perhaps—the walls of indifference would crumble, and injustice fall broken to the ground. Perhaps Wagner, dressed in his usual confusion, would flee. Perhaps Moses would agree to be sheathed in concrete and set in Central Park as a monument of some kind or for pigeons to breathe on. De-Sapio, being a shrewd man, would doubtless take off his dark glasses and join the line of march. And, thus, at last, the back of the Tammany Tiger would be broken.

Alas and unfortunately, this is all nothing but fantasy. I'm sure the beats would be no more effective with their general strike than we politicos have been with our general elections. Still—they might be more interesting.

In any event, having spoken my piece, I am now waiting for the first warm day of spring.

(1959)

The Bomb in the
Brooks Brothers Suit

There are ways in which Soviet and American society increasingly resemble one another. Both are highly industrialized; both have subordinated human values to technology. Both have secret-police agencies and, at times, have used prison to silence the opposition. But prison has never been widely used as a political weapon in the United States except during war, and the slave labor and mass executions of Stalin's period have largely been abolished in contemporary Soviet society. The usual punishment —even for such wily old Stalinists as Molotov—is simply removal from office and loss of status. In the United States, we employ black-listing. Both societies are governed by men who may (or may not) have the real interest of their people at heart, but who who have demonstrated a disregard for the meaning of truth similar to that found in *1984*. Both societies have their crackpot fringe—here, it consists of groups like the John Birch Society and Young Americans for Freedom, whereas, in Russia, it consists of the remnants of the Stalinist leadership. Both societies are essentially bureaucratic, and the means of production both here and in the Soviet Union have been largely collectivized. (The Soviet economic system works somewhat better than ours, because their bureaucracy is centralized, whereas ours is divided among several major corporations, and the Russians have accepted the need for economic planning which we still largely reject—but the effect on the individual worker is much the same: He finds himself alienated from an industrial process directed from distant sources, a process that directs his life, but over which he has little, if any, real control.)

In both nations, the mass of people are manipulated and persuaded rather than directly coerced. Most Americans honestly believe they are free and that they live under a democracy and have a free press. Most Russians believe they, also, are free. The complex of forces responsible for maintaining this set of illusions, for manipulating and persuading the masses, is centralized in the Communist Party in the Soviet Union. Our counterpart to the Communist Party is Madison Avenue. When I say "Madison Avenue," I refer to the whole complex of opinion-makers and communications experts, ranging from the public relations men working for the Pentagon, through the Rand Corporation, down to "Madison Avenue" in its visible, geographic form in midtown Manhattan.

What is significant is that, in both nations, there is an increasing sense of alienation and betrayal felt by elements *within* this ruling bureaucracy. There is a disaffection and dissent that is semi-secretly expressed among small sections of the educated middle class both here and in the Soviet Union.

Most Russians do believe in Khrushchev, just as most Americans do believe in Kennedy. But most is not all. And that small section that disbelieves, that feels the Emperor is, in fact, naked, forms a kind of Underground running through the upper levels of American society. It is to this Underground that I address myself. I write to those who, even in the absence of effective democracy, retain their personal sense of freedom. It is an interesting commentary on the state of our society that, to speak to this Underground, I choose *The Village Voice*, which ostensibly has nothing to do with politics beyond the DeSapio level, and appears, at first glance, as a hip sheet for would-be beats. But, in fact, the *Voice* is a journal for the American Underground. (It even has an occasional department entitled "Notes to the Underground.") There is no other publication through which I could hope to reach those I have in mind. The publications of the radical movement—*Liberation, Dissent, New America, I. F. Stone's Weekly*—not only have smaller circulations but also are largely directed toward the converted. The unhappy fact is that, while the pacifists and democratic socialists have kept alive certain moral concepts about man and his society, our publications are too small to serve as a forum through which to address the general public, and our organizations are too weak to serve as the center for an effective opposition to the system.

The thing that excites and encourages me is that, despite the weakness of the organized Left, there remains a pervasive and healthy sense of heresy and subversion just beneath the seeming conformity of our society. And, if I mourn because I write publicly to persons whose names I do not know, I am comforted to think how much more must the various inquisitors in our society mourn, and how great must be their bafflement and confusion in trying to trace down and smash a conspiracy that, because it does not exist in organized form, is largely safe from investigation and cannot be smashed. In one respect, the American Underground is the perfect underground—there are no membership lists to be revealed, no files to be seized, and no leaders to be jailed.

Who is the Underground? Are you in it? This private letter, publicly published, is addressed to those who wept openly when Budapest fell to Soviet tanks and who wept again with unspeakable shame, when Stevenson rose in the U.N. to declare the United States was in no way involved in the military intervention in Cuba; who were shocked at the executions of both Nagy and Lumumba; who believe in freedom to travel into Berlin but put free access to Jackson, Mississippi, a little higher on the agenda of action; felt America's errors did not justify the crime of Soviet resumption of testing, nor the Soviet crime serve as an excuse for the American resumption. I write to that significant handful of Americans who do not believe freedom can be defended by mass murder through nuclear war, to those who have realized they can pass a necessarily harsh judgment on American society and on American policy without feeling some confused intellectual obligation to become pro-Soviet in the process.

Or, to put it another way, I write to those who realize Jules

Feiffer and Bill Mauldin are more significant than Herblock, that Joe Barry and Murray Kempton are more vital than Max Lerner. I write to those who are not afraid to express their doubts about orthodox liberalism. (The bankruptcy of orthodox liberalism, and its amoral pragmatism, is great enough that one must mourn the fact that the honorable tradition of Robert Taft is now "represented" by such a collection of Edwardian catholics, political degenerates, and ideological incompetents as is grouped around the *National Review* and Barry Goldwater. There is so much that an authentic conservatism could have contributed to American life!)

This "disorganized disaffection" of which I write—and to which some of you belong—is expressed at different levels. Sometimes very quietly, as when one of the top television stars wrote to a pacifist organization sending a large check and asking for a hundred copies of one of our more radical pamphlets to "mail out to some of my friends in the TV and communications field," or when one of the box-office Hollywood star made a substantial contribution to a pacifist publication, or when one of the "sick" comedians sent a wad of money to one of our radical civil rights projects. These things sound minor, but they aren't. People with money don't give it to radical groups lacking tax exemptions. They give to respectable groups like the NAACP or SANE or the Quakers. It has been a long time since people in key positions knocked at our doors with money in their hands.

The Underground has a special nihilist branch centering around *Mad* magazine. (Did you really think *Mad* was just a comic book?) The "sick" comedians reflect this Underground, appeal to it, and, in one case at least, speak directly for it—one of the most brilliant of these comedians is simply a radical, belonging to no organization, who is using humor as a tool by which to help screw up the Establishment. It is an important (if sad) commentary on our democracy that political protest is now channeled through comic books and night-club comedians. What is even more significant is that protest sells. There is the joke that "rebellion is a hot item" on Madison Avenue. Granted—but *why?* Rebellion "sells" because there is a market for it—and that is what is significant, no matter how cynical is Madison Avenue's use of nonconformity ("Brand X" cigarettes) to help sell products.

There are two other examples of this Underground worth mentioning. One is the Committee for a Sane Nuclear Policy. SANE is a moderate group—too moderate in fact—but it was also the first widespread and open opposition to the arms policy of the U.S. Government. And who in New York is active in it? Young middle-class professionals, people from Madison Avenue. Here are people who, day after day, play roles in the "persuasive machinery" that keeps the system going—people who polish the mirrors that sustain the illusions—who then, at night, come to committee meetings and throw themselves into activity in opposition to the very machinery that employs them. The same men who spend their daytime hours grinding out copy for the Luce machine spend their evenings busily refuting it.

The other example is the "reform movement"—broadly considered. In the 1960 campaign, those of us in the Socialist Party mistakenly assumed the left-liberals and "independents" would go through the usual ritual of saying, the day before the nomination, that, unless Stevenson got it, they wouldn't vote. Then, two weeks after the nomination, saying that, after all, this was a real world we live in, and what was the alternative to Kennedy? And, then, six weeks later, saying that, next to Roosevelt, Kennedy was the best man we ever had, and that America's whole future, indeed the future of all mankind, depended on Jack's making it. Radicals have, after all, watched liberals go through these gyrations every four years for as far back as we can remember. But 1960 was different. There was a ragged, but determined segment of independents who never fell in line at all, and others who had to be whipped into position and whose conscious doubts and angers were expressed right up to and including the day of voting. It was the incredible year for slogans like "Vote NO for President," "Keep the White House Empty Another Four Years," or—best of all—for wearing plain white buttons, without any name or symbol.

The same surge from the Underground can be seen in New

York, in the recent primary, where it took two forms—those who finally backed Wagner only in order to smash DeSapio and those who refused to buy Wagner under any conditions. One finds similar expressions of the Underground in California politics and in Oregon and Washington.

I have also noted that an increasing number of those taking part in the mass demonstrations against Civil Defense stand on the edges of the crowd a little proudly, a little shyly, dressed in Brooks Brothers suits, clean shaven, and bearing themselves with the wistful dignity of Madison Avenue. There are other manifestations worth a note in passing—the occasional show on TV which slipped past somebody, the bit on the radio which is unexpected, the quiet news from some of the major book publishers that, if anyone on the Left can get together a book, they will publish it, the formation of "Committees of Correspondence" among academic figures.

The Underground comes to the surface briefly, somewhat like a Poznan riot, during something like the Freedom Rides when suddenly all kinds of nonpolitical people find themselves in jail and thousands of other nonpolitical people find themselves throwing cocktail parties to raise funds to get more nonpolitical people down to Jackson, because a symbol has been raised, and we have glimpsed some meaning in the chaos and wreckage of American democracy.

And because this Underground is not Communist, or pro-Communist, or Communist-inspired, the Establishment doesn't know how to handle it. The best that the worst among us could do in attacking the Freedom Rides is admit defeat—as Senator Eastland did when he was reduced to the pathetic level of charging on the floor of the Senate that the Freedom Rides were Communist-inspired and for proof pointed to the battered face of Jim Peck, the pacifist who was smashed by Southern hospitality on the first such journey. Those who know Peck's record on Communism know how frustrated Eastland must have been to level that charge against him: William Rusher, of the *National Review,* lacking senatorial immunity to libel charges, had to content himself with calling the Freedom Riders "hoodlums," which says far more about the moral level of Rusher and the *National Review* than about the Freedom Riders.

As someone who is part of the organized radical movement, I have a better right than most to be discouraged—for I know how weak our organizations are. But I am not as discouraged as many others, because I know how widespread is the alienation moving through American life. In one respect, the Birch Society is absolutely correct—subversion is rampant at the highest levels of our society. But what threatens the *status quo* in this country— as it threatens also the *status quo* in the Soviet bloc—is not some alien conspiracy, but a sense of human values, obstructed but not quite silenced, repressed but not yet destroyed.

At the beginning of this article, I pointed out the existence of an American Underground—a profound disaffection and alienation moving through the groups that manipulate and control our society, the groups that can broadly be termed "Madison Avenue." There are two questions that come to mind immediately. First, do we *need* an Underground? After all, we "never had it so good," so why gripe? Second, what is the basis of the Underground—where are its roots in our society? Is there any chance at all of the Underground affecting the course of national policy, or is it instead a last gasp of democracy, a kind of rear-guard action before we pass blissfully into the total garrison state and, thence, into fiery oblivion?

Do we need an Underground? I suppose one's view depends on whether one is a *Time-Life* reader, in which case we know that not only are things damn good, but we also know that, when the war does come, we'll only lose 8 per cent of our population. (A reader of the "new, daring, outspoken" *Satevepost* would arrive at the same conclusion; the first "new" issue contained a piece by Herman Kahn telling us we really shouldn't worry so much about war.) On the other hand, anyone with the least information is aware we are in a hell of a mess, that an absolutely terrifying shift of power toward the Pentagon is taking place behind the scenes, that we are continuing to lose the cold war, and that the likelihood of war breaking out in the next ten years (or ten days) is probably greater than the chance it will not break out. And, Luce notwithstanding, we shall be lucky if 3 per cent survive.

Given a social crisis and the need for social change, those of us trained in Marxism have looked for some "motor force" within society—some group that was willing to support drastic social change because it had more to gain than to lose from such an upheaval. Traditionally, labor filled this role in American society. But, today, labor is part of the *status quo*. Its wages are fairly high, and its leaders are men of prestige. Old Sam Gompers's dinner pail is full. On the single, dominant issue of our time—preventing war—the trade-union movement stands somewhat to the right of the late Mr. Dulles. Even the 7 per cent rate of unemployment has failed to push labor toward radicalism; and, in fact, it is precisely this continuing rate of unemployment that keeps labor in line, because a very large percentage of labor is involved in arms production and, therefore, has a vested interest in a *status quo* that includes massive preparations for nuclear war. In a situation where 7 per cent of the labor force is already out of work, labor can hardly afford to demand that military spending be cut.

Thus, the old Marxist motor force has run down and stopped— or, in some cases, following the leadership of men like Jay Lovestone and George Meany, it is running in reverse. Orthodox Marxists, who have delayed or sidetracked so many revolutions by their orthodoxy, continue to prod and kick labor, since, over 100 years ago, Marx gave the word that labor was the motor force, and he isn't around to revise his theories. Unfortunately, while labor does remain important, crucially important, it is not only tied to the *status quo*, but it continues to shrink in size as automation takes over.

And yet the Marxists are basically right: Society doesn't change simply because it should; social change requires a motor force, a dynamic, of some kind. The question, then, to ask is where is the Underground coming from. If it isn't coming from labor, where is its course and what is its potential? The Underground is coming from the middle class; it is emerging from directly within the power structure itself. If this idea shocks orthodox Marxists—who probably don't read the *Voice* and so will be spared—it must be even more shocking to the middle-class readers who compose the bulk of the *Voice's* audience. "Who, me? a Revolutionist? God forbid!"

It is not because I like the middle class that I pick it as a possible force for social change. I do not like it, despite (or perhaps because of) my own reluctant membership in it. At first glance, no group in America seems less likely to push for social change than the middle class. But let's remember that, when Marx first suggested the emerging proletariat would be a revolutionary force, it seemed sheer madness. In Marx's time, the workers were disorganized, ignorant, superstitious, and more often than not they were drunk on cheap gin. They were the last place one would expect to find a social dynamic. And yet Marx was absolutely correct: Given the social conditions created by capitalism, the workers eventually organized and educated themselves, and, in Europe, they even formed their own mass political parties.

The middle class is, by its nature, insecure, threatened always with being forced back to the bottom and, yet, aspiring always to the top. As a result, it has historically found refuge in conservatism, trying to hold on the gains it won in the struggle against feudalism. It was the base for Hitler. It once backed McCarthy and today supports Robert Welch. It listens to Fulton Lewis, Jr., and donates money to Young Americans for Freedom. It belongs to the American Legion and wants to invade Cuba. It thinks Goldwater is sexy.

And yet the middle class has another side. The increased leisure and education of the middle class, the very fact of its emergence from the relative anonymity of the working class, has historically confronted its more sensitive members with the problem of self-discovery. If it has served as the bastion of orthodoxy, it has also provided the recruiting ground for revolutions. If it has given us *Life* magazine it has also given us *The Village*

Voice. Its troubled conscience finances and staffs the ACLU. It gives money to the NAACP and SANE. It wishes it could want to have a Negro live next door. It goes on Freedom Rides.

Most important of all, in the present situation, the middle class is educated. It is trained to act in the present on the basis of what it wants to happen in the future. The working class spends its money. The middle class banks it. Education by itself does not produce miracles—one has only to compare Bertrand Russell and Sidney Hook to realize what different conclusions brilliant minds can reach. And, in one sense, we in the middle class, because of our rational education, distrust our intuition and try to rely upon logic, rather than combining the two in a subtle relationship.

And still . . . and still the "mind"—in the total sense of logic and intuition—may prove to be a motor force. Our minds created the Bomb. Can they now create the social *and economic* conditions required to abolish the Bomb? Historically, people have been moved to action when they were uncomfortable—specifically when their stomachs were empty. A revolution represents the triumph of sheer physical need over the inertia natural to man, over man's inherent resistance to social change. Is it possible that man may have a moral hunger which can drive him to action? Is it possible that men who are not hungry, who are well clothed, socially secure, and emotionally stable, may yet —incredibly—risk a great deal, including their security and freedom, simply because of a moral hunger and alienation from the organized social evil of which they find themselves a part?

Ordinarily, the answer would be no. But these are not ordinary times. It is the future of the race that is imperiled by our smugness and conformity, and no group is in a better position to see this than our educated middle class. Can we apply our training and realize that our present comfort is an illusion if we look ahead a bit in time? It is impossible to answer this question yet. It is true that a small handful of the middle class is shifting from vague liberalism toward a radical break with the present social system, but how far this will extend I don't know.

My objective in writing this article is partly to point out to the members of the Underground that, in fact, the Underground does exist, and by stating publicly a silent fact thereby to reinforce every member of the Underground, leaving him feeling less alone, less isolated and frustrated. I've written in an attempt to strengthen the will to action of those who are in a position to throw a monkey wrench into the war machine. History and politics is a funny combination of material conditions plus the will to act—the intervention of the nonmaterial into history. Marx could not have had an effect on history if he hadn't been basically right when he said the working class would transform society. At the same time, if Marx had not announced this fact and codified it into *Das Kapital*, it would have taken the workers much longer to exercise their power. They had power, true, but they did not use it until someone pointed it out to them.

What I am suggesting is obvious: The men and women who compose "Madison Avenue" have enormous power if they are prepared to use it, if they are prepared to act seriously. One can evade the situation and escape responsibility with analysis or alcohol, with orthodox religion or with mildly liberal politics (which leave us feeling clean but don't get us in any serious trouble), and yet the problem will not go away. And the problem is whether or not man is going to survive, whether life will be on a new and higher level than what has gone before or whether we are doomed to a "Soviet-American" variety of society in which we are manipulated by impersonal bureaucracies.

Finally, I have written the present article for a very practical reason. I want "Madison Avenue" to know that, for all our attacks on it—and I speak of the general radical assault on this symbol of a manipulative and suicidal society—we know we have many friends within the framework and structure of Madison Avenue. Our groups may be very small and seem ineffective. But we are not always as ineffective as we seem. Some of our leadership has a vast amount of practical organizational knowledge as well as a clear sense of political morality. Those of you in the Underground need our help just as we very much need yours. It is time and past time for an informal dialogue to begin and for the Underground to discuss the practical question of how we can transform ourselves into an open opposition to the "community of fear" that dominates this nation. Reform liberalism or personal protest or nihilism is not enough. In the time remaining, let us mobilize our morality, give it organizational form and political direction. Let the frustration of our alienation and disaffection be replaced by action. There may not be enough time left to do a job that is already terribly complex and grows more so every moment. But what a glorious fight we can make if we so choose. We shall neither run nor hide but stand our ground and fight. If you are interested, then, as the saying goes, "Our name is in the phone book . . . Give us a ring."

(1961)

The Majority Generation

I don't know when social commentators began trying to identify each new "younger generation" as it marched by, but I do
know how surprised I was, back in the early 1950's, when I was up
to my neck in radical politics on the campus of the University of
California at Los Angeles, to find I was part of the "Silent
Generation." Just after me, separated by only a year or two, came
the "Beat Generation." More recently, one has heard reference to
the "Rebellious" or the "Angry" Generation. Labels such as these
cover everything—but reveal nothing.

Let me begin with the absolute truth. And the absolute truth is
that no one understands the youth of today. We take it for
granted that their parents don't understand them. But neither, in
fact, does anyone else. Neither religious counselors nor college
deans nor psychiatrists nor even, for that matter, the youth themselves. If I, too, choose to label, the label is not one that attempts
to define the youth but, instead, defines the problem we face
when we try to put "youth" into a category. Today, we confront
the "Majority Generation." For the first time in the history of
the United States, incredible as it may seem, those under twenty-
five years of age now constitute an absolute majority of our
population.

A fact as startling as this defies all attempts to classify and categorize. The Majority Generation is a vast wave of young people that includes everyone from the Peace Corps volunteer to the heroin addict; from the High School "dropout" who has joined the army of the permanently unemployed, to the graduate student heading for a life in the academy. It is a generation that is both silent, satisfied, conformist, and obedient, and, at the same time, troubled, rebellious, impatient, confused, and alienated. Those who try to define this entire mass of young people are like blind men trying to describe an elephant.

Let me stick with that part of the elephant I know best—which is the alienated section of the younger generation. I am aware that this is only a small part of the total youth population. I know that, for every young radical whose picture makes the front page of the paper, there are a hundred young conformists whose lives flow along the well-greased tracks of normality toward the usual quiet personality disorders and tranquilized oblivion of middle age. But, granting this, it remains true that "alienated young" represent the most creative and brightest minds of the younger generation. And it is no less true that, for the past fifteen years, such alienation has characterized the best minds of the college community.

In the mid-1950's we saw the Beat Generation shock the United States by its deliberate rejection of success as a value worth striving for. The beats were saying—quite clearly, if one took the trouble to listen—that American society wasn't honest enough or human enough to make success, in terms of that society, a reasonable, decent goal. They opted for poverty, marijuana, religion, sex, books, travel, coffee shops—for everything except money, success, an expense account, and a membership in the country club. They went even further—by their refusal to engage even in protest political action, the beats were saying that, in their view, American society wasn't even worth saving.

There were good reasons for this alienation. The beats reflected the age of death ushered in by Hiroshima. For the first time in the history of the world, it was possible that all mankind —everyone—would be killed. So why get hung up on things—

particularly material things? Why get married or build up a business or be socially responsible? What was the point when, somewhere out there in the mad reaches of the Pentagon or the Kremlin, some idiot was waiting for the chance to push the ultimate button.

There was also the shock of disillusionment. By 1950, it seemed that everyone had betrayed everything decent. The Church preached brotherhood, but, at 11 A.M. on Sunday morning, it was the most segregated institution in the country. The State told us (1940) that Russians were evil, then it told us (1942) that Russians were good and democratic and religious; then it told us (1947) that Russians were again evil. In 1947, the State told us that the Germans and the Japanese, who, until 1945 had been barbarians, were now, in fact, civilized. Even the radicals were compromised. The Communists had defended the indefensible when they preached—right up to the twentieth Congress and the Khrushchev speech—that Stalin was a decent man and Russia a workers' paradise.

America in the mid-1950's was a society without heroes, ruled by a President whose only visible asset was a grin, wildly arming itself in order more effectively to follow the moral Mr. Dulles to the brink of desolation. It was this lack of a future, this sense of being caught up in some massive technological-industrial machine that had somehow managed to grind up everything of value from the past and to spew it forth as highways and automobiles and TV sets and that gave promise shortly of grinding up the future as well and spewing it forth as a radioactive cinder of a planet— it was this that drove so many students, a decade ago, to seek some personal meaning in their lives, since they could find so little in their society. In a world where so much was false, they wanted the reality of knowing who they were, why they were here, why everyone had to die, and why, through it all, Eisenhower could grin. And there was no one around to provide the answers. The State was dishonest. The Church didn't believe its own sermons. The Left had forfeited its integrity.

And so they took off on their own, these lost and alienated

youth, in a desperate search for some reality in their own lives. Some, thinking orgasm might be the key to reality, explored sex. Others turned to serious—and often Eastern—religion. And it was at this period, too, that drugs first came into wide use among campus bohemians and nonconformists. I don't mean heroin, (though that is used more widely than is admitted) but marijuana and peyote and LSD—the hallucinogenic drugs. A few took these drugs for escape. Most took them because it was another way of exploring reality, of seeing the world in new and almost magical ways. The most ordinary things became transformed. A fistful of sand turned suddenly into an infinity of boulders rolling silently in the hand of a giant. The flesh of one's body becoming a strange new geography.

This was the alienation of the beats—personal, private, non-political. But, starting in 1955 and continuing to the present, a change has come over the campus. Students stopped being beat and became committed. Though they remained fully as hostile to the world of adults, rumors drifted onto campus that heroes had appeared in the outer districts. Reports circulated that, while all was truly lost, one could still take the existential path, could engage in struggle and, thus, give one's life a personal dignity. Students read about Martin Luther King. They watched the student sit-in movement begin in North Carolina. And they were fascinated by the courage, the romanticism, of Castro—the existential hero of our time.

Instead of a Beat Generation apathetic to politics, there now emerged a new generation whose alienation took new forms. Hundreds of students began drifting down to Mississippi, to Georgia, to Alabama—risking and, in some cases, losing their lives. There is, about these students, a bitterness that I have not seen before in the student Left. They are concerned with direct action —existential action—even where it may not seem politically realistic, and despite personal risks they may run. They are courageous—sometimes desperately so. And if, in this country, they support nonviolent methods, it is also true that the late Malcolm X was widely admired and outside of the United States the students think of Castro or Ho Chi Minh as their heroes.

From traveling widely on the campuses, I know how small a minority these students are in the general student population. Yet they are the largest radical student movement we have seen since the 1930's. They may be only a handful on each campus, they may be disorganized, lacking in clear leadership, terrified of elites and bureaucrats, and devoid of a guiding ideology—yet they came down in carloads, over 1,000 of them, to Mississippi last summer; they nearly closed down the University of California at Berkeley with a massive student strike in December; and, on April 17th of this year, they poured 17,000 people into Washington, D.C., to protest the war in Vietnam. No more than a few hundred of these students have affiliated themselves with the organized Communist, Trotskyist, or Socialist groups. Most of them gravitate to amorphous "frameworks of action" such as the Student Nonviolent Coordinating Committee (SNCC) which has over 200 full-time field workers (and no official membership), or to Students for a Democratic Society (SDS), a large, almost formless grouping of student liberals and radicals. They favor *ad hoc* organizations. The historic Free Speech Movement at Berkeley began as a loose grouping including everyone from Communists to Goldwaterites. They organize the "Teach-Ins" on an *ad hoc* basis, with almost no national coordination.

This generation of alienated youth has heroes. They range from folk singer Joan Baez (who refused to pay her federal income tax, because of the war in Vietnam, and who openly urges young men to refuse to serve in the armed forces) to Robert Parris of SNCC who has repeatedly risked his life in Mississippi. They respect men like Norman Thomas, Martin Luther King, Bayard Rustin, Paul Goodman, and Mike Harrington—but it is a distant respect; these men are too reasonable, too practical, and too old to serve as true heroes for this generation.

This new radicalism among students is not simply a repeat performance of the student movement of the 1930's. Those who talk darkly of Communist influence on the campus only reveal how distant they are, in years and understanding, from what really moves students. Many of these students are more radical than the Communist Party, which they tolerate but do not admire, or follow. The handful of "official" Communists left in the United States are considered personally and politically "square" by students. On the matter of sex, for example, in the old days, radicals might use it to recruit members, but the key word is that they *used* sex. It was not seen as an end in itself. In this, the Communists and Trotskyists of the 1930's were truly kin to the Puritans, who tolerated sex, because without it the race would perish, but who felt that to enjoy it was to sin. Students today think sex is its own justification. They are not hung up on questions of what is sexually moral and what is tabooed. They may even, for example, "try homosexuality" if they meet a homosexual they like, but they try it without becoming involved. (If anything, there are fewer homosexuals in the radical student community today than there were fifteen years ago, because homosexuality is not a product of sexual freedom *but of sexual repression.* Among other young Americans, where sexual repression continues and the problem of "masculine identity" is important, I think homosexuality is increasing—but not with the young militants.)

This is a generation of rebels who also insist on their right to experiment with drugs. I'd estimate that, at some larger college campuses, as many as half the students have tried marijuana, while among campus nonconformists the big thing is no longer marijuana, which everyone has tried, but the "mind-changers" like LSD. No one is likely to put this generation in harness. Not long ago, I interviewed William Epton, one of the leaders of the Progressive Labor Party—a split from the Communist Party that tends toward the Peking line and has a certain following on the campus. I asked Epton if the fact that the average age of his members was 25 didn't pose problems of discipline. Somewhat to my surprise, he not only agreed but went on to bemoan the looseness of morals today, to complain of the wide use of drugs by young people, and their casual attitude toward sex. It was clear that Epton was having a hard time bringing his young revolutionists to heel.

I don't know if anyone can control this generation of alienated radicals. Ten years ago, it was rare if a student could boast that he'd been jailed. Today, virtually all young radicals have been arrested at least once (in Berkeley during the Free Speech Movement, over 500 students were arrested in a short space of time). This is a generation that is hostile not only to the "Establishment" but to older radicals as well. And older means anyone over 25. They trust no one except themselves. They accept no ideology, choosing instead to act out an existential radicalism. I think they have the Establishment worried. The Beat Generation was fun—it made the comic strips and the TV shows. It passed into the culture, despite itself. But this generation today—the section of it that has turned to politics—disturbs us all. We do not understand it. We are jealous of their sexual mores. We are angered by their use of drugs. We are terrified by their effective use of direct action. We are dismayed to find they can't be bought off, that they can't be intimidated by jail, and that they aren't even interested in talking to us.

Perhaps our only consolation is that the United States is not alone with this problem. When Allen Ginsberg went to Czechoslovakia recently he was crowned "King of the May" by nonconformists, rebellious, and alienated students there, after which Ginsberg busily educated the enthusiastic young Czechs into all manner of "decadence" until the Czech government finally picked him up and deported him in haste to London.

Whatever else may be true of this generation of students, they are decent as well as rebellious. They may not have a clear idea what kind of society they do want, or how to achieve it, but they know what they don't want—the conformity of either Russia or the United States; the racism they have grown up with and by which they have been wounded; the false emphasis on material possessions as the criterion of success. Most American students are satisfied with things as they are and, given their way, will bring forth a computerized culture. But, if the alienated segment of the Majority Generation has anything like its way, it will produce a culture like nothing the United States has ever seen before. And that, I rather think, would be a good thing.

(1965)

In Defense of Butter

Last year, I spent two weeks with the Polaris Action project in New London, Connecticut, where pacifist youth have been swimming out to climb onto the Polaris submarines (our "fish of death" for the seas of the world) in an effort to arouse the moral sense of Americans. This is, perhaps, a lost cause, since Americans seem to have very little moral sense—or even common sense —left. But the Polaris Actionists did manage to arouse me, if not morally, for I found that to save money the project had abandoned butter for oleomargarine, whole milk for powdered milk, and—as a crowning insult—had substituted instant coffee for the real thing.

I was cheerfully told that all these things tasted at least as good as the originals. I know better, having been forced to experiment with poverty once or twice in my life and having discovered "existentially" that one can survive on plain boiled potatoes with fresh butter but that it is quite impossible to survive with margarine. Poverty is bad enough—margarine makes it intolerable. Rather than argue the case with my pacifist comrades, I simply explained that my religion requires fresh butter, whole milk, and real coffee and proceeded to add my private supplies to the communal icebox (and noted with interest that, while everyone insisted that margarine was as good as butter, no one used the margarine until my butter was gone).

Since that grim two weeks, my work as field secretary for the War Resisters League has taken me across the country and confirmed my fear that many pacifists and other radical elements in our society have a tendency to avoid good food. At one breakfast with pacifists, nothing was served but health foods—the orange juice was so thick, I think they may have ground the orange up entire to capture the vitamins. The salt they used was a healthful product, combining bananas, kelp, carrots, and alfalfa. It had a vague greenish color, and I can testify that alfalfa has an extraordinarily strong flavor.

Now I do not raise these points because I want to engage in a sectarian argument, but because the blind spot of radical pacifists in regard to food exemplifies how even the best element of our population has succumbed to the wiles of technology. It bothers me that the same people who demand moral responsibility and "human values" in our technological society, then sit down for a slice of bread spread with margarine and drink a glass of powdered milk or sip a cup of instant coffee or even (God forbid) instant tea.

My own revolt against the mechanization of my food began some years ago when I heard Henry Morgan joke about a mythical breakfast cereal known as "Fluffies," which was shot from trench mortars and which, the manufacturer asserted, was delicious when served with fresh raspberries, cream, and sugar. Commented Morgan: "Anything—even mattress ticking—would taste good with fresh raspberries, cream and sugar."

Oleomargarine, powdered milk, and instant coffee are symbols of the gradual dehumanization of our food. There are few things man can do that give him greater pleasure than preparing and eating a good meal. It is no accident that we judge how cultured a society is in part by how well it prepares its meals. Life is so short that it is close to criminal to take from it those elements that make it a richer experience. I have been told that butter is not healthy and I assume this is true, but I think I prefer living well to living long.

I suppose most readers will think I am really joking about the question of eating well. After all, what radical would seriously argue the case for butter and whole milk? But I am quite serious, and while food may seem trivial to many, it strikes me as an important symbol of what is wrong with our society. Part of our problem is our Puritan background, which helped create the industrial revolution and now leaves us peculiarly open to its unrestrained rampage through our culture. The pacifist, for example, is concerned with living a moral life, which demands that he not waste money that might be used to further many good causes. And so if powdered milk is cheap, then it should be used, and if margarine is cheaper, it becomes a moral imperative to forgo butter. This is a disturbing concept of morality, in which every moment spent viewing a sunset is time robbed from the Revolution, every penny spent on any "luxury" such as pepper is a penny stolen from the mouths of the starving children of India. Unless we are cut out to be saints, we soon find ourselves torn between enormous guilt for moments stolen here and there and pennies wasted in frivolity or, if we conserve our time and money rationally, we risk that deeper conflict of a spirit trapped by a totalitarian, essentially Bolshevik, "antihuman" ethic.

The health food addict has not—on the surface—given in to the machine, but appears to be fighting an endless struggle with it, battling against radishes grown. with "inorganic" fertilizers, pamphleteering against food additives, white bread, and so forth. But, in fact, he has adopted the values of the machines, for his prime consideration is not to enjoy his food but to consume just that food that will keep the machine of his body in good repair without regard for the rites and rituals and pleasures with which mealtime should be approached. Some of the insights of the health food addict are sound—such as eating vegetables raw or undercooked. (They taste better that way.) But, generally, a health food meal is a trial and tribulation through which only the faithful can hope to pass—and then the only reward is a sense of accomplishment, not of gastronomic pleasure.

Finally, the vast majority of Americans have been tempted by the machine on the ground that it saves time. We have, as a nation, a preoccupation with saving time, as if it were something that could be banked and then drawn against at some later date. And so the various instant foods appeal greatly to us. But, with all our rushing about, do none of us ever pause to ask what we shall do with all the time we have "saved?" Or does no one realize that there is no better way to "spend" time than in preparing a good meal?

The machines, which could be our servants, are becoming our masters. We all know this and we all say it, and then, after deploring the fact, we individually submit to it. For the sake of a few pennies or a few moments saved here and there, we are willing to impoverish our lives. We are a nation of vast wealth that seems determined to see how poorly it can live. The question for a society centered around human values is not whether powdered milk is cheaper but whether it tastes better. And if it doesn't taste better, then put the machines to work on something else and for heaven's sake take them off the job of dusting up more powdered milk. If our job as pacifists—or socialists or liberals—is the construction of a truly human society in which the individual life takes on greater meaning and in which our technology is finally subordinated to the interests of humanity, then let us strike a solid blow for such a society by setting a good table. There are so few of us seeking to humanize our society that we form a kind of Gideon's army, arrayed against the massive inertia and apathy of our times, but let us never forget the ancient maxim that an army travels on its stomach. Even a Gideon's army.

If we expect to change our society, we shall have to make some sacrifices. Let us, therefore, look upon the purchase of butter and spices, whole milk, real coffee, and unprocessed cheese as a necessary expense involved in our struggle for social sanity—an expenditure as necessary as the dues and contributions we pay into our various cause organizations. The time spent preparing good food is not wasted but is as important as the time spent at committee meetings. Gandhi had his spinning wheel—perhaps the American radical should emphasize the kitchen as a symbol of resistance to rampant technology.

In all of this, I have not touched on vegetarianism, because I have no quarrel with it. I am not a vegetarian myself, but I have always felt that the moral case against eating meat is so very strong that, if I must sin, at least I will not compound my sin by trying to defend it. I suspect that, as the sensibilities of society progress, we will eventually become a race of vegetarians. Though I think vegetarianism can be carried too far—I remember one boy, at a pacifist project, who felt it was wrong to eat anything with the *potentiality* of life, which includes nuts, grains, and beans. Somehow, he survived on a combination of powdered milk and seedless grapes—or at least he was still alive when I last saw him.

In my attack on machine foods, I want to make it clear that machines are not the real enemy. If anything, I am a genuine enthusiast of technology. The problem is that Americans have a sense of inferiority when dealing with machines. Little by little, we are giving way and the fault is ours for failing to insist upon the best the machines could offer us. In fact, I do not really care whether my food is canned, frozen, powdered, or fresh. The one and only basic question for me is—does it *taste good?* And, thus far, very few machine foods do taste good. We have simply rushed in, without waiting, and bought what the machines offered us.

In the most radical wing of the pacifist movement, a few people carry their own food with them to conferences, fearful that they won't be able to get exactly that healthy and economical combination of powdered milk, dried lettuce, and flaked wheat germ that they feel is essential. Perhaps the answer is for some of us— a kind of secret society devoted to eating foods that taste good— to devise a portable icebox into which we can pack our butter, whole milk, a small shelf of spices, fresh coffee, a few vegetables, and, perhaps, a bottle of white wine. With such a traveling case, I think I would be prepared to withstand the grimmest of radical conferences.

(1962)

Notes for a
More Coherent Article

Months ago, before this issue of *WIN* was being discussed and before the "Gay Power" street action in the Village and before the trees were cut down in Queens, I had decided, for reasons that remain as mysterious to me as the seasons, that I had to make public the fact that I am homosexual. Originally, I was simply going to "drop the remark" into a longer political article, noting that times had changed so greatly that I could deal with my own sexual life thus briefly. But things are not, after all, that easy.

The kids could not care less, either about any personal statements I might make or about this issue of *WIN*. They are neither more nor less homosexual than I recall them twenty years ago, they are just far less hung up about the matter. But, tolerant as the kids may be, they do not pay my salary at WRL, and they do not, by and large, send in the extra contributions needed to keep *WIN* going. That money comes from an older generation. Do I have the right, as a staff member of WRL and an associate of *WIN,* to threaten the public image of one of America's oldest and largest pacifist groups, or make the raising of funds more difficult for WRL and *WIN,* by a "personal honesty" of this kind? Am I not imposing upon the WRL and *WIN* a burden that it would be better I did not impose?

I have a hunch that younger people will not even grasp my

qualms at this point—*and they will be right*—for they have not yet confused a concern with honesty and directness with a concern for preserving an organization committed to honesty and directness. And so, even at this late moment, I choose not only to be more open and honest than I have been, but, to stretch *WIN* and WRL a little, also, as they are, willy-nilly, forced to deal with my "irresponsibility" on this matter.

It is not, of course, that I have been dishonest. There is not a single one of my friends who is unaware that I am queer. Nor did I ever hide that fact from the WRL staff and Executive Committee. But I held back from a public statement because (a) my private life is my own business and (b) I didn't want to hurt the organizations with which I was involved. The entire matter of my queerness would be much safer to discuss if I were not *really* queer, but neatly repressed, confessing to a life of sin buried in the past. Happily for me, but perhaps not so happily for those groups with which I am associated, I am an active, unsublimated homosexual whose private life is such that it entitles me to something close to an infinity of prison terms. I am a walking ton of potential prison terms. I come into your church to talk to your youth about morality, and they have a right to have the goods on me. If the law is no damn good (and, in this case, it is neither good nor effective—I feel no guilt at all for my sexual conduct, which is everywhere illegal except in Illinois—yet often feel tremendous guilt for being lazy, wasting time, and so forth, activities that are everywhere legal, including Illinois), let us violate it with a certain honesty. And I do not find it honest to let my personal friends and working associates know I am queer, while keeping that fact a secret from those to whom it might matter most deeply as they seek to evaluate my advice and counsel—the youth I urge on to action against this government. My life must be all of a piece, or it is shoddy.

As for the argument that every man's private life is his own to live as he chooses, I am not sure that applies to public figures, and I know it does not apply to a pacifist who believes in truth and honesty. I have to say to you, the congregation of men and women that I encounter day by day, that I will be perfectly happy to live my sexual life in secret at such time as it is legal, but it is impossible for me, finally, to continue to play a game which makes me a kind of Establishment Queer, keeping silent in public because I know I shall be left alone in private.

(These are notes: They will weave in and out. I have found myself unable to write an article on any other topic, once I had determined to write this. At first, I said I would wait until after the WRI conference was over, then I said I would just wait until my speaking trip for the AFSC was over. And now I know that I had to write this before I could write anything else. The Crazies have erupted, SDS split, the Panthers been subjected to murderous government persecution, the Middle East tottered on the brink of a new war, soldiers jam the stockades—and, yet, my head, my pen, my typewriter are stuck with this stupid, bourgeois article, which, having finally begun, has taken two weeks to complete. And, even so, it is not, at the last, an article at all. These are notes to be shared with the brothers and sisters of *WIN*. Perhaps later, I'll polish them and my thoughts and do a proper article for some magazine.)

It is hard to write this. It has become a three-Miltowns-a-day article. I find myself waking each morning at 6:00 or 7:00 A.M., caught up in dreams and occasional nightmares. To dredge into sexuality of any kind is to touch an area of guilts and loves and memories we have buried in our minds; a sea wind sweeps up from the unconscious; a night breeze wakes us from sleep.

How do I explain that I am not sophisticated, but part of Middle America; that my religious life began in the fundamentalism of the Baptist Church and the temperance movement; that I am part of that America that elected Nixon; that my grandparents, still alive, came to California from Kansas by covered wagon at the turn of the century; that my great-grandmother was an evangelist to the Mexicans, and my father and grandfather are both colonels; that I was not raised on Dr. Spock; that I am of American stock so old and proper, even in its poverty, that my late aunt Ettamae was the first of the family ever to be divorced; that no one smoked, and the family was privately scandalized because my aunt Alice and uncle Don were known to serve an occasional glass of port to friends and had once even offered it to Grandfather?

That is my own universe, where I was the first-born child on both sides of the family, destined to be all those things the first child of two large families must be, and becoming instead pacifist, socialist, and queer. That universe of childhood is light years distant, but I am bound to it by singular ties, so, when I move to make public my failure as the first-born son, my mind is caught at, snagged in a host of old guilts, of those private prayers for salvation uttered when, in my youth and confusion, I knew I found young men attractive, that I had to lay my hands on them, but could not bear to believe I was queer—those years of waiting to be 17, then 18, and then 19, because the books on sex told me my homosexuality was a phase and, at some point, I would find women attractive, but my "phase" would not pass and the horror, which I can feel even now, as I realized I *was* queer. A Baptist, first-born son, saved Christian, temperance worker for the lord, old-line American, of decent and honest parents and grandparents and great-grandparents. Queer. To put this in writing is almost to mock my ancestors, but, much more, it is to be cut off from the generations to come. Some will understand. Most will not. It is to hold onto the generations of the future, of life itself, that I accept being queer but refuse to be gay.

This issue of *WIN* will inevitably lead some to think the radical movement—or at least the radical pacifist movement—is loaded with queers. Wrong. We don't have as many as statistics say we should. On the WRL letterhead and the *WIN* masthead, there are a total of about sixty names (weeding out duplicates that appear on both lists). So far as I know, there are only three homosexuals on that combined list, which is below the national average for truck drivers, readers of *Playboy, Esquire,* and *National Review*, members of the Marine Corps, and American Legionnaires. It is just that pacifists are more permissive, making it possible for the individual homosexual to act more openly. That is, the most distant reader of *WIN* knows I'm queer, because I am admitting it in print. But who knew about Johnson's inner circle, until Walter Jenkins got arrested in a men's room? (And J. Edgar Hoover, in one of his few acts of decency and courage, sent Jenkins a bouquet of flowers as he was recovering from the event.) Who realized there were "problems" in the inner circle around Ronald Reagan, until Reagan accepted the resignations of key aides?

I am bored with these notes, with this article. It might be easier to take a small personal ad in *The Village Voice* "I am queer and, perhaps, an exhibitionist, and this ad is irrational. David McReynolds." Below my window, as I type, there is a very attractive kid of 19 wearing an army jacket and smoking a cigar.

Jn—who is in the military, may be on the edge of a crackup, has not slept with me, and has been staying at my place in the evenings when he gets off base—was sitting around the apartment in an almost catatonic state the whole of Saturday. Late in the afternoon, I told him he needed a walk and took him out. We moved up Second Avenue, past a bunch of kids painting some buildings, toward St. Marks where the Communist candidate for mayor was speaking. Then I saw a crowd gathered, not around the Communist, but around a hefty white about forty-five, well-built, most of his teeth out, and flailing the air with his belt. It developed he had come storming out of Olga's bar, after knocking her down three times, had swung into a crowd on the street, and, eventually, moved off to Seventh Street where the cops picked him up. In the meantime, I found Olga—whose bar, along with McSorley's, I count as "my bar"—standing, furious and near hysterics, talking to the cops on St. Mark's. I kept telling Olga to come back and I'd buy her a drink; the cops told her to move into the bar and they would get a description of the man; I explained to the cops I had already seen the man picked up by the cops on Seventh Street; Olga broke down and started crying, and I scrounged her kitchen, in which I'd not been before, for an old bar rag I could dampen and bring out to her. Off she went with the police, leaving me in charge of the bar. Fortunately—because it develops there is a knack to drawing a stein of beer, which I don't have—her relief bartender, who had also been out on the street, came back almost immediately. Anyway, this explains why I went back to Olga's late that night.

I had been, for dinner, at Ann Slavitt's. An elegant dinner and very nice people. I got far too drunk. Peter Kiger, who had been there, asked me on Monday if I had gotten home okay, since I had almost been falling-down drunk when I left Ann's. As a matter of fact, the rest of the evening is vague. I called Jn from Ann's, asked him if he wanted to meet me at Olga's where we did meet, and the last thing I recall is seeing two guys in the bar— one a young, white, short, nasty guy with a broken nose; the other a black guy, good-looking, to whom I said something like, "I trust you" or "I have no choice but to trust you." That is it. The next thing I know, it is Sunday afternoon, 3:00 P.M., I am home in bed, feeling all right. I get up, go into the back room to ask Jn if he wants a Bloody Mary for breakfast, I mix them up, and find out from Jn that I had invited both guys home for coffee, that Jn, myself, and the two of them had come home, I had collapsed into bed with the black guy, and, I assume, both of us passed out, while the white, who turned out to be a Marine in civvies, asks Jn how much money I've got and why don't the two of them roll me. (No money, was the answer, but Jn talked him out of it and, I gather, stayed up till 8:00 A.M. talking with the guy, when he and the black kid both finally left). Of all of this, I remember nothing. Jn said the Marine was sitting quietly on my sink, tossing one of my kitchen knives in his hand during their discussion.

By the time I pieced this all together, I felt ashamed and terrified. This is the first blackout period in many years, and the first really suicidal risk I had taken in even more years. The bad taste in my mind got much worse during the night. I woke very early Monday morning, trembling, on that brink of madness I sometimes touch, took a Miltown and tried to sleep, realized I was terrified of being awake but even more frightened of moving back into the forest of nightmares that sleep would be. Jn had left for his military base. I lay in bed, shaking, holding one of my cats when, about 8:00 A.M., there was a fumbling at the door, the lock turned and P. came in. God, I felt saved. Only those who have lain close to madness know the relief. I had not dared believe that P., who so rarely comes by, would show up. He asked if I wanted coffee. I said, no, for God's sake, just lie here with me, I'm frightened as hell, and I told him about Saturday night. The only reason I think P. and I are hooked together even against our wills is something like this: At a moment of desperate need, he comes without warning. Early this summer, I came down with a fever and, for the first time in years, was delirious, and, being delirious, I was frightened. By dawn, a heavy rain came, the sound of it merging into the delirium, and at 7:00 A.M., P. walked in the door, soaked to the skin, having decided to take a walk that particular morning, in that particular cloudburst, at that extraordinary hour. He was drenched from the rain, and I from the sweat of the fever, and he stripped free of the wet clothes and climbed into bed to hold me and, later, made orange juice.

This last is—or is it?—a foolish intrusion. Should I not know by now that P. is gone, his life safe now from me, secure, his own, and that I am really alone. Carson McCullers thought—half-correctly—that love was a process of trying to possess someone else, that the drive to love was really greater than the drive to be loved. I am no longer so sure. I know only to whom I belong, and that is more important than knowing who belongs to me. Some guy asked me the other night, as a group of us were rapping about the "problem" of homosexuality, whether guys really get involved with other guys like they do with women. Yes.

The homosexual minority is different from any other. It is a basic mistake to think of the queer as another variety of Negro, Catholic, or Jew. Other minorities are *visible*. Blacks stand out, can be segregated, kept from certain jobs. Even Catholics and Jews *choose to be identified*. We know these minorities because of which holy days they take off, which food they eat and which they forgo. Of course, Jews and Catholics *can* "pass" into the general population, and blacks cannot, but, if Jews and Catholics "pass," they have been assimilated and cease being Jews and Catholics.

Now we come to queers. Everyone—hopefully—realizes by now that most queers are not obvious. I mean, if you met Paul Goodman walking down the street, would you know, or even suspect, that he was queer? With the exception of a small handful of homosexuals, we are invisible. We are not black. We eat fish on Friday. Pork doesn't bother us. We wear no yarmulke, no cross. There is literally no personality test most of us could not pass. Therefore, we are unique as a minority. We are—in five out of six cases—absolutely normal in appearance, invisible, omnipresent, occuring in upper and lower classes, among blacks, Jews, Catholics, Puerto Ricans, and so forth. (With the exception, it seems, of the Asians, among whom I have, in this country, encountered few homosexuals.) We do not, contrary to belief, even recognize each other on the street by some secret sign. Often, it is only in the bar that we meet an old high school or college friend and turn, saying, "My God, Frank! I never thought I'd see you *here!*"

Some of the militant gay kids think the cause of queers *must* be linked with that of blacks, because "if they can cut down the blacks now, they'll get us later." Nonsense. Homosexuals have survived the most rigorous of persecutions without difficulty. It turns out we always have friends in very high places. The brotherhood touches everywhere. One supports black liberation because it is moral and right to do so, but never because these two minorities are almost the same.

Homosexuals are a reminder of the dark side in every man, the repressed parts of his psyche. We know from a study of psychology that men have homosexual drives, that these are generally absorbed into nonsexual channels, such as male friendships, men's clubs, and so on. The homosexual makes visible this hidden aspect of every man, and he is, therefore, feared precisely by those men who cannot come to terms with their own inherent sexual ambiguity.

Homosexuals do not, incidentally, represent the "feminine" in men. It is a myth that homosexuality is feminine. Homosexuals represent a wide range of male and female characteristics, not only as a group, but within each homosexual. The man who is today, in one relationship, aggressive and dominant (that is, "masculine"), may be, the next day with another partner, passive and yielding (that is, "feminine"). The reason drag queens don't convince us they are women is simply their failure to project the veiled strength that is a basic part of "womanness," just as the "bull-dyke" lesbian strikes a false note because she is too tough and misses that which is essential in the normal male—a strange, astonishing gentleness.

The normal male wants to think queers are feminine, because that reassures him of the distance between himself and the queer. The race survives and the family exists because, early on in the man's life, there is a fixation on the sexual role he will play, which is that of husband and father. Playing that role demands that most men repress other possible sexual roles. The "straight" or normal male can engage in homosexual relations only with a very feminine man—someone so obviously a faggot that the "straight" man does not feel threatened.

The homosexual minority disturbs men therefore, because it is, in a certain way, part of every man. We are not simply 10 per cent of every individual man. We may, as WASPs, hate Jews, Catholics, and Negroes, but surely not because we secretly believe we may be, or may be about to become, Jews, Catholics, and Negroes. But the queer we hate precisely in order that we not become him. Why does William Buckley so deeply fear and hate Gore Vidal? . . . (After reading their *Esquire* encounter, where incidentally, Gore Vidal copped out, I suddenly stopped hating Buckley. I realized that Buckley had destroyed himself utterly. It is not anger I feel now, but pity.)

Do we, perhaps, hate queers simply because they are "different?" May I not be making too much of the "queerness potential" in each man? No, I don't think so. Cripples are different, but we don't spit at them. Blind men are different, but we don't smash their balls in the alley.

There is a common joke (which is not, of course, a joke but a true story endlessly encountered) in the homosexual community of the handsome young sailor who was picked up by the queer, and, as he stripped off the last of his clothes before climbing into bed, he said, "I'll do anything and everything you want—only please don't kiss me, I'm not queer."

Warning: Never call a queer a queer unless you know for sure that he knows he is queer. Otherwise, he will try to kill you. One of the two times in my life I came close to being killed was when, having been involved, quite reluctantly, with an older man who had "led" all the way ("Do you mind if I take off my coat," "Do you mind if I take off my shirt," "It's hot here, don't you think, I'm going to take off my shorts—why don't you," and so forth), and sitting stark naked in a room with him, the two of us at opposite ends of the room, he had said, "Boy, wouldn't it be nice if we had a couple of broads here." I was furious, and said "What do we want women for—we are both queer." He sprang at me from across the room, hit me twice, hard, and said "You're queer, baby, you're queer. I'm not queer. You're queer, you queer faggot, and don't you ever forget it." I survived that evening only because I can run very fast.

The reason that charges of homosexuality are not used in politics, even though such charges would be effective, is simply that all sides, left, right and center, are vulnerable. During the most bitter days of the Old Left in the 1950's, the Communists called me an FBI agent, but never once did I hear them rumor that I was queer. The only group I know of, in twenty years in politics, that tried to deal with my politics by slanders on my personal life is a tiny sect of prowar ex-socialists called Shachtmanites that momentarily controls the Socialist Party. I was amused that they, of all groups, would dare to dabble, haunted as they have been by this very matter in their own organization. Max Shachtman and William Buckley would make a great comedy team, but it is a pity either of them is in politics. (This is a catty remark, but I hope I may be permitted one in the course of this article, and I could not, in fairness, do less for the Shachtmanites after all they have done for me).

It will be charged that this article is nothing but personal therapy. Of course, all life is personal therapy. Therapy is trying to come to terms honestly with reality. The only time I ever saw a psychiatrist was at UCLA where I went to the shrink and told him I had nightmares, occasional hallucinations, constant thoughts of suicide, terrible feelings of guilt about my homosexuality, and an inability to wake up on the mornings of my final exams. He said (I am *not* kidding), "Ah, yes, those are symptoms, without a doubt. But as long as they remain only symptoms, we should not worry." I have never since had any interest in seeing a psychiatrist and cannot honestly urge confused young men to visit them, though I suppose that psychiatrists cannot do much harm. A number of the psychiatrists I have known have been queer themselves; most of the rest have been crazy.

At the moment, the best science can suggest is (a) homosexuality tends to be caused by variables in the family pattern rather than by hormone inbalance or genetic factors; (b) there is no effective cure for homosexuality, nor does it seem desirable to make a neurotic homosexual into a neurotic heterosexual; (c) there does not seem to be any "neurotic homosexual pattern" that shows up on tests.

Homosexuals do not need to be forgiven. To forgive them is an insult, for it assumes that sin is involved. There is a notion in some circles that most homosexuals rather willfully "choose" to be queer, the implication being, oddly, that queerness is really more fun than straightness. Most of us didn't choose this particular bed of nails and would have preferred it otherwise. We have come to terms with it.

The tragedy with most homosexuals is that they do not trust their friends or family enough to be honest with them.

I went to sleep last night listening to a tape of Bessie Smith—Jn has temporarily fixed the tape recorder; I slept very badly, waking twice in the middle of the night and taking a Miltown. Js came by this morning, soaking wet from rain. It seems he and Rn had been up all night at a coffee shop, and Rn was still there. Js takes off his shirt, is disturbingly well built as ever, and climbs into bed while I leave for the office—he plans to sleep all day and do I have carfare for him back to Brooklyn? Js is part of a small gang of kids that hang around my place, coming by once a week or so to talk, drink, listen to records. Have I gone to bed with them? Yes, in the beginning, but time has passed, and Rn and his girl friend come by now with love beads for me, and An came over a couple of times with some airline hostess. I serve as a kind of father figure.

This article does not aim at converting anyone. In any event, one does not convert with words, nor save with laws. This article is not even an article. It is a set of notes, a statement of becoming.

One major point I had meant to make in this nonarticle is an attack on gay society. "Homophiles" and gay publications are always compiling lists—Socrates, Caesar, Alexander the Great, Hadrian, Leonardo Da Vinci, Michelangelo, Walt Whitman, and so on, who were queer. Yes, sure, and so what the hell. I can make up a list too, of A. J. Muste, Norman Thomas, Ernest Hemingway, Albert Einstein, Sigmund Freud, Karl Marx, Charles Darwin, Eugene O'Neill, George Bernard Shaw, Pablo Picasso, and they weren't queer, and so where does that leave us?

When homosexuals compile themselves into a ghetto they are sterile. The black ghetto had, and still has, tragic power, because it is involuntary, coerced from outside, and out of the rage and sorrow of what blacks faced in white America came—among other things—jazz. There is *nothing* in the history of mankind that homosexuals *as a group* have contributed. Allen Ginsberg is a poet, and his homosexuality is not central to that fact. Allen's poetry is not homosexual poetry, but the poetry of a homosexual— and there is a world of difference.

There is a boring sameness of bad taste to the writing, poetry, painting, and so forth, produced by gay society. To the degree that interior decoration is dominated by gay society, it is deadly. One can barely breathe in a living room which has just won the design prize for its too-much curtains, its utterly darling sofa with the divine little rug. To make love in it, or to die in it, is forbidden (see Kenneth Patchen's poem on this). Gay society isn't meant for living, for dying, or for creating. Do I dig gay society? Sure.

When I get tired of life and the struggle I retreat to a gay bar, secure that reality will never penetrate there.

I said earlier that every man had a queer lurking in his brain somewhere. But I did not mean that in the sense one hears it from gay society. Bar talk will persuade you that every man is queer, while the fact is that *every queer is fighting against his heterosexuality*. Women either terrify him or his relations with them must be on a very "safe" terms—I confess this is true of myself. If every man potentially is participant in a homosexual act, then every queer is potentially able to make love to a woman and is terrified of that.

Once I came home and found my roommate P. lying on the bed, naked, with a girl, also naked, not quite making love, but moving together to the music. I was not betrayed since P. never said he was queer nor that he loved me. I backed out, closed the door, went downstairs to get a pint of rum, came back, drank half of it straight down. P. and the girl were dressed by then, said hello, and went out. And, after they left, I realized what had hit me like a wave was the trauma of realizing it was the naked *girl* on the bed to whom I had been attracted. For twenty-four hours afterwards, I could, I think, have made it with any woman of any age. Heterosexuality made absolute sense to me, in thunderously clear ways, for the first time in my life.

But the days passed, the old repressions returned, and I am again a queer. Not that I didn't, years ago, make it a couple of times with women, but somehow that hadn't turned me on. Perhaps it was seeing P., whom I love, with the girl that allowed me to transfer sexuality for those few moments. I have always been sorry that I didn't, when I first came in the room, simply ask, "May I join you?"

The black ghetto is alive, even if brutalized and repressed. Life flows from it. Children are conceived in it. The gay ghetto is a voluntary separation in which nothing lives, nothing is painful or dirty or gives birth. Gay Power is a plastic flower. Gay is *not* good; it is boring. It is sick in a way that queerness is not. And, yet, I wonder if my hostility toward faggots is not a secret statement that *I* am a faggot and am holding back that element in myself.

I don't even find the gay ghetto particularly repressed or persecuted, and the cry for "Gay Power" is, in a way, an effort to draw on the strength of the blacks, and, in a way, that is good. Kids who struggle openly to be gay may find, in the course of that struggle, that their own "masculine" nature has been strengthened. I know faggot eyes too well, tragic cows seated on bar chairs, with smooth, vacant faces. They are not hunters, not in those bars. They are frightened, huddled together for strength, biting each other, turning to one another for bovine comfort. Eyes of terror, turning, watching, never focusing. Eyes without sexuality or sex. If gay power can give any inner power to those eyes, those desperate eyes that I've seen in the bars of this nation, then, okay, I'm for the slogan. But I'm not for the gay ghetto. I may visit it. I found Cherry Grove fun when I went there several years ago. Riis Park is, as they say, kicky. But, while it might be fun to visit, you wouldn't want to live there, and you don't really go there for sex.

Do I realize what I have done in this article, an article in which I have said everything except to confess I've had VD (which, incidentally, I've had, several times)? Does this mean I'm out of politics? No. I don't think so. I am betting on the kids. Almost every pacifist my age and older will be upset about this article and baffled at why I choose to write it and why—in their view—I choose to destroy myself and harm the organization. After all, leaders don't write frankly, except for Gandhi, who is dead and was an Indian and Indians don't count.

But I think those under twenty-five, if they read this at all, couldn't care less. They will, if anything, respect the honesty and the courage that went into these notes.

Look. First of all, why do we expect honesty only of poets and crackpots and misfits like Allen Ginsberg and Paul Goodman and, then, excuse the bureaucrats and politicians like myself? Why should we preach honesty but fail to practice it "in order to protect the organization." If the Aquarian Age has begun it has to liberate and touch even us.

Second, I don't believe in leadership. We need fewer leaders and more leaders. If that makes sense. I was criticized when, some years ago writing in *Liberation,* I admitted to being a coward. "Leaders," I was told, "don't admit such things." Right, I said. They don't. The point, friend, brother, sister, is that, if cowards and queers can be in the movement, so can you. If I can somehow find the courage to write this article, which is one of the genuinely courageous things I've done in my life and one of the very few things of which I am deeply proud, then why not you? The job is to open the radical movement to all of us. To normalize radicalism. To humanize resistance to inhumanity.

Do I want, with this article, to help liberate the closet queens? In part, yes. They are terrified, and I would like them to risk telling their parents (who probably know), their associates, their friends. But only in very small part is the closet queen the person in whom I am interested.

I don't want to see every queer in the theater, in publishing, in the military, and so forth, announce themselves tomorrow, because the problem is elsewhere. I am concerned with the 15-year-old boy who may be queer and terrified of it. It is desperately important that he has relatively masculine models, such as Paul Goodman, to reassure him that queerness is not disaster. But I am equally concerned with the 15-year-old boy who is *not* queer but might be driven into it because he grooves on a certain guy. Bisexuality is not homosexuality. He should trust the beauty of his own instincts.

I want older men, now raising sons, to be honest and say "By God, he's right—there was a guy, years ago, in high school, and we fooled around a little, went everywhere together, and then his family moved away, and I met Karen. It's been years, and I'd forgotten. Maybe love comes in different packages, and I will have to let my kid go his way, also."

I am not pushing for special tolerance for queers. I am asking all

of us to be easy on each other, to let our love move less fear-
fully, to let the homosexual realize it isn't that everyone is gay, but
that everyone is a sexual animal, which means that everyone can
be a loving animal. And love has no boundaries.

(1969)

Comments on Notes for a More Coherent Article

This is *the* article—I will not take the time for a more coherent
one. But I must correct some errors. My grandparents traveled
by train, not covered wagon, when they came to Los Angeles. My
father is not a military man—it played a small role in his life. I
regret the degree to which, in those autobiographical notes, I
slighted my mother's side of the family.

Those are minor corrections. I did not know, until after the
article was written and out of my system, the degree of self-
hatred my homosexuality had involved. It shows through in part
in the bitterness of my comments about gay society. In fact, I had,
over the years, largely accepted society's definition of the homosexual as queer, pervert, and sinner.

Life can be hard for all of us, and one reason I'm never much
impressed when some black militant says, "You shouldn't talk—
you have no idea what it is to have a black skin," is because I
want to say back, "And you have no idea what it is to be queer."
But the lesson that every minority should learn (and we are all
part of some minority) is that the human condition is such that it
involves great (and usually hidden) pain for all of us and, in different ways, for each of us. Life is a joyously hard, painfully
sweet, bitterly happy experience. You are black; I am queer; she
is ugly; he is a moron; his wife got killed on their honeymoon—I
suggest we all bear such a freight of pain with us, that no one,
poor or black or queer, should dwell too long on his own problems.

My article was profoundly in error in suggesting that persons
past 25 would not understand it. No article I've written brought
more comments, all but a very small handful being sympa-

thetic. (One of the hostile comments being from a homosexual who suggested that I ought to kill myself if I was going to be so negative.) But the response from those 50 and over—including a treasured note from Ammon Hennacy, written not long before he died—made me much more humble about writing off those of us who have passed 25. I was also proud of the War Resisters League, which did not even discuss firing me.

I realized after writing the piece that the remarks about gay society need to be amended. When I was younger, "gay" meant a secret, exclusive, and sick subculture. Today "gay" can also mean the militancy and physical courage and absolute openness of the Gay Liberation Front. I do not agree with the Gay Liberation movement, am not part of it, and stand by the essential line set forth in my article, but do want to retract the intensity of my comments against gay society.

Finally, sexuality remains a mystery to me, as to all of us. Once we truly open ourselves to sexuality, we find it a door to a greater mystery, a wild garden where both sun and moon hold sway; a beach with a midnight tide sweeping our dreams to sea; a meadow where we sit shortly before noon; the sun, fiery, but distant; the wind moving nearby; and the mere touch of our hands is more sexual than pornography. Sex is tedious. Sexuality is Bessie Smith, Janis Joplin, the songs of Randy Newman. *Bolero* is sex, but the close of Beethoven's Ninth is sexuality.

Love is an irrational thing—perhaps our only proof of God, because it is so strange, so pointless, so necessary. We could make the biologically necessary fuck without the confusions of love. The race would survive. But, painful as it may be, we love one another. Sometime those loves do not even make biological sense, but they are no less valid.

(1970)

IV
Everything Revolves
Around Vietnam

*"It is a major confrontation
between the machinery of war
and members of my own
generation."*

Vietnam Is Our Hungary

I have listened to the experts and read the government reports on Vietnam. And I have a curious feeling of *déjà vu*. When I started college in 1948, the French had just begun their task of "pacifying" Indochina, following the Japanese defeat. Month after month and year after year, that war went on. And always, in *Time* magazine, the war was almost won. Every two or three months, *Time* came very close to simply declaring the war over and the Viet Minh defeated. One had the impression that Ho Chi Minh must surely have had his bags always packed and that he waited nervously for each week's issue of *Time* to see whether or not he had, at last, to flee swiftly across the border into China.

And, then, quite suddenly, *Time* magazine lost the war. How this came about, after the brilliant campaign *Time* had waged steadily for nearly ten years, is still not clear. But it is obvious that it was some great act of treachery that, on May 7, 1954, led to the final victory of the Viet Minh, undoing all the good work of *Time* magazine. The French, of course, had no choice but to leave.

I have the same feeling again, watching Vietnam. Kennedy told us, at one point, that all our troops would be out of Vietnam by 1965. Now, it is conceded we may have to stay a bit longer, or even send more troops in. And, by some odd twist of the military mind, having lost the game in South Vietnam, they want to expand the war into the North.

But the war is over, all except for the killing. The Viet Cong can strike with impunity at our "secret" air base just twenty miles outside Saigon. It was way back in April that Walter Lippmann wrote, "The truth, which is being obscured for the American people, is that the Saigon government has the allegiance of probably no more than 30 per cent of the people and controls (even in daylight) not much more than a quarter of the territory." Things have, by all accounts, gotten a good deal worse since April.

Reviewing all the material on Vietnam, it seems to me that the emperor is absolutely naked but the public, including, oddly, the experts on Vietnam and most of the usually sophisticated intellectuals, has been quite unable to spot this nakedness.

Why this should be so, I do not know. The facts have appeared in the press. True, they have not always been featured, and, sometimes, one must follow a news report to its very last paragraph or learn to read between the lines. But the facts have been published widely. We cannot plead ignorance. The statements issued by Dean Rusk, President Johnson, and other officials are so directly contrary to these published facts that one would think that someone would make note of the divergence between official statements and press reports from Saigon.

For example, while Kennedy was in office, there was frequent reference, both by him and by Dean Rusk, to Diem's regime as being an "outpost of the free world." Today, government officials (*Life,* November 27, 1964) admit Diem was quite a brutal little tyrant. But no one in the government seems to blush over this contradiction between what the government said two years ago about Diem and what it says today. No effort is even made to explain the contradiction. Do they think we have all forgotten and and are now prepared to trust the same government that indirectly admits it was lying to us two years ago? Perhaps they do think this, and, tragically, they are probably right.

The government has made constant reference to the "massive

shipments of men and supplies" being sent into South Vietnam over the fabled Ho Chi Minh Trail. Dean Rusk even had the effrontery to announce to us that he had personally asked the Soviet Ambassador to bring pressure on North Vietnam and China to cut off these supplies. One cannot really believe that Rusk actually told the Russian Ambassador any such thing. Rusk knows perfectly well there are no "massive shipments" coming in from North Vietnam. My guess is that he and the Russian Ambassador discussed their families, the weather, and the relative merits of Russian versus American vodka. Contrary to Dean Rusk's statements, only a trickle of military supplies have ever been sent down from North Vietnam. *The New York Times* reports that 75 per cent of Viet Cong weapons are American-made and captured from the forces of Saigon, and most of the rest are manufactured in primitive "jungle factories." *Business Week* puts the figure even higher, saying up to 90 per cent of all Viet Cong weapons are American-made. If the government really wants to cut the flow of weapons to the Viet Cong, I respectfully suggest that it bomb our own ships as they put into the harbor in South Vietnam.

On this matter of learning to read between the lines, I cite the report in *The New York Times* of December 11, 1964. Peter Grose, reporting from Saigon on a recent Viet Cong military victory, wrote: "The loss of the two mortars, along with 300 rounds of high-explosive ammunition, was particularly unnerving to American and Vietnamese officers. . . ." Now, why should the capture of two mortars "unnerve" us? If there is such a flood of matériel pouring down the Ho Chi Minh Trail, surely it makes little difference whether the Viet Cong captured two mortars or twenty mortars.

The government not only cannot document the amount of military aid from North Vietnam, but it also cannot document the presence in South Vietnam of North Vietnamese military advisers. The government may well think that if it makes a statement it will be accepted at face value, even when the press is reporting contrary facts. And the government may well be right—thus far, almost everyone seems to accept the myth of massive North Vietnamese intervention. Certainly, North Vietnam is not innocent, and it has given certain aid that can be pinpointed fairly closely. Radio Hanoi gives daily support to the Viet Cong. North Vietnam maintains a close link with the Communist element in the Viet Cong. Some South Vietnamese doubtless slip across the border for military training or for political discussions. But that is about the extent of it.

There has been increasing talk about our need to "go North" to deal with the "source of the problem." This is less than honest on the part of the government, since we have been sending military expeditions into the North since 1961 (see Sulzberger, *Times* of June 27, 1964). The problem is that our "counterinsurgency" forces have been cut to ribbons. *Aviation Week* (April 6, 1964) reported, "War against the Communists has already erupted over the borders of South Vietnam with raids and infiltration moves as far North as China. . . . Despite Defense Secretary McNamara's implication in Washington (March 26) that the decision has not yet been made to extend the war, it is known here that guerrilla strikes against the Communists have been increasing since last summer." Given these facts, surely we ought not to have been surprised when some of our ships got fired on in the Gulf of Tonkin—particularly since the government later conceded the North Vietnamese might have confused our ships with some South Vietnamese ships that were then raiding the coast of North Vietnam!

We are still being told that South Vietnam is a democracy, even though no free elections have ever been held, and even though the United States intervened to block the free elections that had been pledged at Geneva and that were to be held in North and South Vietnam in 1956 to unify all of Vietnam. The United States, correctly enough, I think, realized that Ho Chi Minh, who was a national hero because of his victory over the French, would easily win a free election.

We have been told repeatedly that, if the United States gets out of Vietnam that the Viet Cong will win. That statement is a little naïve, since the Viet Cong has already won everything except the cities, and the real question is not whether the Viet Cong will win, but why they have won. The Saigon government will collapse the moment we leave. But why? The Saigon government has an armed force of over 600,000 men, well equipped and, by Vietnamese standards, well paid and well fed. In addition, Saigon has an air force, a navy, 20,000 American military advisers, and, over the past ten years, several billions of dollars of American aid, both economic and military.

In contrast to this, the Viet Cong has no more than 100,000 men in its army—and the vast majority of these are part-time soldiers. The Viet Cong has no air force, no navy, virtually no artillery (note again the importance the United States attached to the loss of two mortars), no tanks, no trucks. The Viet Cong must live on the rice the peasants are willing to provide. And, still, they have won most of the territory of South Vietnam. Why is it that, in South Vietnam, guerrilla war works in territory held by the Saigon government, but it doesn't work when Saigon tries to use it in areas held by the Viet Cong? Has it not dawned on anybody that the people of South Vietnam do not support their own government; that, denied any chance to vote against it with the ballots, they are voting against it by supporting the Viet Cong?

The emperor is naked, but none seem able to see his nakedness.

I skip over the various violations of international treaties involved in United States actions in Vietnam. Treaty violations do not really interest liberals. Dean Acheson, just this week, assured us all that we were much too concerned with morality as it is. People who are unconcerned with an almost unbroken record of broken treaties with the American Indians will hardly cavil at a few international treaties being broken.

But there is a crucial point that might, if pressed hard enough, bother liberals. It is the fact that our actions in South Vietnam are criminal. They are also tragic, dirty, blundering, confused, and stupid. But they are, above all else, criminal. They are not a game, though too many American "experts" seem to treat Vietnam as a kind of game. They are not experiments to test new methods of killing people, though the Pentagon is on record as expressing its satisfaction that it can make such tests. They are not designed to produce new officers for the General Staff, though most of the American officers in South Vietnam view their role there in this light. They are, I repeat, criminal actions.

The Viet Cong is not innocent, and let me record that here. I hold no brief for the terror used by the Viet Cong, for the kind of repressive regime I think they will establish when they take over the cities. But all the terror of the Viet Cong is as nothing when held against the terror the Americans have brought to South Vietnam. We have dropped napalm bombs on villages all over South Vietnam hoping to kill a few Viet Cong in the process. We have machine-gunned a good many people from the air— some of whom have been Viet Cong, a great many of whom have not been Viet Cong. We have sprayed rice crops with chemicals that destroy those crops, so they cannot be used to feed the Viet Cong. The catch is that peasants and their children also run short of food. They starve. In areas where peasant support for the Viet Cong is heavy—in other words, in most areas—we have rounded up thousands upon thousands of peasants at the point of a gun, we have burned their villages to the ground and herded these people into dirty little barbed-wire encampments "for their protection." We are permitting the torture of captured members of the Viet Cong—many of them young boys still in their teens. And every reader of the *Voice* has seen these photographs in *Life, The New York Times,* the *Daily News,* and so forth. We have even, in our marvelous American enthusiasm, bombed villages in Cambodia, across the border from South Vietnam, killing a fair number of Cambodian peasants, and then been terribly indignant because Cambodia has accused us of aggression.

I think, My God, what facts have to hit us in the face before finally the American liberal community will move? We moved fast enough when the Russians went into Hungary or the French into Algeria. It was proper for us, as liberals, to move then in condemning those actions. Nor were we alone. Many Communists, even though aware of the real military and political threat that a free and independent Hungary might pose to Russia, joined us in condemning Russia. And many French intellectuals risked (and, in some cases. endured) prison to attack French policy in Algeria, even though a French withdrawal meant abandoning one million French citizens.

But where is the intellectual community today? Aside from groups of radicals like the War Resisters League, the Socialist Party, and the Fellowship of Reconciliation, the liberal movement is less worried about the crime of what we are doing in Vietnam than about the danger that the war might get "escalated" and thus hurt some Americans. In acting as coordinator for the December 19 Vietnam Protests, I received answers from a number of decent, liberal men who declined to join in sponsoring the protest because they felt U.S. withdrawal would be "irresponsible." I do not have time to argue with them here, but I wonder how many of these same intellectuals hesitated before condemning Russia or France? I would have to ask whether, like the Communists they oppose, they do not really have a double standard. The Russians, after all, only killed 25,000 Hungarians. Already, more than 79,000 Vietnamese have been killed.

What is one to say when a man like George Kennan, who is inherently decent and generally somewhat aware of moral issues, can argue in *The New York Times Magazine* (November 22, 1964) that we ought not to joggle the elbow of the government just now in regard to Vietnam, while our men out there are risking their lives. Yes, Mr. Kennan, but what of the lives our men are snuffing out? We have lost just over 200 men—all of whom are volunteers and many of whom were eager for service in Vietnam. But the Vietnamese have lost over 79,000 lives, very few of them volunteers, a great many of them women and children.

Vietnam is the American Hungary—or Algeria, whichever you prefer. It is the test of our intellectuals. Our present silence is deafening. We need the kind of resistance, even if it lands a number of us in prison, that will do something at this point to redeem our national honor, now so badly tarnished.

(1964)

Author's Note: I must note—and do later in this collection—that the Socialist Party very early ceased to be a part of the struggle against the Vietnam war. But the intellectuals that I here so bitterly excoriate were to prove the great strength in the resistance to this war, their relentless efforts exceeding those of similar groups in any other country in modern times. For my part I am sorry to see, looking back, how long I insisted on using "Viet Cong," how slow I was to refer to the National Liberation Front.

(1970)

Open Letter to RFK: What Is Loyalty?

Dear Senator Kennedy:

The *New York Post* of May 6 quotes you as telling reporters (in answer to a question about whether you would fly a plane bombing North Vietnam) that "I will do anything my country wants me to do . . . I will go where my country sends me." It is, I suppose, unfair to expect you to say that you would not do anything your country asked you to do—that would probably mean the sudden end of a promising political career. Yet perhaps the greatest service you could render the nation just now would be to lose your political career by a consistent, forceful opposition to Johnson. The nation looks down on men who avoid the draft— yet they are trying to save their lives. Why should we excuse political leaders who avoid risks in order to save their political careers?

Is it, in the deepest sense, patriotic for you to say, "I will do anything my country wants me to do?" What, in fact, is the role of the patriot during this uneasy time? A number of us will probably have to be rounded up by the government if Johnson insists on continuing this war. The technical charges placed against us may be something as trivial as "disorderly conduct," but the charges the government apologists will level are going to be more serious: treason, sedition, subversion. For we do propose to impede this war. We propose to aid men in staying out of the army, and in sheltering those who leave it. We propose to encourage citizens to refuse payment of taxes. We propose to do what we can to slow down or prevent the production of napalm.

I am writing you partly to suggest that you consider whether your place may not be on "our side of the line." But I write also to provide the ideological basis for those direct actions being undertaken. I am fundamentally a conservative radical. I am unprepared to rush into confrontation with the government until I have thought my way through. I am troubled about pitting myself against a state that won power in a democratic election. The problem is simple: Can a loyal American engage in acts of overt disloyalty to the state? One can also turn this around and ask if an American who cooperates with this state is loyal. When Americans say, "my country, right or wrong," they really mix together, as if they were one, the two distinct concepts of the state and the nation. The state is a set of machinery, while the "nation" is really the traditions, the culture, the whole people, and the landscape on which they exist. We may not realize that occasions arise when loyalty to one concept involves disloyalty to the other.

Let me cite some examples. The men who established the United States had been bound to the King by solemn oaths of allegiance. They were subjects of the Crown and citizens of Great Britain. To wage war on England meant sedition, subversion, treason, and terror against their country, England. Our founding fathers excused all these sins by citing certain moral laws that justified their rebellion. Thus, loyalty to conscience meant war against the state.

Let us look at the situation of a farmer in Southern Illinois in 1859. At midnight, an escaped slave knocks on his door and asks for help in getting North, into Canada. To aid that slave is a flagrant violation of federal laws covering fugitive slaves—democratic laws passed after full debate and sustained by the Supreme Court. Does the loyal American farmer obey those laws and call the sheriff or does he place his own sense of the rightness of things above that of Congress and the Supreme Court, give the slave food and lodging, and send him on his way North?

Or, more recently, Martin Luther King led mass civil disobedience projects against local and state segregation laws in the South at a time when those laws were constitutional. King was not arguing for test cases and a court victory. He was saying, "Brothers and sisters, racism is contrary to what this nation is or *should be*—stand loyally by the best in America and break the law."

Let's look at Germany. Every American (including the Freedom House liberals who have taken full-page ads to remind us that our dissent must be "responsible") would agree that the "good Germans" were not those who supported Hitler but were those who opposed him—even to the point of trying to kill him. Hitler came to power democratically. The clear majority of Germans did not hate or fear him—they supported him with enthusiasm to the very end. But, we are told, the "good Germans" were the ones who sought to strike down Hitler. They tried to do so because they felt that, regardless of how popular Hitler was, his policies had soiled the culture or traditions of Germany. To the mystique of the state (that is, Hitler) they opposed the mystique of the best aspects of German tradition. They sought, out of loyalty to that tradition, to destroy the state itself.

I suggest loyalty is rarely as simple as it may seem. There are times when one organizes mass civil disobedience actions against certain aspects of a democratic society. There are times when loyalty to the concept of the nation drives one into bitter struggle with the state. What the "country wants me to do" may be different from what the "government wants me to do," and it may also be different from what "I ought to do."

To the "state"—the machinery of government—we owe nothing. But to the nation, the culture, we owe everything. Even our ability to protest and disobey is derived from this culture. And, when I say we owe this culture "everything," I mean we owe it our very best. And the very best is not blind obedience to the state, but rather it is obedience to our own sense of right and wrong. It is this that serves as the final check on the state—even more than the Bill of Rights. The one unwritten part of our Constitution is the concept that not even a democratic state may coerce a man's loyalty for actions he finds immoral. It is this unique aspect of America that I find very much worth defending.

The tradition I choose to follow is not the only tradition in our history. But I think it is the best one. It holds that our nation is never completed, that it is always in the process of being consciously formed, as it was consciously formed in the beginning. For the American who accepts this tradition, the present is not inevitable. The future can be shaped. The war in Vietnam does not "have to go on," simply because we are in it. I choose the tradition of giving greater loyalty to my conscience than to the state precisely because I am an American. I do not fear the charge of sedition or treason, for, as I argued earlier, it happens from time to time that loyalty to a nation may demand "treason" to the state. In my willful, deliberate, joyous encounter with the state and in my open resistance to it, I assert my Americanness. My roots are here, and no one, *certainly* not as shoddy a piece of goods as Johnson, will drive me north to Canada. Nor shall any man, nor any act of Congress compel from me obedience and loyalty to that which I believe evil, as I believe with all my mind and heart and soul that our military presence in Vietnam is evil.

It is in the very instant of our cheerful disobedience and disloyalty that, faulted and imperfect as we ourselves may be, we find ourselves standing on the same ideological ground as Martin Luther King, A. J. Muste, Eugene Victor Debs, Henry David Thoreau, John Peter Altgeld, William Lloyd Garrison, John Peter Zenger, Mary Dyer, the men and women of the Underground Railroad, and the subversives of the Boston Tea Party. It is good ground to be on, and there is room enough here for a great many of us— even for a United States senator.

(1967)

A Letter to the Men
of My Generation

This is an open letter to the men of my generation. I think of
my generation in political terms—comprising all those who were
part of or were influenced by the democratic Left in the period
between the purge trials and the twentieth congress. We are
those who not only opposed fascism but also opposed Communism. It is a generation that covers a broad range, from Bayard
Rustin to Norman Mailer to Mike Harrington to Irving Howe to
Mary McCarthy. Twenty years may separate some of us, but we
shared a common experience.

We twice confronted profound and organized evil. On both
occasions, that evil was not located within our own nation but at
a distance from our shores. Only in a very indirect way, can
America be blamed for the rise of Stalin and Hitler. These were
events we did not basically create but to which we had to respond.
They were events that exceeded any evils in our own country at
that time. To say that Jim Crow was a ghastly institution is an
understatement, but to compare the treatment white America
inflicted on its Negro citizens in those years with the slaughter
instituted by Stalin and by Hitler is simply to argue that one
Negro is worth 1,000 or 10,000 Jews and Slavs. Also, even though
we were a Jim Crow nation, we, the white ruling class, had already admitted segregation to be evil and, in a ponderously

slow way, were moving against it. The German rulers were not moving away from murder—they embraced it as a state policy. The Soviet rulers were not ashamed of their purge trials—they staged them as public events. The America in which we grew up is gone beyond recall. But, for all its faults, it was clearly preferable to Hitler's Germany or Stalin's Russia. Steinbeck's characters in *The Grapes of Wrath* were victims of an irrational economic system, not victims of some decision of a central committee. And, even as the Oakies struggled to keep alive, Steinbeck was there to record—and to publish—their story. Neither Russia nor Germany permitted any Steinbecks to record the plight of the gypsies, the Jews, the kulaks. In the midst of our lynchings, Langston Hughes and Richard Wright were able to cry out. In Germany and in Russia, millions died in silence.

I put all this down because we—those of my generation—share two problems. The first is our anti-Communism, which was, in a sense, our unique mark. Germany sought bad ends by bad means, and it was easy to stand in judgment on it. Russia sought good ends with bad means, and it was difficult for many intellectuals to see what a perversion this created. But our anti-Communism, born out of our commitment to humanity, has now become utterly dehumanizing. Too many of us have forgotten why we became anti-Communists. We see the NLF and the North Vietnamese not as living creatures but as abstract symbols holding guns, ideological puppets directed from Moscow or Peking or both. And we are prepared, some of us, to sacrifice them on the altar of an anti-Communism that has become as much a god for us as Communism was for some in the 1930's. Be wary of gods, for they kill people. The Vietnamese peasant is, first of all, human, and, only secondarily, is he a Communist, a Buddhist, or a supporter of Ky.

We must recognize that the struggle of the Vietnamese has long since transcended politics and even its own violence and has become an existential statement about man and his willingness to suffer and to endure. Even if the NLF lost the war tomorrow, they would have won it, for they have become a legend that will last 1,000 years—a legend rooted not in their Communism but in their raw courage. We have dumped more bombs on Vietnam than we dropped in all of World War II. We have total control of the air over South Vietnam. We have everything: clean hospitals, hot meals in the field, regular mail from home. They have nothing. And they fight. It does not matter what happens now. We have lost, and they have won. They might not have been a nation before we came, but they shall be a nation when we leave. Hubert Humphrey likes to say we are engaged in "nation-building" and indeed we are—we have unified the Vietnamese because there was no other way they could get us out.

That is the first point. Anti-Communist that I am, I salute the NLF and Hanoi. Not their politics, which I loathe, but them—as people. The world may someday forget what we have done to this tiny nation, but the world will never be able to forget what they have done for themselves.

The second point is that we find it all but impossible to realize that, this time, the evil we confront is here, at home. Always before, the massive evils have been at a distance from our shores. Now, it is within our boundaries. We are not ruled by Hitler, as the New Left seems to think. Hitler had style, brilliance, and courage. (Some murderers and madmen do.) Johnson simply has cunning. He is neither Hitler nor Stalin. He is a Mussolini with hydrogen bombs. But a criminal? Yes, he is that. We know it in our hearts, but we cannot bear to say it. And the war? That is criminal, too. It started as a mistake, but it long ago became a crime against humanity. The New Left is wrong when, with its crude approach to Marxism, it thinks of all evil as being contained within this nation. But they are correct in judging that we have become an outlaw nation today. Our troops and tanks and planes march and clank and blast from Santo Domingo to Saigon. Nothing that Russia or China has done in the past fifteen years compares to what we have done in Vietnam. Hungary, 1956, now looks like a mere exercise in riot control, if contrasted to Vietnam.

Now, God help us, we know what it must have been like to have been a true Bolshevik in Russia after Stalin took power—

the sense of guilt and confusion and complicity. Now we know how German socialists felt after the attack on Poland, knowing their own beloved Germany was embarked on a criminal course. Some of you—good friends and old associates—suggest we will lose our effectiveness if we speak the full truth about the war. I suspect that the only thing that may save us now is the full truth. One reason the kids don't listen to us—or listen only with contempt—is precisely because, in our concern to be politically effective, we have spoken lies and left truth to the poets. We organize a "Negotiations Now!" movement because we think "Withdrawal Now!" would fail to win support. And, yet, what have we left to negotiate, except the roads our troops will follow as they withdraw? Do we have any right to negotiate the kind of government we shall leave behind us? God knows, I'm not against negotiations, yesterday, now, or tomorrow. But let us be honest in public and say we do favor withdrawal and are simply searching for a politically expedient solution. In short, I ask from all of us some adherence to that sense of morality which brought us into the democratic Left in the first place. The same moral perception that led us to attack Stalinism as well as fascism must now lead us into an equally committed struggle against our own government.

In this context of trying to face our moral responsibilities, I want to take up the meaning of December 5. When the young men of the Resistance began to burn draft cards or return them to their boards, several adult "support groups" were organized. Noam Chomsky's article "The Responsibility of Intellectuals," helped spark this, as did the work of Dwight Macdonald, Paul Goodman, Mitchell Goodman, Karl Bissinger, Grace Paley, and others. Signatures were gathered on various "statements of complicity" in which adults declared they had encouraged and supported these young men in their illegal actions. Technically, such statements are a violation of federal law. I know the courage it took various faculty members and ministers and writers to sign statements that might land them in jail for five years. The problem is, the government has refused to prosecute. It wants to avoid a confrontation. Paul Goodman is absolutely correct when he points out that the government, by refusing to move against us, has declared its moral bankruptcy. But it still holds power, drafts men, and wages war.

But what does happen is that kids, seeing these statements, are encouraged to burn draft cards or turn them in. And they *do* get arrested. I don't suffer for signing these statements—but some eighteen-year-old may. He will go to jail, and I can send him a Christmas card assuring him of my continued moral support. Look, if we are right in pointing out that it is obscene for old politicians who never saw combat (Johnson leaps to mind) to send thousands to their death, is it not also wrong for us to settle for signing statements of complicity, which tend to encourage young men to take risks for which they—not we—shall be punished? Do we not have to move beyond statements of complicity to *acts* of complicity?

There is another problem. I think it is wrong for us to take our moral cues from the youth, which is what the complicity statements are about. The kids took a courageous stand, and we moved in to stand behind them. I submit we should stand *with* them and, in some cases, we should stand in front of them. If the struggle were violent, then youth would have to take the lead, because their physical strength would carry the day. But the struggle is not violent. It is a nonviolent moral confrontation. We, therefore, have an equal right to be on the front line—and the kids have the right to expect us there. I don't accept the notion of a kind of thirty-year-old barrier that keeps each group in a little age-ghetto of its own. We need eighteen-year-old men in the front lines, and they need fifty-year-old men (and women) right there beside them. Why let SDS, which increasingly sounds like the Old Left, tell us we aren't needed? Since when do we abdicate such decisions to SDS? Is it because it was comfortable, in a way, to be told we had to stand on the sidelines?

The third problem is that I don't think the guys in the Resistance need our support. They can take care of themselves, better than we realize. They are middle class, with all the resources (and contacts) that go with that. They will survive prison, and they will get good jobs afterwards. I'm not being harsh if I say I don't want to waste time supporting the Resistance—I'm stating a profound confidence in these young men.

But who does need our support? Here, to be allegorical for a moment, the Jews need our help. I'm not a Jew, and so I'm safe. You're not a Jew, and so you're safe. Jews don't read *The Village Voice*. The Jews live in Harlem, in Brooklyn, and in my own neighborhood. We think of them as Negroes or Puerto Ricans or poor whites, but they are really Jews. While we sign statements of complicity and support for middle-class kids who could dodge the draft if they wanted and who can survive prison if that comes, the government is rounding up hundreds of Jews every day— every day—and, by dawn's early light, within view of the Statue of Liberty, it processes them and sends them into camps from which they go forth to die.

The average poor white or Negro cannot refuse induction. What do you think happens to a black man with a felon's record? For any Negro to risk prison is an act infinitely more courageous in our society than for a middle-class white to risk prison. The poor not only have no choice but to submit to induction, they must often volunteer, for where else can they get jobs? What, then, is truly the responsibility of the intellectual? What should a good German do, knowing he and his children are safe but knowing that the Jews are collected every day from the ghettos of his cities? The good German obstructs the trucks carrying Jews to training camps. He blocks the doors of the induction center. The good German says very simply that the Jew is my brother, and, there- fore, you shall not take him, thinking to buy my silence by granting me personal safety.

Can we stop this war? I don't know. I think Johnson will survive our complicity statements, and I'm pretty sure he can handle Jerry Rubin's call for revolution (*Voice*, November 16). But I am not really sure what happens if you and I—the men and women of this particular generation—with our middle-class respectability, must be jailed, in order to keep the doors of the induction center open. How many writers can Johnson jail? How many priests? How many professors? If I urge civil disobedience, it is because I believe in America, because I believe the way to reach the conscience of America is not through bombs and terror but through civil disobedience, the ancient deadly, radical weapon of the democrat.

The intellectual community demands responsibility of Johnson. We expect him to simply withdraw from Vietnam and commit political suicide. In the security of our cocktail parties, we say terrible things about Johnson, because he will not act responsibly. But which takes more courage—risking ten days in jail (and the subsequent status of hero to our friends and associates) or risking the destruction of one's political career? Johnson was never a man of courage, and yet we demand great courage of him. We speak as if we ourselves had no power, as if Johnson was a Czar or Kaiser, a natural event, perhaps, over which we have no control. But Johnson got there with your vote—and mine. This isn't Russia, where the intellectual can only talk in privacy but dare not act in public. This is a democracy, where we share the responsibility with the rulers. We do not have a right to ask of Johnson a courage we cannot find in ourselves. So let us act. On December 5 and afterwards. The street is also a ballot box.

The youth have largely lost faith in us. Some of them mutter of violence, of blowing up draft boards and troop trains. And there are always those in the middle class who support such demands, middle-class neurotics, whose self-hatred is so deep they applaud Rap Brown when he calls for guns and blood. (I once thought that these expensively dressed whites didn't realize Rap Brown meant them—I have since concluded that, even if only unconsciously, they know it perfectly well, and their applause is a prayer for their own destruction.) The debate between violence and nonviolence can, logically, arise only when nonviolent opposition has been suppressed. Until that point, we are all, functionally, pacifists. Civil disobedience is simply one aspect of the democratic process, like voting. The whole question of whether the present young generation will turn to violence, or to Canada, or to withdrawal—or to a life-affirming and democratic politics depends on where our mouths are. The youth need a leadership that, in this, the year of our Lord Vietnam, cannot be given through articles, no matter how well written. The youth need proof that you and I still believe enough in our country to take risks for it and to hope those risks will pay off.

Next Tuesday, December 5, at 6:00 A.M., some hundreds of New Yorkers, including Dwight Macdonald, Susan Sontag, Nat Hentoff, Jane Jacobs, Paul Krassner, and Paul Goodman will be at the Whitehall Street Induction Center, in the old part of Manhattan, below Wall Street. Dozens of persons will move toward the doors of the Induction Center, there to sit down and physically block them. Nonviolently. Gently. But firmly. Hundreds of others will join a supporting picket line. There will be students there, but it is not a student demonstration. It is a major confrontation between the machinery of war and members of my own generation.

(1967)

Answering McReynolds:
A Question of Philosophy,
a Question of Tactics
by Michael Harrington

David McReynolds's letter to "my" generation—to "those who were part of or were influenced by the democratic Left between the purge trials and the twentieth congress"—is a thoughtful statement of some of the agonizing issues posed by the tragic war in Vietnam. This answer is intended in the same generous, unpolemical spirit in which he wrote.

I begin with a personal anecdote, not to flaunt a venerable credential like an American Legionnaire of the antiwar movement, but to make a point about my own ambiguities.

In 1950, when the Korean War broke out, I joined the Army Medical Corps Reserve, thinking that noncombatant status would satisfy my conscientious objections to American participation in that conflict. When I enlisted, both the Army and I thought I was to be sent to Korea, but there was one of those sudden changes in policy and I was only required to go to biweekly training sessions. In 1951, I went to live at the Catholic Worker house, a spare-time soldier dwelling in a pacifist community. When I had to go to drill, I waited until everybody was at dinner, since I didn't want to be seen uniformed in the livery of my compromise. Eventually, I went on the annual two weeks of active duty with a firm promise from the officers that my principles would be respected. As soon as we got to camp, I was sent to the infantry;

next day, they tried to give me a rifle and march me to hand-grenade instruction. I refused the gun and the grenade lesson and, after some very anxious moments and due to good luck and sympathetic superiors, was sent back to the medics.

After all the turmoil—and fear—of thus defining my position (I later severed all my connections with the Reserve, but that is another story), I was walking along a road in the camp. A column of marching men came by, and suddenly, even though I had fought grimly for my right not to be among them, I felt lonely and left out and wanted nothing more than to get into step.

That is how I often feel these days when I watch, or read about, the antiwarriors in some new confrontation. My heart, my emotions, my instincts are with them; but, in a good many cases, my head will not allow me to join up. I truly wish that I could see the issues as sharply defined as Dave McReynolds does. But I can't. My ambiguities are in no sense a function of doubts about the wrongness of the evil war in Vietnam. On the contrary, I believe that politics and morality require that all our energies be devoted to ending this abomination in Southeast Asia at once. That is precisely why I cannot participate in some of the demonstrations.

At the beginning of his letter, I think Dave McReynolds introduces something of a red herring. I am talking about the issue of Communism. Since I have written so extensively on this point, I would just as soon leave it alone, but McReynolds puts it first among his comments and uses it to explain the failure of my generation to respond with sufficient militance to the war. So I have no choice but to deal with it once more.

His meaning is clear enough: that some of us on the democratic Left mute our opposition to the war because of an obsessive concern with Communism ("We see the NLF and North Vietnamese not as living creatures but as abstract symbols holding guns, ideological puppets directed from Moscow and/or Peking"). Yet I do not know of anyone on the democratic Left who views the struggle in South Vietnam as the result of a Russian, Chinese, or any other kind of conspiracy. That is a view that is still entertained in the State Department and on the American

Right, but it is not to be found anywhere that I know of among "my" generation of the Left.

Secondly, the issue of Communism influences my attitudes on Vietnam in two very specific, and I believe, unobsessive ways. First, often it relates to how one goes about the imperative task of organizing a movement to end the war that will be politically effective within the United States; secondly, it touches upon my solidarity with the anguish and suffering of the Vietnamese themselves.

The American people are not going to be persuaded to end the war by fellow citizens who favor a victory for the Viet Cong. On the contrary, I believe that every Viet Cong banner in a peace demonstration drives people toward the hawks, and, were I suspicious by nature, I would consider the flag-waving contingents as CIA plants (in fact, they are usually composed of middle-class activists who regard venting their alienation from American society as more important than stopping the bloodshed in Vietnam). For these reasons, the American antiwar movement must make it politically clear that it is for peace and not victory for one side or the other. This does not mean that Communists, or anyone else, should be "purged" from the line of march. If the Progressive Labor Party, or any other Communist group, is willing to march in a demonstration with the clear policy I have just described, they are welcome. If they want to have their own Victory-for-the-Viet Cong parade, I will vigorously defend their civil liberty to do so.

The position that I have just stated does not strike me as obsessive, particularly since it is aimed at stopping the slaughter in Vietnam.

But then, how does one face up to the issue of Communism in Vietnam itself? McReynolds writes, "We must recognize that the struggle of the Vietnamese has long since transcended politics and even its own violence and has become an existential statement about man and his willingness to suffer and to endure." This is a tragic half-truth, and I can sympathize with the emotion that led both to the perception and the distortion it contains.

The average Vietnamese wounded, maimed, or killed probably knows little of the great ideological struggles of this century. Many of the cadres of the Viet Cong are moved by a genuine nationalism and thirst for social justice and not by admiration for totalitarianism or the ambition to become privileged bureaucrats. The peasant caught in the fate of war is a witness to the indomitable resilience of man; and the militant, however much one disagrees with his politics, is touched with heroism. Given the technological savagery that the United States has loosed upon these people, I can understand Dave McReynolds's reacton: to forget all the ideological disputes in the presence of their suffering, rebellious humanity.

I can sympathize with this response—but I cannot agree with it. For even the sacrifice of blood in Vietnam has not exempted that land from politics. Indeed, I think that McReynolds is not existential enough, for he does not carry the tragedy that he evokes to a quite possible, brutally ironic, conclusion. Suppose that finally peace does come to Vietnam and that the Viet Cong take over, and the new government then turns upon the peasantry, as it did a decade ago in the North, to force collectivization; suppose that the dying leads to a betrayal of what the men—and the women and children—died for.

In saying this, I am not arguing that one should, therefore, support the war because the peace might—or probably will—end in a Communist regime. Two years ago, in the *Voice* (November 11, 1965), I advocated self-determination for Vietnam, even though this involved "the probability that a free election might result in a Viet Cong victory." The point I made then, and repeat now, is that French and American imperialism have created a situation in which a peace that will probably lead to dictatorial Communist rule is preferable to an "anti-Communist" war that ravages the land and people of the country we are supposed to be protecting, threatens World War III, and corrupts the moral fabric of American society. (I put "anti-Communist" in quotes, because Paris and Washington have since 1945, been the most effective recruiting sergeants for Vietnamese Communism. Somewhat similarly, I did not favor armed Western defense of the Hungarian uprising of October, 1956, against the Russians, even though I regarded the revolution as Democratic Socialist. Magnificent as that uprising was, its destruction was a lesser evil than the nuclear war that intervention would probably have provoked.)

But, even though one could thus conclude that a policy which would probably lead to a Communist victory in Vietnam is a lesser evil, it must be made clear that such an outcome is still an evil. And an emotional solidarity with a people that has been subjected to almost a quarter of a century of war must not blind us to the fact that, even after all that misery, they have not escaped from politics. I insist on this point not out of scholarly fanaticism but because understanding it is the prerequisite to struggling for a world in which peasants will have more meaningful alternatives than submitting themselves either to Western domination or to the totalitarian accumulation of capital.

The analogy of Algeria might make this point even clearer. During that country's struggle for independence, there was no serious issue of Russian or Chinese involvement since the Algerian Communists never really recovered from the fact that their French Communist comrades supported the repressive colonial policy in North Africa right after World War II. There were romantic revolutionaries in the West—and particularly in Paris, where some of them risked their lives for their convictions—who were so outraged by French brutality and humbled by Algerian courage that they viewed the National Liberation Front (FLN) as the vital cell of a new socialist society. Those of us on the democratic Left who campaigned in support of the Algerian demand for independence were often asked if the FLN would set up a dictatorship (rather than a socialist utopia) once it triumphed. We answered honestly that it probably would, in considerable measure because the French had made democracy impossible. But, we said, even though the right of self-determination would lead to this unhappy conclusion, it was preferable to the continuation of French rule.

Five years after Algerian independence, the bourgeois leaders have been purged by the militant politicals, the militant politicals have been overthrown by the army, and many of the young Frenchmen who engaged in the clandestine struggle would probably be deported as subversive from the nation they helped to

create. The point is not simply that we were right and the ro-
mantics wrong. It is that the Left cannot ignore these complexi-
ties if it wishes to transform them. And that means that the
Communist leadership of the national movement in Vietnam
must be recognized and analyzed so that we might someday offer
the poor of the Third World a positive good rather than a lesser
evil (in the September-October issue of *Dissent,* I described at
some length what this might mean).

But, as a final word on the Communist issue, I hope that Dave
McReynolds's letter is not a sign that he is buying the newly
fashionable devil theory of an international anti-Communist conspiracy. This view notes that the most right-wing, vicious elements in the country are anti-Communist, sees that democratic
leftists are anti-Communists too, and then proclaims that these
antithetical political tendencies are, therefore, part of a single,
sinister movement. Joseph Stalin once operated on a similar
illogic, declared that the German Social Democrats of 1932–33
were really fascists in disguise, and thereby made a major contribution to Hitler's rise to power.

But the issue of Communism is really not the central one I want
to raise. For, in his defense of the tactics of nonviolent resistance,
McReynolds is talking about the best tactics to employ in
ending the killing. For me, as for him, that is the crucial point:
How can we stop the war in Vietnam? And it is from the standpoint of this common goal that I disagree with at least part of
his analysis.

In the December 7 issue of *The New York Review of Books,*
Noam Chomsky put it this way: "Resistance is in part a moral
responsibility, in part a tactic to affect government policy. In
particular, with respect to draft resistance, I feel that it is a
moral responsibility that cannot be shirked. On the other hand,
as a tactic, it seems to me of doubtful effectiveness, as matters
now stand. I say this with diffidence and considerable uncertainty"
(emphasis added). Basically, I agree with Chomsky's assess-
ment of the practicalities, but this leads me, as will be seen, to
conclusions that differ from his.

To begin with, there is the individual, moral level of draft resistance. On this count, I have the same attitude as McReynolds, Chomsky, and other advocates of resistance. I was a conscientious objector during the Korean War and was willing to go to jail rather than to serve in the army, and that would be my position now, were I of draft age, but with even greater emotional certitude. I think that the young men who are voluntarily giving up their (middle-class) deferments and handing in their draft cards are making a courageous witness. I would, incidentally, like to put the public prosecutor on notice, in writing, here and now, that I support them in their conscientious decision, and if this is a violation of the law on my part, so be it.

At the same time, I do not believe that such a highly motivated form of resistance is going to create a mass movement that will end the war. The great bulk of the draftees, as Dave McReynolds notes, come from working-class and impoverished backgrounds and, for a number of reasons beyond their control, are simply not able to take such a stand. On this level, then, draft resistance is a moral imperative by which the individual conscience enjoins a man to refuse to take part in violence he considers immoral; and it is a moral and political witness by a minority, which could possibly touch the hearts and minds of some of the uncommitted. But it is not, as Chomsky notes, an effective method of winning peace.

Dave McReynolds then proposes a certain way of implementing our support of these young men—by closing the doors of the induction centers—and here we part company. This tactic is urged with the greatest seriousness, yet I think it contributes to a confused, self-indulgent, middle-class, and even antilibertarian tendency that is coming more and more to the fore in the peace movement. I am not, as will be seen, heaping all of these adjectives upon McReynolds's ideas for action—but I am asking him to see where his strategies could lead.

In the struggle to end the war in Vietnam, political effectiveness is a major determinant of morality. The activist who maximizes his own sense of dedication, exhilaration, and righteousness *and* alienates his fellow citizens from the cause of peace is immoral (I judge here objectively; whether he is actually guilty depends, of course, upon his individual subjectivity). If a person is commanded to kill in an unjust war, I believe he must refuse no matter what the political consequences; but if he undertakes a demonstration against the war, he is morally obliged to act with a view of how he affects others.

Thus, when Dave McReynolds proposes to block the induction-center door in support of the draft resisters, the relevant question is not "is draft resistance right?" but rather "will this action hasten the end of the war?" In my opinion, the rising sentiment against the war has come about in spite of, and not because of, tactics of civil disruption. The horror and ugliness of what is happening in Vietnam, not the kamikaze tactics of a minority of the protesters, have incited revulsion.

But, McReynolds might reply, "What should a good German do, knowing he and his children are safe but knowing that the Jews are collected every day from the ghettoes of the cities?" This analogy, as McReynolds himself admits earlier in his letter, is dangerously inexact. In a fascist dictatorship where there are no other means of changing a murderous policy other than illegal opposition, that is, in Germany under Hitler, the good German uses all available means to fight genocide, including non-violence, guns, bombs, poison, and so forth, but not including nuclear weapons. In a country that, for all of its obvious, tragic faults, is still democratic enough that the government negotiates details of a protest march with organizers who call that government's leaders moral monsters, it is still possible to change policy democratically and nonviolently. Under such circumstances, an elite minority cannot impose its will upon the nation.

I can understand youthful impatience toward my insistence on democracy and democratic forms. The war is daily more monstrous and the political process seems so insensitive, slow, and indifferent to basic moral issues. I cannot here detail all of the reasons for my advocacy of democracy, but let me state only the most pragmatic and least transcendental: If the Left leads in an assault upon civil liberties and democratic norms, it will unleash the Right, which is much more skilled in and has much more support for such tactics. George Wallace is every bit as fervid as the peace activists, and he has a simple answer to their protests: Jail the dissenters. There are, to be sure, some militants who are under the impression that America is already a fascist country. They lack, of course, any sense of what fascism is (the armed dictatorship of the Right does not confer with opponents who have announced the intention of carrying on civil disobedience; it shoots them), but even more than that, they have no sense of how real and tough the American power structure is. Even Senator Joseph McCarthy was only a despicable, demagogic reactionary, not a fascist, and I shudder to think what would happen if the paranoids of the Right really armed themselves and took to the streets.

In short, I believe that a leftist attack upon democratic legality, a leftist championing of elite decision-making by students and professors, would prolong the war in Vietnam and push domestic American politics even further to the right. It is a responsible tactic to block a door as a witness as long as it is done without any intention of really depriving others of their civil liberties to enter a building (I did exactly that when I was arrested on the opening day of the New York World's Fair) and quite another thing to try to "close down" an induction center. Does Dave McReynolds really think that his demonstration will move the uncommitted? Or might it not make them more sympathetic to Johnson?

In McReynolds's case, I am quite sure that the door-closing tactic is urged from within a democratic perspective, even if, from my point of view, mistakenly. But an ugly tendency toward anti-libertarianism and elitism is developing among some of the resisters.

For instance, Jerry Rubin urges "a nationally coordinated strike (that) will paralyze the major knowledge factories of the nation —shut them down for good with one national demand: America, dismantle your massive murder machine" (*Voice,* November 16). The dumb workers, the stupid farmers, the ghetto dwellers, the overwhelming majority are not going to be consulted; the pure, moral, "leftist" youth are going to decide. Instead of the dictatorship of the bourgeoisie or proletariat, we are to be treated to the dictatorship of the graduate students, the knowledge-factory hands.

In all of this, there is a strain of youthful middle-class petulance and self-indulgence. "The worst thing you can say about a demonstration is that it is boring," Rubin says. (The worst thing you can say is that it does not bring people to oppose the war, I would say.) "Good theater is needed to communicate radical content." And, most precisely, candidly, and exactly, "The youth movement should not judge actions on the basis of whether or not they will alienate the American middle-class mass, but whether or not the actions liberate the imagination and energy of youth." A Vietnamese peasant who is being shot at because of the policies supported by the American middle class might disagree.

Rubin concluded that article with a proposal to disrupt the Democratic National Convention: "Bring pot, fake delegate's cards, smokebombs, costumes, blood to throw, and all kinds of interesting props. Also football helmets." On the most superficial level, I wonder, if it were shown that *not* smoking pot, wearing costumes, throwing blood, and so forth, would hasten the end of the war, whether Rubin and his cothinkers would subordinate their free middle-class spirits to the necessities of a political struggle.

On a more serious level, I am disturbed when the Left proposes to break up public meetings. For Lyndon Johnson and Dean Rusk—and even the Joint Chiefs of Staff and General Westmoreland—have a right under the Constitution of the United States to peaceable assembly. One of the many reasons I am in favor of their right to advocate their wrong ideas is that I want them to respect my right to advocate my (to me) right ideas. There used to be a militant antiwar socialist slogan, "Those who begin this war shall not end it." I would suggest to the social disrupters that if they take a calm look at the relationship of forces in America today, and particularly at the control of the forces of repression, they will see that they are creating a logic whereby "those who break up meetings will not be able to hold meetings." Mark you, I support the right of people to gather together to discuss disrupting meetings. I am just not sure that the power structure will be quite so libertarian as I am.

Finally, let me take up the famous opposition of "negotiate now" and "withdraw now." Dave McReynolds says that the slogan of "negotiate now" is a "politically expedient solution" to the tactical problem. Of course it is! And I would add, in terms of my previous distinction, that antiwar activity that is not politically expedient, that is, that does not mobilize Americans to end the war, is objectively immoral in the light of the tragic urgency of Vietnam.

When I went down to Washington with a Negotiation Now delegation to present some hundreds of thousands of signatures to a meeting of congressmen and senators, the chairman was Bishop Shannon, a Roman Catholic ecclesiast from the Midwest. In his statement, the Bishop, while saying that he was forced to oppose the war, commented that he prayed nightly for the President. To a good many of the militant confronters, such a sentiment would probably seem either funny or obscene. But to the corny, dialectical, and very human American people, I suspect it had the ring of authenticity. I even think that such a quiet statement coming from a Catholic bishop who is against the war might even have more political effect than resisters pissing on the Pentagon steps.

But finally, Dave, I confess once again to being emotionally dissatisfied with my own position. This war is so ugly and horrible that I want to do something more personal, more involved than simply being rational and political. But I can't participate in demonstrations that will alienate people from the antiwar cause: I can't condone "leftist" attacks on the First Amendment freedoms; I can't endorse middle-class elitism or regard middle-class psychodrama as a substitute for serious politics. In a way, it would be a relief to get arrested again and feel that I had put my whole being, and not just my political thinking, on the line. But I insist that every action be related to the supreme task of ending the war. If I have an obsession, that is it.

(1967)

Philosophy and Tactics:
Answering an Answer

But finally, Dave, I confess once again to being emotionally dissatisfied with my own position. This war is so ugly and horrible that I want to do something more personal, more involved than simply being rational and political. But I can't participate in demonstrations that will alienate people from the antiwar cause; I can't condone "leftist" attacks on the First Amendment freedoms; I can't endorse middle-class elitism or regard middle-class psychodrama as a substitute for serious politics. In a way, it would be a relief to get arrested again and feel that I had put my whole being, and not just my political thinking, on the line. But I insist that every action be related to the supreme task of ending the war. If I have an obsession, that is it.

Thus Mike Harrington ends his reply to my article in the November 30 *Village Voice*. But it is not a reply at all, for I agree with every point in Mike's summary. My original letter to the men of my generation—such as Mike—was not an appeal to violate the First Amendment, nor to engage in psychodrama. It was a simple suggestion that we use our bodies, without hatred or violence, to block the doors of the Whitehall Induction Center.

The public may well have been alienated by some of the events of the rest of the week, but I don't think Tuesday was "counterproductive." Nor was it psychodrama. It was not a game. When you are arrested, you have no way of knowing you will be out the same day. And those of us who were arrested have no idea what will happen at our January trials—suspended sentences or jail terms. The rest of that week was a game, one which turned bloody and showed that our cops can be as brutal as any in Mississippi. It was a game in which, theoretically, everyone might get away without being beaten or arrested. It was a game of tag with the cops, and I have some deep reservations about those three days. I did not sponsor them, nor did the War Resisters League. But my open letter had not invited Mike to take part in those three days. The invitation was to December 5. It is a weak answer, indeed, for Mike to list the reasons he could not join the activities of the 6th, 7th, and 8th as the reason he was not present on the 5th.

There was, for example, something forced about explaining his unease in the presence of the NLF flag when no such flags were carried on the 5th (so far as I know) and when those of us who organized the 5th shared Mike's feeling about the value of the NLF flag. But, since Mike did raise the question, I think it a tragedy if the one or two NLF flags that do appear in mass peace demonstrations are what keeps him out of the line of march. Since it is obvious by now that such flags will show up and can be removed only by physical violence, I propose that Mike join with me and others in dealing with the "flag fetish" at the next demonstration by carrying a sea of flags: Cuban, Spanish, Russian, American, Saigonese, French, South African, and so forth. So many people have died for flags it is time for us to carry *all* flags and let people see them for what they are—pretty pieces of cloth that flap in the breeze.

Mike feels I dragged in a red herring in suggesting that some on the democratic Left had been slow to respond to the war because of anti-Communist hangups. He wrote that such a reactive view "is not to be found anywhere that I know of among 'my' generation of the Left." I am both sorry and unhappy to say it, but that is a disingenuous statement by Mike. I doubt if *Voice* readers want a blow-by-blow account of the internal struggles that have taken place in the Socialist Party and *Dissent* magazine and the Fellowship of Reconciliation and SANE—to name just four groupings—but those of us who have been willing to march in demonstrations despite NLF flags, or who have raised the demand that the United States withdraw unilaterally and unconditionally from Vietnam, have been accused, and by personal friends of Mike Harrington, of being soft on Communism, of supporting Hanoi, and so forth. I won't pursue this here, but I am certainly prepared to pursue it if necessary. (And, as Mike must be aware, I've tried for over a year to engage his one-time mentor, Max Shachtman, in a public dialogue on Vietnam and the socialist position—thus far I've had no luck.)

There are several substantial questions Mike raised, and they trouble me as much as they clearly trouble him. First, I had argued that the struggle of the Vietnamese had transcended politics and become an existential statement about man and his willingness to suffer and endure for what he felt was right. Mike gently expressed sympathy for the emotion that led me to make that statement but argued that I wasn't existential enough, because I failed to point out that after the NLF wins it may turn on its own people just as the government of North Vietnam turned on the peasants in 1954 and compelled a program of collectivizing the land, which may have cost as many as 50,000 lives, and that the suffering and heroism will be mocked by events. Mike is right. I was not existential enough, nor was he. He sees clearly the betrayal that lies in wait for violent revolutions—the rise of a secret police, the concentration of power into the hands of a new elite, the rigidity and puritanism of the new regime. But what he does not see is that he, too, has been betrayed in the course of winning his victory. Both Mike and I and many others on the democratic Left voted for Johnson. Our support was critical and limited, but it was real. We broke our backs to get as heavy a vote as possible for Johnson because Goldwater was the front man for the radical right: the military, the racists. We believed that a broad coalition of civil rights, peace, trade union, and liberal groups could compel Johnson to embark on a serious program of social reform at home, while restraining the military from adventures abroad.

God help us, Mike, we won. We fought our good and rational political fight and defeated Goldwater's war policy. We got Santo Domingo, Stanleyville, and Saigon. We defeated the reactionary domestic policy of the GOP and have seen the poverty fight cut to shreds. There are now 500,000 dead Vietnamese and 15,000 dead Americans—most of them killed since we won our striking victory at the polls. A victory "that clearly proved" that democratic political processes can defeat reaction. Let us pray God we never endure another such victory.

Here is truly the existential tragedy. Bayard Rustin, like some hero in a Greek tragedy, broke off personal and political ties of decades to make a courageous effort, through direct cooperation with the power structure, to get some real action on the ghetto problem. That action never came, and Bayard, whom I admire because he was willing to walk through the deepest shit of politics because he genuinely cared more about the slum kids than about his reputation as a radical purist, now must surely rage in the silence of the night, knowing what he has lost and at how great a cost, and how little, how terribly little, he won. And you, Mike, who know poverty as few other intellectuals, and who, like Bayard, truly cared about poor people, seeing them as human beings trapped in futility and not as statistics or as an excuse for slogans, you saw a chance, after a life spent in socialist sloganizing, to actually *do* something about poverty. Like Bayard, you went "into the camp of the enemy"—as the sectarians might say —hoping to find there enough decency and common sense to make some kind of program possible. And now the war on poverty is over, its forces demoralized and in retreat, for the energy of the nation is involved in Vietnam.

All of us in our generation have made our compromises. Not one of us is a political virgin. But we may, all of us, have learned from 1964 that, at the core of radical politics (and not incidental to it), is a sense of morality. That year should have reminded us that we cannot really predict the results of our acts, and that, for the radical, it is essential to judge the value of the act itself. Means are in the hands of men—the ends are in the hands of God.

I do not mean we abandon logic or rationality, but I do suggest that our rational actions should be infused by a certain moral daring.

Turning to the question of the conflicting slogans "Withdraw Now" and "Negotiation Now!" Mike says he is for "Negotiation Now!" because it is more likely to end the war. I think that point can be debated, but the important question, which Mike leaves unanswered, is whether he personally believes we should withdraw. It is one thing for a man to say he supports "Negotiation Now!" because it is a politically expedient and face-saving device to get the United States to withdraw from the Asian mainland, and it is quite another thing for a man to say he supports the slogan because the United States has some kind of moral right to help lay down the conditions under which we will leave Vietnam. What does Mike think we have to negotiate in Vietnam except the routes our troops will take getting to the ports of embarkation? Does he think we have a right to demand free elections as a condition of our leaving? (And does he believe free elections are possible as long as our troops remain or, for that matter, would occur if our troops withdraw?) Do we have a right to shape the future political system of Vietnam? (And, if so, why only Vietnam? Why not free elections in Taiwan, Spain, South Africa, and the Soviet Union?)

Let us suppose that, for tactical reasons, "Negotiation Now!" is our best slogan—and then let us suppose that, driven by fury and rage, the Vietnamese refuse to negotiate. Would Mike then finally join in urging the unilateral and unconditional withdrawal of U.S. forces?

Let me make it clear—as I've tried to do so many times—that Vietnam is a tragedy that cannot be redeemed, cleaned up, and given a happy ending. If the war stopped this instant and all the Americans went away leaving flowers and candy behind, and all the corrupt Saigon politicians were touched by Buddha, and all the supporters of the NLF were weaned from violence to being gently democratic and compassionately revolutionary, Vietnam would still be a tragedy. More than half a million persons have died thus far, leaving behind women without husbands, mothers without children, infants without parents, all of whom must ache with their loss into the years to come. And there would be the tragedy of the hundreds of thousands of Vietnamese who would have to make their way through even the best of all possible postwar Vietnamese societies minus arms or legs or hands or with napalm-smeared faces. That is what will haunt us even if all goes well.

The problem is that all will not go well. If we win and organized violence stops, Vietnamese self-respect will be destroyed by our occupation, there will be a Saigon-Hilton, the Peace Corps will move in, and the peasants will continue to live in disease and ignorance. If the NLF wins, there will be an end of government corruption, there will be education for the people along with adequate food and medical care—and, also, unless I am greatly in error, the introduction of systemic coercion into the daily life of the individual, the absence of those personal freedoms I greatly value, and the jailing and murder of political opposition. If anything, I have even fewer illusions about totalitarian and violent methods of social change than Mike. Vietnam is a tragedy we may mitigate but cannot erase. That "third solution" for which both Mike and I have worked over the years, a democratic and noncoercive socialism, is not now possible in Vietnam.

Mike is concerned about politics being conducted by an "elite minority" and views the December 5 Whitehall action as an effort by such a middle-class elite to impose its will on the nation. Nonsense! It is one thing to argue that a man has the right to enlist—I agree he does—and another thing to say the government (this government or any other) has the right to compel men to kill and be killed against their will (particularly when most of those being drafted can't even vote yet). To go back into our own history, it is one thing to argue that a Negro had the right to move from the North into the South and sell himself into slavery and that I ought not interfere with that decision. But, if a Negro escaped from his master and moved from the South to the North, I emphatically deny that I should have to cooperate—as

Mike would seem to suggest—with the police under the terms of the Fugitive Slave Act and help return the Negro to his "owner," accepting the law as valid until I could change it by existing "nonviolent and democratic methods."

Mike understands that refusing induction is a moral imperative that may not win the peace but is necessary for the individual. But when it is suggested we block the doors of an induction center, he feels the relevant question is no longer moral but political—that is, "will this action hasten the end of the war." May I suggest that what is politically sound is generally morally defensible and what is morally imperative generally proves politically sound in the long run. All actions, personal and collective, must be judged by moral as well as political standards. It seems to me Mike is trapped in a confusion. If I must examine my political actions in terms of how effective they are (and, if they are "counterproductive," Mike feels they are immoral), why the devil are my personal actions exempt from the same scrutiny? If Mike's approach helps us examine *all* our actions thoughtfully, good, but his approach can be dangerous and ultimately antidemocratic if it opens the way for us to behave as moral creatures only in our personal relations. Mike says closing an induction center may prolong the war by alienating people, and, therefore, it is an immoral action. But quite possibly it will also alienate people (and prolong the war) if I personally refuse military service. Mike opens a Pandora's Box by so sharply dividing personal from collective action.

Mike should not be too worried by public reaction to peace demonstrations nor too eager to keep them respectable. The history of social change shows that any action that brought a controversial issue to the attention of the public aroused tremendous negative reactions. The reactions were more violent and negative if the actions themselves were violent and negative. But even the gentlest action, if it truly forced the public to "see the issue," would arouse storms of anger. Think of the struggle against slavery, the struggle for women's rights, the struggle of labor, and the Negro struggle. In 1955, Martin Luther King was considered a flaming

Communist radical and bitterly hated by the South for the simple action of not riding a bus. He had compelled the South to face a difficult issue, and they hated him for it. Moderate civil rights leaders in the South warned King he was sweeping away, in a matter of days, all the "progress" they had made over the years.

A final point: Mike expresses the hope that I am not "buying the newly fashionable devil theory of an international anti-Communist conspiracy." I'm not sure what Mike means. If he means the theory that America is the root of all evil, it is clear from my November 30 article that I reject that theory. Both as a Marxist and as a pacifist, I believe that men and nations are products of history, as well as the makers thereof, and that if there is any devil, it is neither in the Kremlin nor in Wall Street, but lurking in the hearts of us all, and buried in that series of past events which shaped our minds. But, if Mike is wondering if I think America is, at this moment, the greatest single threat to the peace and well-being of humanity, then the answer is an emphatic "Yes, I do," and I assume Mike does also. Yesterday, it was Germany and Russia and Japan. Tomorrow, it may be China. But at this moment, the "problem nation" is our own. Having said that, I would add that yesterday, today, and tomorrow, the true enemy of mankind is no single nation or ideology but is man himself, just as man's only hope rests in man, and not in any single nation or ideology. It is a hard and lonely position, but the devils and the gods are in us all, all here and nowhere else.

(1967)

Let the Punishment Fit the Crime

On October 27, 1967, Father Philip Berrigan, a Roman Catholic priest; Thomas P. Lewis, an artist; and two other persons invaded a Selective Service office in Baltimore and poured animal blood over the files. On May 17, even before he had been sentenced for his first offense, Father Philip Berrigan, accompanied this time by his brother, Father Dan Berrigan, and several others invaded another Selective Service office, seized draft records and burned them.

On May 24, Father Philip Berrigan and Thomas P. Lewis were sentenced to six years in prison for their action of last October 27. In the meantime, on the other side of the continent, Rap Brown was given a five-year prison term for carrying a gun across state lines while under indictment.

There will be those who will rush to the defense of the Brothers Berrigan (or is it "the Fathers Berrigan") on the ground they are priests acting out of conscience, just as there will be those who will rush to Rap Brown's defense on the grounds that, since he is black, any action he takes is white and exempt from the law. It is clear, however, that, in a democracy, there must be limits on how dissent is to be expressed. Letters, speeches, resolutions, even public demonstrations (providing they don't block traffic and interfere with the rights of others) are valid, constitutionally guar-

anteed methods of expressing protest. The most obvious and forceful method of protest is, of course, the political process itself,
voting for a man and a program that will express one's views.

But when one moves beyond these forms of dissent to direct
action against property, particularly against the property of the
Federal Government, there is no question whatever that such
acts are not constitutionally protected. Federal property (such
as draft cards and draft boards) is—in a democracy—property
that belongs to the whole people and that no small group has the
right to destroy. If these acts of violence against property go un-
punished, they open the door to anarchy and, by encouraging
others to violate the law, create a situation in which the rights of
the dissenter are threatened. The same is true of Rap Brown
and his rifle—the law protects us all, black and white equally,
but if we take the law into our own hands by arming for self-
defense, then the security of the entire community is undermined
and we move backward toward a frontier mentality.

I have, therefore, not the slightest sympathy for Father Berrigan, nor for Rap Brown, just as I have no sympathy for Messrs.
Coffin, Ferber, Goodman, Raskin, and Spock, who ought not to
be surprised to find themselves on trial after their open conspiracy to support those who refused military service.

There is, however, one problem. It is not with the arrests and
convictions—those are absolutely necessary if the democratic
process is not to break down and if respect for the law is to be
maintained—but with the length of sentences. Does the government feel entirely easy about giving Brown a five-year term and
Father Berrigan a six-year term? It is a question I raise out of a
sense of personal concern for the leaders of the government.

Brown, for example, transported an unloaded rifle across state
lines, a gun that he was prepared to use in self-defense. That was
a violation of law and must be punished. But then what shall we say
of men who transport guns not only across state lines, but across
international boundaries, and not for the purpose of self-defense,
but for the purpose of illegal armed intervention in the affairs of
another nation? For example, several years ago, Johnson ordered

30,000 troops into the Dominican Republic, in violation of the treaties that are binding on all members of the Organization of American States. A number of persons, both citizens of the Dominican Republic and citizens of the United States, died as a consequence of that illegal transportation of guns across international boundaries. And, in Vietnam, the President has transported or caused to be transported 500,000 men across international boundaries for the purpose of an illegal, armed, and violent intervention in the affairs of another nation. (The illegality is based on the violation of the Geneva Accords and the violation of that section of the U.N. Charter that requires member states to take any threat to peace to the Security Council for action before proceeding on its own.)

The late Dr. Martin Luther King, Jr., estimated that a million persons had been killed as a result of our intervention in Vietnam. Now, if we assume that a human life is important enough that those who conspire to kill or do actually kill a human being should be punished, and if we set the punishment as low as is reasonably possible—let us say that those involved in planning the war would serve one minute in Federal prison for every person who had been killed—then we have a situation where the President and such associates as have been directly, explicitly, and publicly involved in conspiring to carry on the war (this would include Humphrey, Rusk, Rostow, the Bundy brothers, McNamara, Westmoreland, and so on) would each serve just under two years in jail. If, of course, we decide that a man should spend an hour in prison for every person killed, then those involved would each be sentenced to something over 100 years.

I raise this because of my deep concern with seeing the law enforced. I believe in the majesty of the law. I am not interested in "punishing" people, anymore than the judge who sentenced Rap Brown or the judge who sentenced the Fathers Berrigan was trying to "punish" them. It is the majesty of the law itself that is at stake, as well as the need to deter others from criminal acts. If it is absolutely intolerable to have guns transported across state lines and if it is absolutely intolerable to have blood spilled on draft records or to have those records deliberately burned up (and, in my view, these acts are intolerable), then obviously it is even more intolerable to engage in the burning of people or in the act of shooting them.

The majesty of the law and its power to bind together a democratic society depends on the assumption that justice is blind, seeing neither wealth nor power nor social status. Justice sees only the crime itself. It is perfectly obvious that if the law begins to "see" a priest or a black man and on that basis begins to hedge its indictments or modify its sentences, the majesty of the law is unhorsed. I am certain that men with the keen democratic perceptions of Abe Fortas, Grayson Kirk, and Sidney Hook will agree with me that the law should not "see" the office of President, or Vice President, or Cabinet member, but that it must act on the basis of the crime itself, indicting and sentencing solely on that basis, lifting its blindfold only after sentence is passed, to see whether the man being carted off to prison for conspiring to kill is in the Mafia, the Black Panthers, or the President's cabinet.

Some would suggest that to talk about indicting government officials is unrealistic and that we should therefore content ourselves with indicting priests, black militants, baby doctors, and so on. But these critics are faint hearted in their commitment to law and order, and, by their willingness to see the law only partially enforced, are as great a danger to the majesty of the law as priests who pour blood on draft files or blacks who carry unloaded rifles across state lines.

This brings us back, finally, to the matter of having a punishment that fits the crime. If the courts eventually decide to sentence the present government leaders to one minute in prison for every person killed as a result of their Vietnam policies (and I do not reasonably think we can expect the court to impose a lighter sentence), then six years in prison for merely bloodying draft files seems rather excessive. Even six months would be pretty stiff, and, actually, even a sentence of six minutes would be out of proportion. May I submit that the majesty of the law might best be upheld if the sentences for these men—Father Berrigan and Rap

Brown—were something in the neighborhood of one or two sec-
onds? If the majesty of the law is to be sustained, and the law to
be respected, the punishment must fit the crime. If, on the
other hand, Father Philip Berrigan is sentenced to six years and
Rap Brown to five years, it is clear that the President and his
chief advisers will need to be locked up and the jailer will have
to throw away the keys. Let the punishment fit the crime.

(1968)

V
Black on White

*"To the degree that the
Negro accepts himself he no
longer needs our 'acceptance.' "*

*"Without a coalition, we shall all
die in spirit, and the ghettos will
become ready-made concentration
camps."*

Baldwin Versus the White Negro

A Review of Nobody Knows My Name, *by James Baldwin*

There are books that entertain and books that bore. A few books instruct, but fewer still are those books that force the reader into a dialogue not only with the author but with himself. Such a book is James Baldwin's *Nobody Knows My Name*. It is probable that the work is too alive to be reviewed, that any review may reflect more of the reviewer's own internal dialogue than what Baldwin himself was saying. If so, this is a high tribute to Baldwin.

This slim collection of thirteen essays is enormously stimulating. The writing is lean and clean: the kind of writing that must take an agony of work to produce, because it appears so simple. But, behind the uncluttered approach, there is a razor-sharp mind at work, probing deftly and with depth. The book contains, among other things, Baldwin's essay on Norman Mailer ("The Black Boy Looks at the White Boy"), three essays on Richard Wright, an essay on André Gide ("The Male Prison," a somber study of Gide and homosexuality), and an essay on Ingmar Bergman. I found these interesting, but, because my field is not literature and the arts it would be both unfair and unwise to venture comment on the discussions of Wright, Mailer, Kerouac, Gide, Bergman, and others (though I must say I think Baldwin is too hard on Kerouac and does not fully grasp the significance of the "beats," who are both better writers and more important than he realizes). The book, for me, comes most profoundly alive when it turns to the problems of the Negro minority in this country.

Mr. Baldwin suggests we have overdramatized the sexuality of the Negro, and I agree. Some Negroes are sexually exciting, and some are not, but, taken as a whole, I think there is little basis for the folk myth of the sexuality of the Negro. What I think we do see in the Negro is the *élan vital* traditional to the lower class and reinforced in the Negro because his "primitive" nature makes him more alien, more exciting. But this does not mean he is a sexually unique creature. The young working-class Italians, Puerto Ricans, and Poles I pass in the street also possess this *élan vital* and are as sexually attractive as the Negro. We should remember that the men in the Ozark Mountains have families of ten or twenty (yes, twenty!) children, which should prove something; and the old English folk ballads sometimes have a quality of sexual frankness (for example, "Blow the Candle Out") akin to some of the blues.

The Negro excites the white because of something deeper than sex as the American generally understands it. There is sex as an aspect of romantic love, and there is sex as a physical habit not far removed from masturbation and probably less satisfying than a wet dream. But there is also sex seen as a door, as a kind of opening away from our burden of individuality; sex in the way Otto Rank discussed it, being both a denial and a fulfillment of self—terrifying, essential, and unifying. It is because the middle-class white is so hedged in with taboos, and is "civilized" in such a sharp-edged and pathetic kind of way, that *any* working class is exciting and becomes romanticized as we view it. Not only does the working class seem less sexually repressed; it represents a kind of community feeling denied to us, but one that we delude ourselves into thinking we can achieve through sex. Because we are in the process of moving toward individuality and because this process is invariably painful and even dangerous, we look back (or down) at the working class and see, in its sense of community and in its relative sexual freedom, a kind of Eden lost.

It is easy to fail to see the other side of this "community of feeling" of the lower class—the boredom, the poverty, the physical and mental sickness, the speed with which men age and women wither, the daily limiting and, sometimes, limitless horror. It is only distance that lends romance to the working class. I would even venture the dismal thought that the relative sexual freedom of the working class is paid for by a lack of intensity in the sexual act itself. At least I understand the Kinsey report showed that an extraordinary number of women in the working class never experienced orgasms.

What we see as the sexuality of the Negro is not "sexuality" at all, but rather this sense of *élan vital* plus a disturbing sense of the strength of the Negro (which, in part, accounts for our ambivalent view of the Negro—we both envy and fear him). Beaten by the sheer fact of his birth, he is nonetheless not defeated. We have taken everything from the Negro except life, and, therefore, he has faced life most starkly, most directly. If he has integrated sex into his life in a way that we cannot, it is perhaps because he cannot yet afford our "American illusion" that sex is a fun game. And, so, sex is still tied to birth and dying, still felt as a life-force that may be approached with fear or with joy, with gentleness or with violence, but certainly not with shame (compare Bessie Smith with Elvis Presley).

The Negro, or a member of other lower-class groups, has this sense of integration and wholeness because there is no developed sense of individuality. It is Baldwin himself who points out that "primitive" art is social, not individual, in character, and that the role of the artist in African culture is vastly different from that of the artist in the West, where he is an isolated individual speaking to a small and scattered collection of other individuals. It is the middle class that is forced to grapple with the question of individuality, a question forced on us by our freedom from poverty. But we have no desire for that exploration into and toward ourselves that true individuality demands; we avoid the search by conforming to the standards of society around us. The problem is that our conformity is voluntary, and, thus, our failure to become individuals is a personal failure and a defeat. The conformity of the working class—and particularly of the Negro—is not voluntary, but is forced on him from above, as well as being a natural development in a situation where life permits little time for transcending the narrow limits of "necessity." As a result, the Negro is without that sense of failure that haunts white society. The life of the American Negro is hell—but it is a hell without shame, without the burden of failure and of guilt.

But what happens to the Negro as he seeks to end his status as the "American proletariat?" All other working-class elements—Irish, Italian, Polish—have passed into society despite every barrier we Anglo-Saxons could erect. The Negro cannot pass because his color betrays him. But why do we need this barrier in the first place?

Baldwin, with brilliant insight, drives into the heart of the matter by pointing out that the "materialism" of American society is not essentially materialism at all but an effort, through material objects, to assure ourselves and our neighbors that we possess certain intangible and immaterial qualities. We do not even enjoy our material wealth—we use it, in the old Calvinist sense, to demonstrate to our fellows that we have found favor in the eyes of God, that we stand among the elect. In a society that, lacking any common standards, adopted money as the universal mark of success, we have also used the Negro to guarantee us against failure. Because we lack any clear notion of who we are, the Negro serves the effective purpose of reassuring us of who we are *not*. We are not on the bottom of the ladder, because that is where the Negro is, and that is exactly where we want to keep him. The Negro is proof, tangible evidence, that, even if we have failed, we have not failed totally, because there is someone lower than ourselves. No wonder intermarriage terrifies us. It is one thing to have a sexual liaison with a Negro, but intermarriage means we have lost our place on the ladder, the bottom has been taken out from under us, and we risk infinite "free fall."

And so our insecurity is inflicted upon the Negro. I know from my brief stay in jail how shocking it was to see this insecurity of the whites so visibly and *physically* slashed on the faces of the Negroes. There was hardly a Negro in jail whose face was not weathered by the horror of police violence and the violence that Negroes inflict on one another as a blind expression of their own frustration. (As, in an earlier age, the Irish spent Saturday night beating each other up.)

The American Negro faces a second problem that we have created and imposed on him. Not satisfied with barring the door of the larger society in his face, we have barred him also from himself, from his own roots. We have told the Negro that Africa was a dark and primitive continent, a murky past from which he must somehow liberate himself before we would accept him. And the Negro, looking up from the gutter we had assigned him, wanting the better things of life, believed us, accepted our standards, and sought, not only to be treated as a human, but to become white both psychologically and physically (skin-whiteners, hair-straighteners, and so on).

The Negro is primitive by Western standards. There is no point boggling around about this. Rather than the old argument of the white liberal that, given decent housing and education, the Negro would be as white as any of us, let us re-examine the concept of primitive. And, in doing this, we will find that, without exception, the West as a whole has considered every culture it ever encountered a "primitive" culture. The Aztecs were primitive, as were the Mayas and the Incas, so we destroyed them. The Africans were primitive, so we despoiled them. Because the West first hit upon the scientific method and applied it with vigor, we rose to power and managed to impose our standards on the world. And the world, defeated by the gunpowder and hard steel of the West, half-believed us when we told them they were primitive. After all, we had achieved power, and they had lost it, and this is almost universally accepted as a kind of pragmatic proof of superiority. (Looking back on it, there was an almost incredible arrogance in the West, which was so essentially barbaric, daring to write off the rest of the world as pagan, primitive, inferior.)

In any event, the Negro found himself a minority in a white nation, and he was told that, being an African, he was primitive—which is only another way of saying that Africa is different, which is self-evident. The Negro has spent most of his life in this country trying to live down and forget his African roots and become "truly" an American. But this has simply proved impossible. Had the Negro ever been accepted into the full American society, his African background would long ago have become only an echo, a faint shadow across his interior life. But the Negro was closed out and pressed down. Because he could not be assimilated into our society, he assimilated our culture into his own. He borrowed our language, adopted our religion, took freely from our musical forms—but he shaped these things in a special way, in a way profoundly related to his African past.

However, the problem is again complicated by the fact that, while Africa shaped and continues to shape his thinking, he is no longer an African. He has been in this country longer than most white Americans. He is not an African in America. He is an American influenced by an African past. He cannot become African. The Black Muslim movement would be foolish, if it were not essentially tragic. If it was wrong for the Negro at one point to deny his African heritage, it is also wrong for him today to deny his American heritage. (One must add that, even racially, the Negro cannot claim to be a true African, thanks to the racial mixing carried on by the high-minded southern whites.)

And, so, most Negroes, as they try to rise from the cellar of American society, face a confusion. They seek to be white, but we won't let them. Yet, even if we let them, they still could not be white, for the real job of the Negro is not to become white but to become himself. It is as foolish for me, discouraged by white society, to try to become black, as for the Negro to become white. We shall never make it, either of us. Our only hope is to give up the color game altogether and concentrate on becoming human.

And, so, Baldwin forces us back again to his central point, which is that our task is to be men—not black or white, not Africans or Americans. And being a man involves accepting what and who we are without either shame or pride. I am neither proud nor ashamed of my Scotch-Irish ancestry. What right have I to be proud? What reason for shame? Neither Baldwin nor I should have to bear the responsibility for our ancestors, nor can we take credit for them. They are simply a condition of our being, and the necessary starting point, which we must accept, in our search for our own personal "self." Our ancestors will make a difference between us—but it is a difference and not a division. It is pointless for me to ask if Baldwin is or is not my "equal," as if he were a separate object apart from myself to be measured, weighed, counted out. If I value Baldwin, it is precisely because he is not my "equal" but, far more important, because he is an aspect of myself, and I of him. As Kenneth Patchen has said:

> . . . the white man and the black man,
> The Englishman and the German,
> Are not real things.
> They are only pictures of things.
> Their shapes, like the shape of the tree
> And the flower, have no lives in names or signs;
> They are their lives, and the real is in them.
> And what is real shall have life always.

The white must abandon his romantic image of the Negro as a sexual figure or a dark mystery, fearful and fascinating, and see him as another man, both very like and very unlike himself. This we can do only when we whites know our own identity— when we do not need a segregated Negro to assure us of our place in society. We cannot liberate Eastern Europe until we liberate the South. We cannot liberate the South until we have liberated the North. And the North shall not be liberated until we ourselves stand free and sense, beneath the chaos and terror of our freedom, a meaning and a purpose to our lives.

Nobody Knows My Name will irritate some and baffle others. And certainly this review does not do justice to the book for the reasons stated in my opening paragraph. But the book's value lies exactly in that Baldwin does not merely confirm what we already believe to be true, he forces us to think. In insisting on plunging beneath the surface of things, he has guaranteed that his audience will be limited, but also that, in the long run, his writing will have a profound impact.

One final comment. I have heard that some reviewers were unhappy because Baldwin was so "bitter," and they felt he didn't really appreciate America. Now I do not think Baldwin is bitter as much as he is sad—and angry. And, so, perhaps I should make a point very clearly that Baldwin never makes quite explicit. The American Negro—both North and South—has less real human dignity granted him than the average citizen living under Soviet domination. He is dismayed to find Kennedy prepared to blow up the world for the right of free access to Berlin, while Bobby tells the Freedom Riders to cool off. He is painfully aware that the very same liberals who justified Kennedy's violent adventure in Cuba (or who condemned it only because it was badly handled) would be the first to turn their backs on the Negro if, in his search for freedom, he were to use violence. I cite these things not as an apology for tyranny elsewhere, but only so as to put the appalling racial tyranny in this country in its true perspective. The American people prefer their justice anywhere except at home and prefer their Negroes white and polite. We want to "accept" the Negro on our own terms and in our own good time. Baldwin reminds us how out of date we are. To the degree that the Negro accepts himself, he no longer needs our "acceptance." Baldwin's anger at American society is evidence of an underlying and very real love affair with America, and his ability to reject the standards of white America is proof that, while no one else may, Baldwin does know his own name and has found his own identity.

(1962)

Automation: One More Headache for the American Negro

It is a fact about revolutions that none, save prophets, can see them coming. We can distinguish between the prophets and crackpots only after the event. Revolutions are like earthquakes: They are caused by vast structural changes that occur so gradually they escape notice until some very slight additional stress causes the most extraordinary reaction. All seems calm until the very moment when old patterns shatter and new forces stand revealed.

Almost ten years have passed since Rosa Parks sat in the white section of a bus in Montgomery, Alabama, and by that slightest of strains suddenly unleashed the upheaval we know now as the Negro revolution. Already the name of Rosa Parks is fading into history. The year 1955 seems distant, and it is hard to believe that Martin Luther King, Jr., was just twenty-six years old when the leadership of that local struggle was thrust upon him and he became, overnight, the leader of his people and a world figure. Yet all vast changes have origins, and, in this case, it is important to track those origins down, because the origins of the Negro revolution may now prove to be its stumbling block.

Until 1955, all but a handful of the American liberals and radicals who were concerned at all with civil rights had settled for *pro forma* attacks on southern racism. Groups like CORE (Congress of Racial Equality) limited their work entirely to northern

189

states not because the problem of racism in the North was greater, but because such work in the South was suicidal. It was widely assumed, even on the very eve of December 1, 1955, when Rosa Parks sat down in the "wrong" section of the bus, that "not in our lifetime" would we see a real change in the racial patterns of the South.

I do not mean to paint an inaccurate picture of the southern states before 1955. A Canadian motoring through the South at that time would have seen no Negroes beaten to the ground by southern cops. He would, on the contrary, have seen a society with a grace and charm lacking in the North, a society where Negro and white children played together and where genuine good will seemed to exist between the races. The South was not cut off by a barbed-wire fence running across the continent, nor was segregation maintained by visible terror. But the appearance of calm would have been deceiving. (As, indeed, it did deceive those whites who had lived all their lives in the South and claimed to know it best; as it turned out, they were truly strangers in their own house.)

Segregation was enforced by the whole population, black as well as white, and, therefore, did not require constant and visible police action. In a state like Mississippi, *any* white hoodlum could shoot down an "uppity nigger" and be absolutely confident no jury would convict him—in the extremely unlikely event he was arrested and brought to trial. And, for their part, the Negroes, having learned that even the *appearance* of rebellion could mean death, had long since learned to smile through masks that hid their deepest feelings not only from whites but even, in many cases, from themselves. Negro children were schooled early by their parents in these techniques of survival.

Two forces were at work, however, that spelled the end of this pattern in the South and that made possible a nationwide revolt against all forms of racism. One of these forces dates back to the nineteenth century, while the other is located more than three thousand miles away. This second force was African nationalism. The American Negro had long ago not only been forcibly stripped of his African culture but had willingly yielded up whatever "Africanisms" he could root out on his own. Far from having any pride in his origins, he counted them a mark against him. He generally accepted the white myth of African inferiority. Then, very suddenly, with the rise of African nationalism, the Negro regained a pride in his own origins. (His culture he could not regain; the American Negro remains more American than any other immigrant to these shores.) As the American Negro saw nation after nation emerge to freedom in Africa, as he saw the United States seeking their favor, treating them with ostentatious "equality" in the councils of the mighty, he "reclaimed his past." And, in finally accepting and *exalting* in this past, he gained the psychological footing to struggle for his own future. There is a sweet irony in this. The United States is a *status quo* power today. It opposes social revolutions everywhere, and yet the story of the American Revolution has never ceased to agitate and inspire younger nations. In an odd sort of way, the Negro Revolution is the American Revolution of 1776 coming home to roost, being, in no small part, a reflection of African independence.

But the more important revolutionary force in the South is that of industrialization, and this dates back to the nineteenth century, when, as the Civil War drew to a close, the industrial system was in full flower. Free at last, thousands of Negroes moved north to seek their place in industry. At first, this migration was fairly limited, but World War I saw tens upon tens of thousands of Negroes flow north into war industries. Then, in World War II, hundreds of thousands of Negroes (and poor whites) moved north and, almost for the first time, to the Pacific Coast. But the migration was not simply an exodus from the South. It was also a migration away from the farms and plantations and into the cities, and, as the South developed an industrial base, Negroes moved into these new industrial centers, too.

This shift in population meant three things for the Negro. It meant the development of a small Negro middle class, which could afford to educate its children and, thus, probably quite unintentionally, provide the leadership for a revolt against the racial pattern. Second, it meant that, in the North, where the Negro was allowed to vote, he began to exert his influence on local and national politics. Third, it meant the old traditions of terror that the southern white had used to subdue the Negro would no longer work. It did not matter that the Negroes in the southern cities were demoralized, uneducated, leaderless, and, often, unemployed—the important thing is that they were now an "urban mass." It is one thing for a band of hoodlums to put on white sheets and terrify some Negro sharecropper in the sweet and ominous darkness of the southern night. But, when the same men dress in white sheets and invade a Negro slum, they not only look foolish, they expose themselves to physical attack. To sum up, industrialization gave the Negro a chance to get off the farm and, in some cases, to get out of the slum. It made possible the creation of a group of educated youth, potential leaders who were no longer prepared to accept racism. And it provided physical protection for the rebel and nonconformist.

There was charming historic justice in the fact that, while southern industry was built by an extraordinarily reactionary combination of venal southern politicians—who sought the wealth that industrialization would bring their states—and northern industrialists—who sought to exchange the burden of unionized labor in the North for compliant southern labor—this very coalition of reaction was largely responsible for creating the conditions that meant that, when Rosa Parks sat down just when and where she did, an explosion took place that is still rocking the United States.

There are other roots to the Negro revolution. Ethical impulses were a very important factor. Integration of the armed forces, starting in 1948, gave both Negroes and whites practical experience with integration. The cold war made it necessary to "clean up" America's image in order to defeat Communism. These were all factors, but African nationalism and the American industrial revolution were, I think, the prime movers.

Now, however, the very process of industrialization that helped lift the Negro up threatens to dash him down again. The factory has long been the road out of bondage. Now, this road is closing, for automation is wiping out those relatively unskilled factory jobs that the Negro, with his inferior education, was able to fill. The jobs being created by automation are not ones that uneducated persons can handle and to move out of the "labor force" entirely, into the professions and services (doctors, dentists, lawyers, teachers, and so on) requires a degree of education that very few Negroes have and of social "openness" that American society does not yet possess.

The industrial revolution was the economic base for the Negro revolution. Now the technological revolution—automation— threatens to destroy all the Negro has gained by wiping out that economic base. The question of how the Negro will deal with this threat must be left to another time, but one can only understand how serious a problem new industrial developments pose for the Negro if one appreciates the role industrialization has played in making possible his partial liberation. We are seeing two revolutions moving toward conflict.

(1965)

In Coalition with
the Black Panthers

This article has been written in my mind for two years but, somehow, never got onto paper. It must now be written down, as I find myself entering electoral politics in coalition with the Black Panthers.

On Sunday afternoon, July 21, I was, against my will and better judgment, and without any opportunity to discuss the matter with friends and coworkers, drafted as the Peace and Freedom candidate for the U.S. Senate. Eldridge Cleaver had already been designated the Presidential candidate. My own situation was complicated by the fact that Freedom and Peace (a New York splinter group from Peace and Freedom) had already designated Herman Ferguson as their candidate for senator, and, as a consequence, the Black Panthers, allied to Peace and Freedom, found themselves torn between that alliance and the strong community support they found in Brooklyn for Ferguson, a black militant.

Seeking to resolve this dilemma, the Panthers, late Tuesday afternoon, July 30, entered the offices of Freedom and Peace, marched their staff to the offices of Peace and Freedom, demanded a unity of the two parties, my withdrawal as senatorial candidate, and the designation of Ferguson as the PFP candidate for senator. Thus, they reasoned, the Panthers could be loyal to their agreement to support only PFP candidates and could also, by backing Ferguson, hold their Brooklyn followers.

As that curious confrontation deepened, I went up to the PFP office to help seek a solution. I found myself facing a handful of Panthers demanding my instant, on-the-spot withdrawal. There is a rumor that, in the course of that heated discussion, a gun threat was made. The rumor is true enough—one of the Panthers did make such a threat but was calmed down by the other Panthers present. (The threat was brief and emotional but also tragic, because it shows that guns acquired for self-defense against cops can become an instrument for resolving political differences within the radical movement, because word of the threat is much more exciting for white liberals to talk about than the substantial political issues, and because our subsequent decision might unhappily be seen by the Panthers as a victory for the show of force.) The Panthers left without having gotten my withdrawal, and our committee went into session until midnight. The decision is one for which we were all responsible and about which all of us, I know, have doubts. I did withdraw, persuaded that to run for the senate seat with Ferguson also running would tear apart the Black Panthers.

Perhaps we failed the Panthers, who, at some point, must learn that a genuine coalition not only requires us to "sell" Cleaver to the white community, but also requires the Panthers to sell a white radical to the black community. My brief nine-day race for the senate seat and sudden withdrawal indicates the problems of building a serious coalition. Both the Panthers and the white radicals may have failed the first test, and certainly the Panthers aren't happy—if I withdrew, it is also true that we have refused to endorse Herman Ferguson and simply left the senate race open.

On Wednesday night, July 31, the PFP then nominated me for congress in the 19th congressional district, a nomination that, after several days of discussion and thought, I accepted. Why, having been driven out of the senatorial race by black opposition, did I still accept the thesis of coalition with the Panthers and choose to run for Congress? It is at this point that I begin the article that I've had "written in my head" for more than two years.

This is essentially a letter to the community of white liberals and radicals. It cannot be addressed to blacks, because the static between black and white is too great just now for blacks to listen to an argument that responsibility for our situation rests on both sides.

We must begin with the fact that a breach between blacks and whites has now been formalized. It is not that the black militants hate white racists—baby, they hate us all, racists or radicals. If anything on earth is justified, it is that hatred, though paradoxically it is also terribly unjust. Collectively (and largely unintentionally), we have unmanned the black in our midst, made his woman into Aunt Jemima, laughed sentimentally at the pickaninnies, and written our history as if blacks were never involved in it except, briefly, as a "moral issue" in our Civil War. We have variously raped, lynched, patronized, and humiliated the black man. We have, and this is far more unforgivable than anything else, castrated the American Negro in cultural terms. We made it impossible for him to retain in any coherent way his African heritage. He was deprived even of myths that might have sustained him in time of poverty and despair. (Jews should be particularly understanding of the power of myths—the legends of what was, historically, a minor desert kingdom sustained them through centuries of persecution.) There is an irony in the element of anti-Semitism in the black movement today, for the spirituals sung by the slaves touched more on the mythic Jewish leaders of the Old Testament than on the gospel itself—"Didn't My Lord Deliver Daniel?" "Go Down Moses into Egypt Land," and so forth.

Of us all, only the Negro is truly American, having no other history, no other language, no other religion, save what he found here. Yet he alone, of all those who came to this nation, was kept rigidly outside our culture. The black rediscovery of Africa is understandable, but it avails nothing, for the Negro cannot go home again, even less than I could vanish back into Northern Europe. The black man and the white man will make it together in this land, or they will fall together. History has nailed us to this continent, and we cannot change that absolute fact. This is not to mock the current "Africanization" of the American Negro. If he could not save his religion or language, there is still an inevitable even if, at times, subconscious link to the culture of Africa. Overtly, the slave owners destroyed the African roots. Covertly, those roots continued to grow, though the plant that now springs up is a strange hybrid.

As the black American seeks for his identity, he may search in odd places, and the results may astonish us, but we would do well to keep in mind that cultural traits cannot be destroyed easily, not even by slavery, and, just as we are aware that the Chinese- or Japanese-American carries something of the Orient with him to this New World, so the Afro-American carries something of Africa with him, even when he is least aware of it. Our ultimate goal cannot be simply "integration," in which we admit blacks to the dominant white culture as they pass our culturally devised tests, but it must be the striving toward a multiracial society. There is a massive difference between racial and cultural pluralism and a monolithic concept of integration.

I think, really, that very few of us, even when we were fighting the good fight for integration, realized the degree to which we interpreted integration as meaning that the niggers would learn to act like white folks. In any event, a breach between us, long a reality, has been recognized. We stand on different shores, trying to see our common humanity through mists of alienation and raw hatred. The lines of communication have been cut. We whites are speaking to ourselves, and we have a great deal to talk about, for we are being tried, and, thus far, we have been found wanting.

I want to take up the matter of guilt first, for guilt is a hideous basis for building a movement. Are we, for example, guilty of white racism? Of course we are, myself included, in the same sense that we are guilty of speaking English. Not one of us can grow up in a racist society and not be wounded by it. But racism applies to blacks as well. No one—black, white, brown, or yellow—can avoid the stain of racism. Jews, who currently find themselves in a tense situation vis-à-vis black militants, should understand them, for if the WASPs were anti-Semitic, is there a single Jew who can deny that anti-*Goyische* feeling was part of the Jewish culture?

Such cultural racism is something one can be aware of, but not something there is any point in feeling guilty about. The crime has been committed—locating the guilt in an exact way proves all but impossible. Let me say as carefully as I can that the crime that the white culture has inflicted on the blacks of this nation is so cruel, so heart-rending, so far beyond anything for which I can find words, that, if the first-born of every white household were struck dead tomorrow by the hand of man or God, the sorrow of those deaths would not even begin to equal the sorrow that black parents have lived with for more than three centuries.

The problem is that the slaughter of the first-born of every white household would only compound the misery and not erase it, nor would it have dealt with the matter of guilt. Did you bring any slaves to this country? Obviously not. In fact, many, if not most, Americans immigrated to this nation after the last slave had been set free. Is the refugee from the Irish potato famine guilty? The refugee from the Kaiser's militarism? Even in my own case, where I am told I have four ancestors who came on the May-flower, I myself neither imported nor owned nor traded a slave. And if whites in general profited from black labor, I find it impossible to locate my own profit. Guilt is not general, collective, and hereditary. Guilt is limited, specific, individual. Most of us— the vast majority of us—are simply not guilty for slavery, not guilty for ghettos, not guilty for the racism that infects this nation. Even the poor white, who hates niggers and says so, is a product of his situation and only rarely the conscious creator of it. If, for example, the white southerner is to be held "guilty" for racism, do we not also have to hold southern blacks guilty? Every white child in the South grew up seeing blacks move quietly to the back of the bus, laughing easily when the white folks made a joke, seeming in every way to accept their status. Can one blame that white child who grows up and says that "the Nigras love our way of life, y'all just don't understand"? If you excuse the black, arguing that circumstances trapped him into servile behavior (for rebellion meant death), it is just as true that "circumstances" betrayed the young white into believing a lie to be the truth.

Even the origins of slavery are confused, because the Arabs, current heroes of SNCC as it seeks "Third World" allies, helped collect slaves for sale to white slavers, and even some black Africans helped in the collection of slaves and their sale to whites. The point is that guilt is a stupid and rather dangerous gambit to pursue, for either it is limited and specific, as I suggest, or it becomes so diffuse as to involve everyone and to explain nothing. I do not mean there are no guilty men or there is no guilt. Johnson bears great guilt for the war, as do all the members of congress who remained silent so long. Eastland and Thurmond are educated men who know better and yet lend themselves to the brutalities of racism, and they are guilty. Guilt is a reality, not an illusion, but to feel a vague, general sense of guilt, simply because you are white or American, is not healthy. Guilt is not hereditary but intensely individual. Feeling guilty for things you haven't done is a middle-class luxury for those with the time and money for analysts.

The problem, however, is that, even though we aren't guilty, we are either going to accept responsibility for racism and deal with it, or history will hold us as responsible as if we were guilty. "Responsible" has three meanings. In one sense, it is identical with guilt (that is, if a drunken driver kills a child, we can say that he is either "responsible" for the death or "guilty" of it.) But, in the second sense, it has nothing to do with guilt, as when a man takes his child with him into a store, and the child breaks something—the man will "be held responsible" for the damages even though he isn't guilty. (In the matter of racism, it is somewhat as if our great-great-great-grandparents were wandering around the store breaking things, and the children were being held responsible.) In the third sense of the word, "responsible" can simply mean that a man is mature and reliable—he is a "responsible person."

History gives us a choice of voluntarily accepting responsibility for the past, even though, in every moral sense, we are innocent of what had occurred, or, if we fail to accept responsibility, history will hold us responsible. History is a blind bitch, ruthless, collective, cruel, lacking the slightest sense of justice or mercy. Following the Civil War, both black and white children died of starvation throughout the South. Were they responsible for slavery? Hitler launched a war, and our bombers killed hundreds of thousands of German children. The Japanese attacked Pearl Harbor, and we, in turn, wiped out countless thousands of children in Hiroshima and Nagasaki. Who dares to justify the killing of those children? Old men make the mistakes, and young boys get knifed to death in meaningless gang attacks. The men who brought slaves to this country are long since dead, but we, black and white, are now paying the price of that sin. We are innocent, and yet history will hold us responsible, unless we take responsibility.

I can tell Rap Brown that I am personally innocent, that, having had nothing to do with slavery and having made no profit from it, I choose to live out my brief life in ways that are enjoyable to me rather than to involve myself in the problem of the ghetto. I can argue that, since I'm not guilty, I refuse to be held responsible. But the conditions of our times mean that, innocent as I may be, my apartment may still be robbed by a black junkie, and my own throat may be slit one night by a black man driven mad by the ghetto. Ironically, I may even be struck down by a cop's bullet fired at a rioter. My protection, my hope of avoiding the bumbling stupid wrath of history, that miserable collection of passions and wounds that have gone before, is to accept responsibility and try to change the society. If we would avoid history's judgment, then we must make history, shape it, for, otherwise, it shall work its way with us, and that will not be pleasant.

Justice is a term as elusive as guilt and responsibility. Justice can never be fully achieved, and, if we make justice our sole objective, "untainted" by any cowardly and bourgeois ideas of compassion, it is certain that massive injustice will follow from our actions. The Russian Communists sought justice, not mercy, and we do not yet know how many died as a result; we only know the number of murdered seems to be greater than the number of Jews killed by Hitler. Justice is not revenge, with which it is usually confused. Justice is a concept that applies to the living and, particularly, to the innocent. The search for revenge defeats the search for justice. Let us suppose that, "to secure justice," I go and shoot a cop. What have that cop's wife and children done to me that I have the right to inflict on them widowhood and fatherlessness? Why must they suffer? Justice is oriented to the future, not to the past. Our job is not half so much "bringing the cops to justice" as it is to "let justice roll down like the waters"— that is, to house the homeless, clothe the naked, feed the hungry, provide work for the jobless. To create a just society is not a matter of shooting some people and jailing others—it is a matter, rather, of recognizing that we are, collectively, victims of a situation or a system, and to seek our universal liberation.

But, if justice is a concept that is oriented to the future, it is also a concept that is unfair to those within a society who seek to achieve justice. Those who suffer most directly from existing injustice are usually precisely the ones who must pay the highest price to achieve justice. The cause of the working class in its struggle with capitalism was a just cause, but the capitalists did not starve, were not beaten, were not jailed, were not murdered. Those "honors" fell upon the workers. The cause of black Americans is just, and "if there was justice," the full burden of the massive social changes now required would be borne by others, certainly not by the blacks. By senators Eastland and Thurmond, for example. But they are in good health, while Martin Luther King, Jr., lies dead and buried. My point holds true not only for the black community, which must continue to bear the main burden, but it is also true of those of us in the white community who own no slums, make no profit from racism, and who might choose to live out our lives without being involved in this struggle. Goodman and Schwerner and Cheney are all equally innocent, and not one of them is an "artifact" (if there is an artifact around, it is LeRoi Jones). All three sought justice, and their murder is a tragedy that cannot be revenged and can only be absorbed by the movement as we learn to realize that, paradoxically, the just and merciful suffer in cruel and unjust ways in order to bring a new society to birth.

If there is a slogan I would write in neon letters on the consciousness of every radical, it is simply that: "JUSTICE IS NOT A PRODUCT OF HISTORY AND ENTERS INTO HISTORY ONLY AS MEN CREATE IT IN THE FACE OF HISTORY."

Love (embarrassing and nervous term) is all that can bind us together and make it possible to suffer that injustice that must be suffered if justice is to be achieved, and that can make it possible for those who are not guilty nonetheless to accept responsibility and to act responsibly. Love makes it possible to endure the humiliations that must be endured. Love, first of all, for ourselves, and then love for that group of which we find ourselves a part (which means that I do not despise my own "whiteness," nor that of other whites), and, ultimately, love beyond the limits of our own group. It is in this sense that the slogan "black is beautiful" makes perfect sense. It is a way of lifting one's head and saying, "Man, no matter what you do, I will not hate myself any more. I will not knife my brother because I'm afraid to knife you. I will not seek out your white woman because you make me ashamed of my own skin." For a black man to say that black is beautiful is to say that he is beautiful, and it is a step toward that day when we look at one another with wonder in our eyes and realize that love has no color, no color at all. Love is the power of life, the creator of life, while hatred betrays us into the hands of death, our common enemy. It is love that teaches us, slowly, never easily, that we are part of one another. But, if we would love, then we must be prepared to absorb the violence and hatred of an oppressed black society, rather than rushing in the riot squads.

Friend, let me spell out some home truths. The murder of Schwerner, Goodman, and Cheney hit the North so hard because two of those kids were white. When blacks were lynched in the South we talked about the need for new laws—and we *talked* about it for years and years. If a cop kills a nigger, we will form an investigating committee, taking our own sweet, though deeply concerned, time about it. But let a black man kill a cop, and it becomes a national crisis. Do we think the black community doesn't notice the difference in the size of the headlines in the *Daily News* between these two events? Friend, we asked Martin Luther King, Jr., to take on the burden of history and suffer the violence of white bigots. I am asking us to take on the burden of history and suffer the violence of black bigots. Or did we believe in nonviolence only for black people? Are we saying that it is wrong for blacks (such as the Panthers) to possess a handful of guns to defend the ghetto against police, but that it is all right for white America to possess a massive stockpile of nuclear weapons to defend itself against the Russians and the Chinese? My own position is against all guns and all violence, but, if I were forced to make a choice I'd submit that a Eugene McCarthy presiding over a nuclear deterrent was a greater threat to us than the Panthers presiding over their handful of guns.

Do not ask the black man to love us now. He cannot. Whatever psychic energy he has will be directed toward loving himself, his people, his potentiality. Accept his hatred as a step toward his own liberation. The problem is filled with paradox, for those who are innocent must accept responsibility, those who seek justice must suffer injustice, and the road to love involves hatred.

But, if I urge that we accept black hatred, I would also warn against patronizing that hatred. We should try to understand hatred, but we should not flee in the face of it. Above all else, there must not be any more applause or twittering amongst ourselves when we are called "honkies" and written off as "scum." Those "white radicals" who respond to such attacks by screaming "do it again, harder, harder!" are every bit as sick as those blacks who confuse militant black racism with a radical program.

When I say that we don't call in the riot squad, I do not mean that we castrate ourselves. Nonviolence is not cowardice. The "black militant" who thinks he is a larger person by trying to make whites smaller is a small person who can only grow and develop if his smallness is not patronized.

Because we are not guilty, it would be easy, when falsely accused of guilt, to tell the black that, if he doesn't want friends, then he can damn well go it alone. And yet I ask us to take responsibility, rather than shunning it, because we have the crucial power needed to transform the situation. Courageous black militants can, in their rage, burn down the center of every city in this nation. But only the white community controls enough capital to tear down ghettos and rebuild them. We didn't ask for the power, but we have the power, and if we fail to use it, we then do become guilty for the communal violence that lies ahead.

Brothers and sisters, we tried harder than we realize to make integration work. We certainly tried harder than the blacks understand. I don't blame their anger, but I want us to keep our self-respect. I think of my own Republican, conservative, devout parents who did not move from their home nor leave their church when blacks entered the neighborhood but, instead, fought to integrate the church, losing old friends in the process. I think of them, no longer young, living in the curfew area during the Watts riot, hearing machine guns a block away, and still not moving from that neighborhood. If I did not know how many whites had, in similar ways, put their lives on the line, perhaps I would be more impressed by Rap Brown than I have been.

I ask no pity and no understanding from blacks—they have suffered too much, too deeply, and far too long. But I want us, the whites, to realize we did try and that we must continue to try. And we will try to deal with racism, not because we are guilty, but because we are more decent than we sometimes realize, just as we are collectively or historically more barbaric than we care to admit.

It is revolution that can deliver us: nonviolent but real. The longer we discuss the "problems of racism," the longer we put off the real issue—dealing with poverty and unemployment, regardless of color. The more we look at racism the less able we are to deal with it. The more we look at the real problems, the more easily racism will fade away. Together, we may have the power to transform our society and to eliminate that black poverty that leads to rage and that white poverty that leads to George Wallace.

A revolution without violence cannot be achieved by the blacks alone, nor can it be achieved by white radicals alone. It is frankly doubtful if any kind of revolution, violent or nonviolent, can be achieved at all. Our future may well be George Wallace. But if we want at least to try to control our future, if we want to try shaking history by the neck and teaching it a lesson, we will not do it by being put off by the rudeness of black militants, any more than they can afford to wait until we all confess a guilt most of us can never honestly feel. Thus I choose to run on a ticket headed by a black ex-convict, Eldridge Cleaver. I pledge him my full support. Cleaver knows that, without a coalition of blacks and whites, there will be death in the ghetto in which a few cops and many black children will die. And there will be death in the white areas and the suburbs, too, before the iron fist of white fear closes in. Without a coalition, we shall all die in spirit, and the ghettos will become ready-made concentration camps.

In what I have written, I do not seek to excuse us, but to liberate us to act out of a sense of responsibility, which can be genuine, rather than a sense of guilt, which would be false. I want us to liberate the future, not to revenge the past upon the present. Radical politics is an effort to insure that the past does not entirely dictate the future. It is vital we accept responsibility for a situation we did not create but that, in large part, we may have the power to resolve.

(1968)

VI
Neither Run nor Hide

"Democracy is more than a system of majority rule. It is a system in which minorities and, even, individuals accept a continuing obligation to defend their own viewpoint."

Are We Ready for Space?

I am a science-fiction fan. The names of Ray Bradbury, Theodore Sturgeon, Lester Del Rey, Poul Anderson, and E. E. Van Vogt are familiar—writers who have conjured up for me worlds of the possible, lying just a dimension beyond ours, in time or space. Those of us who are SF fans greeted the launching of Sputnik I with extraordinary enthusiasm. I remember walking through Greenwich Village that night in October, 1957, when news had just come in that the Russians had sent a satellite hurtling into the sky. For a moment the bonds that make the race itself mortal, tied to this planet that must someday die, had been snapped. I stopped someone in the street and said, "Have you heard the news! We've done it!" The fellow looked at me as if I were quite mad, and asked just what it was we had done. "Why, we've sent a rocket into space. We've thrown something into the air, and it didn't come down," I said, groping to explain myself. "Oh," he said, "you mean that thing the *Russians* did." I sobered and realized that what for me had been a victory without nationality, a triumph of science to which every race and nation had made its contribution, had been seen by him as merely "Russian."

Paul Goodman, writing in the American magazine *Liberation* in November of that year, put my feelings better and more clearly than anyone else:

A new thing with heavenly motion made by us
flies in the sky, it is passing every hour
signaling in our language. What a power
of thought and skill has launched this marvellous
man-made moon! And suddenly the gorgeous
abyss lies open, as you spring a door,
to enter and visit where no man before
ever came.   It is a mysterious
moment when one crosses a threshold
and "Have I been invited?" is my doubt.
Yes, for our wish and wonder from of old,
and how we patiently have figured out
the laws of entry, warrant we have come
into the great hall as a man comes home.

The year is now 1966. Less than a decade has passed, and already we have weather and communications satellites; we have hit the moon, and photographed it, and probed Mars and Venus, and sent steel balls hurtling into the sun. And, last December, the Americans succeeded in placing two space-ships in orbit, each containing two men, and in having these two fragile specks of air and warmth, spinning through a blind darkness, meet. One of the teams—James Lovell and Frank Borman—spent two full weeks in space before descending. A long step from where we were on October 4, 1957. Within the next ten years, it seems reasonably certain that men will have landed on the moon and walked on its surface. Perhaps, we shall even have landed on Mars. And, possibly within my lifetime, the first starship will be launched.

And now I have doubts; I do not voice them as an opponent of technology. I know we shall explore space, because, for reasons we have never fully understood, man must go where no man has been before. But I have doubts and hesitations, and I am less than proud of our latest space spectacular. A friend of mine, also an SF fan, and as enthusiastic as I had been at the earlier space flights, was glum and unhappy when he came by the night after Lovell and Borman had landed safely. While we sat and drank, he said, "You know what the whites are always saying about the Negroes in Harlem? 'They haven't got a pot to piss in but they go out and buy a Cadillac.' Well, when I saw the TV shots of this last space flight, that thought ran through my mind. I mean, here we are in a nation where every city has a stinking slum, and we shoot billions of dollars into space just for prestige."

We stand now on the edge of space. We have begun to enter it, to swim outward from our own planet into that vast sea. And now the question, which is terribly real, is: What right do we have yet to go anywhere? Suppose, by some odd chance, we find, when we land on Mars, that there *is* intelligent life—the odds are heavily against it, but just suppose for a moment. And suppose we can establish communication with the inhabitants of Mars, and they ask us about life on the planet earth. How can we reconcile our gleaming ship with the slum of Harlem? How can we explain to this hypothetical Martian that, while our technology has mastered the problems involved in penetrating outer space, we have made so little progress in exploring the "inner space" of our own lives and culture that we are still a world divided and armed, poised on the brink of annihilation?

I do not say for a moment that, until each man lives like a king, we have no right to venture elsewhere. But I don't think it is out of place to say that, so long as any of us lives as beggars, we do not have the right to spend billions on space travel. I don't speak here as an American, but, as a member of the species Homo sapiens, and my comments apply to Canada, France, England, or Russia as well as to America. The money going into the space program could easily rebuild every slum and ghetto in the United States. This is no less true of Russia, where, not only are enormous consumer needs unmet, but, as in my own country, the spirit of man is too often oppressed by political restrictions or the dead hand of a computerized technology.

So long as the earth was all we knew or had any reason to know, our problems were supremely important but still bearable. The boundaries that divided us seemed reasonable. The suffering so many endured seemed endurable. But our entry into space opens a whole new dimension of judgment. Just as it was a great shock for man to learn that the earth was round and that the universe did not revolve around him, so—now that we can "see ourselves from the perspective of space"—we are shocked to find the old concepts no longer adequate.

A world that can lift men into space can lift them anywhere, out of disease and poverty. It is not so much criminal to shoot billions of dollars into space while children starve—it is a form of human arrogance that demeans us in this new age.

For an SF fan, this isn't easy to say—but it's necessary: let the Russians land on the moon first. We are not yet ready to go there. (*They* are not ready either, of course. But the beginning of wisdom, in this matter, would be to measure ourselves by our own highest standards, not by the failings of others.)

What I most desire is a realization by all men, everywhere, that the exploration of space belongs to all mankind, not to Russia or America. Why not pool our space projects, thus accomplishing at least as much at half the cost? Can we honestly want to carry the cold war into space? Can we not see that the first person who lands on the moon will be a human being, not a Russian or an American? And even so, consider this: The green hills of earth are all we have and we have blighted them. Are we now to go, barbarians, into the unknown?

On this threshold, we should pause. True, space is ready for us. It awaits us. But *we* are not yet ready. We shall never be fully ready or entirely perfect, and we can't hesitate at the door forever, fussing with our tie and straightening our jacket. But, somewhere out there, as we probe steadily farther, we shall encounter intelligent life. When the encounter comes, I want our emissary to be proud of the world for which he must then speak. And, if, after exploring to the limit of our powers, it should prove that we are, in fact, the only form of intelligent life in the universe, how much more imperative that we make of our loneliness something magnificent, rather than something squalid.

(1966)

A Prophetic Minority

A Review of the Book by Jack Newfield

To understand the New Left is probably impossible, but Jack Newfield is foolish enough to have made the effort, youthful enough to be involved knowingly with his subject, journalist enough to have treated the matter with objectivity, and honest enough to have clued us to his bias so we can guard against it (that is, he is mad at Nat Hentoff, heavily influenced by Mike Harrington, hostile to the DuBois Clubs). He also writes well. In the passages on the civil rights movement, his normally good prose is lifted by a special passion.

The New Left is a difficult thing from any standpoint. It is too young to provide the material for a history, yet it has been around long enough so that we can't pretend it isn't here. Newfield has wisely chosen to write a biography of the movement rather than a history. He has not written a definitive study. No one has—or can. Ten or twenty years from now scholars, distant from the passions of this period, will give us a definitive treatment (it may not be correct or accurate, but it will be definitive). When those scholars, uncommitted and disengaged, dissect this period, Jack Newfield's book will be source material. *A Prophetic Mi-*

nority is a vital book but not an eternal one. It is not a book that staggers under the weight of extended intellectual analysis. (Which is not to say that Newfield does not raise some very sharp and probing questions.) This book is a report about now. It was written by someone who is involved in now. If you want some idea of what the New Left is about, this is a book to be read now.

I would suspect that thousands of young radicals in and around SDS and SNCC will buy the book and read it—not because they want to understand themselves, but because, simply, this is a sympathetic story about them, in which they are the heroes, and in which they will recognize the place names and even the terrain where the great battles were fought.

After a generous introduction by Mike Harrington—who has his disagreements with Newfield and hints at them—Newfield lists some seventeen persons, starting with his mother, to whom he dedicates the book. I think he would have been more true to his own position if he had skipped over the names of individuals, no matter how worthy, and dedicated the book to the person who really inspired him and who won him from the middle-class conformity of Hunter College to active participation in the radical events of our time. That person is not Wechsler or Kempton or Harrington (God love them all) but is the individual, courageous, confused, agnostic, often anonymous kid who, without benefit of ideology and without any meaningful hope of salvation, yet stormed the gates of heaven.

The New Left confuses us because it is not—as Newfield points out—just the Old Left minus thirty years. It is, in fact, new and, therefore, automatically hard for those, like myself, whose roots are in the Old Left, to understand. Our yardsticks were designed in another time, made to be used in measuring other objects. We are like those brilliant, logical, decent physicists who first confronted Einstein's theory of relativity. When the good men of hard logic, like Sidney Hook, attempt to deal with the New Left (and, unhappily, they do insist on trying to deal with it), they are simply baffled and irritated and furious. They are also, when one reads their analysis, pathetic. It is not a question of whether, for example, Sidney Hook is right or wrong in his comments on something like civil disobedience—he has done the best he could, but he is simply irrelevant.

The Old Left, for all its seeming divisions into Communist and Trotskyist and Left Socialist and Social Democrat, shared common ground. And that common ground was Marxist. Which is to say it was a movement with a clear, masculine, rational ideology. Suffering could be abolished. Disorder in society could be ended. Utopia—a rational and scientific utopia—could and would be established through the Party (which was not a moral movement but a scientific weapon of history). The debate was over which Party and which tactics—the common ground of Marx and historic inevitability, and so forth, was taken for granted. (The only group that did not share this common ground was the "kooks" of the socialist movement—who happen also to have been the great men of the American Left. Men like Eugene V. Debs. Because, underneath their Marxism, was an irrational commitment to values, a sense of humanity and its power to transcend any dogma. Debs left us no books of abiding theoretical value. Instead, he left us a heritage to which we can still turn—courage, honor, truth, compassion. The brilliant men of the Left have given us books, but not a legend. Men need books and analysis, but they need a sense of their own humanity even more—which is why someone like Norman Thomas has meant so much more to the Socialist movement than the more logical, more politically astute Max Shachtman. One man stands for moral values; the other represents the world of maneuver and manipulation.)

This common ground was sufficient that, for all the bitter disagreements, there was a dialogue within the Old Left. Reams and reams of dialogue. Books, discussions, bulletins, pamphlets, public debates, forums. But, between the New and the Old Left, there is no dialogue. There is disagreement but no discussion. No New Leftist is writing long articles to convert those of us in the Old Left to their point of view. Nor do we write to them. We write about them, we write against them, but we do not write to them, because we do not understand the new grammar. Because the vocabulary has changed. Because the common ground does not exist.

To be very simple for a moment, and, therefore, less than accurate, the Old Left believed the working class was the force of social change, the Party would lead the working class (democratically or undemocratically), and the victory of the working class was inevitable. The New Left does not see the working class as the main force for social change (if anything, it tends to see it as a reactionary force), it doesn't have a Party to believe in, it doesn't sense that society is likely to be rational, and it is without any theory that would assure it that victory was inevitable.

The New Left cannot be lumped together. It is a mistake even to try, as I just have, to suggest a single theme for it. Its heroes and sources are as diverse as Camus, Sartre, Goodman, Rustin, Malcolm X, Leary, Castro, Ginsberg. The New Left includes Black Nationalists (often "white Black Nationalists") and, also, youth who bitterly oppose this new brand of racism. It includes pacifists and, also, those who urge revolutionary violence. It embraces the user of LSD and those who decry the use of any drugs as a cop out.

But the factions of the New Left do have certain things in common. Where the Old Left played down the sense of individualism or "selfness"—this being a bourgeois hang-up that interfered with one's political reliability—and was suspicious of pleasure and doubtful about art forms that did not advance the revolutionary cause; the concern for the individual, the "self," the discovery and assertion of "selfness," is very important to the New Left. Students did not go south to risk (and sometimes lose) their lives because victory was assured or inevitable but because they felt it necessary, personally, to go south. The courage of the New Left is greater than that of the Old Left in somewhat the same way the Old Left is more courageous than the Christian martyrs. After all, it means little for the Christian believer to risk his life in a just cause—heaven awaits his demise, and a holy death assures his immediate admission. The Old Left had no heaven, and yet it risked death. But at least it risked personal death in a collective cause where the victory was certain (so it was felt). The individual might be imprisoned or killed, but the workers would take power, and mankind would be liberated. The New Left has neither the assurance of heaven nor the confidence of any victory. The workers probably will not take power, mankind may not be liberated, and, yet, on the basis of personal values and individual morality, the New Left radical enters into the struggle.

The New Left believes in pleasure and in spontaneity in a way that terrifies all of us in the Old Left. In sexual matters, for example, I think it would be accurate to say that the Old Left—particularly the Communists and Trotskyists—were puritans. They used sex freely, but they used it to recruit. To "use sex" is instantly and fundamentally to debase it, to take the Christian view of it, as being a means to an end. Whether the end is that of the Catholic Church—that is, conception—or that of the Old Left—that is, new recruits—makes no difference. One doesn't sleep with others because of pleasure in the act of love. The concept of individual pleasure is almost counterrevolutionary. The New Left doesn't, I am sure, "sleep around" any more than the Old Left, but it has the disturbing habit of making love because of the pleasure that act gives, because of the desire to touch, to communicate, to actually love.

And the New Left is also disturbing in its dedication to spontaneity. The Old Left not only had a common ground in Marx, but it agreed on the ground rules for the game. One was loyal to the organization, to the Party. There were fights and arguments and factions, but, once the leaders reached a decision, it was accepted. Gus Hall, the Communist, and Max Shachtman, the anti-Communist, have far more in common than either has with the New Left. Both see the need for obeying the rules of the game, and for accepting the decisions of The Party. But the New Left can't be trusted. One can't make deals with them. No sooner do you think you've reached an agreement with, for example, the SDS leadership than you find their rank and file has overturned the decision. This is chaos, anarchy. It is irresponsible. Those of us who are leaders are terrified lest the same kind of rank-and-file sense of individual power and responsibility creep and seep into our organizations and undermine our authority. (And, in the Old Left, it is the leadership that is important. There is the story I got from Dwight Macdonald about the time a fire broke out in the headquarters of a Trotskyist organization and the leader— nameless here—rushed to the door, brushing aside secretaries and file clerks, crying, "Save the cadres, save the cadres.")

I do not want to be too hard on the Old Left. Brecht, in his poem "To Posterity," told us something of the inner agony of the dedicated Communist, the dehumanization that occurred within him, his awareness of it, and his willingness to make that choice willingly to advance the cause of humanity. Compassion was the trap that led the Old Left into inhumanity. Pity and compassion turned it against the inner self. It was afraid of love, which, being irrational, threatened the whole scientific view of how the world could be changed. Newfield is too harsh in his comments on the Communist Party (comments that could apply as well to the Trotskyists and to a good part of the Democratic Socialist movement). Yes, they were hacks, and bureaucrats. But, at what a cost, Newfield does not begin to understand. Particularly in the case of the Communist Left, which carried the debasement of human values furthest, and was most prepared to "use" human beings, including themselves, I think we see something almost saintly. Catholics certainly ought to understand how like a priest, burdened with antihuman vows, the dedicated Communist can be.

If I have been hard on the Old Left, it is not because I am entirely soft on the New Left or because I think every idiot project of SNCC or SDS has some special blessing because it was conceived by youth. I am furious at the New Left at times. But it seems to me that the real problem of those of us in the Old Left —who are standing on one side of the "generation gap" of which Newfield writes—is to speak to the "men of our generation," who are so caught up in their anti-Communism that they can applaud the slaughter in Indonesia or support the Vietnam policy of Johnson.

I vigorously disagree with Staughton Lynd and Tom Hayden

and Stokely Carmichael. Not on one issue alone, but on several. And, yes, it is wrong for the New Left to find integrity in the hacks of the Communist Party who wrote apologias for the murder of Jews in the Soviet Union or workers in Budapest. But it is more urgent now for us to ask some of our own friends in the liberal and, even, in the socialist movements to break their ties with men like John Roche, intellectual commissar for Johnson, or men like Leo Cherne, Frank Trager, Louis Stulberg, Aaron Levenstein, Sidney Hook, and the others who signed the recent Freedom House ad in *The New York Times* in which they made their apologia for murder in Vietnam and became men as morally corrupted as those intellectuals who collaborated with Hitler or with Stalin (more corrupt—for they live still in a free society and could have refused to sign the ad). Who is the greater danger to American values—a Herbert Aptheker, who defended the Soviet actions in Hungary ten years ago, or the men I have just named who defend a far greater slaughter, which is occurring now? How can we blame the New Left for its bitterness, when we realize that Roche was, until recently, chairman of ADA? I know he does not speak for ADA. I know, in fact, that ADA's position is a fairly good one on Vietnam. But when men like Roche, Trager, Levenstein, and so on, can claim to be liberals and continue to move within that framework, one must not be too surprised if the New Left, observing this, charges that liberalism is morally bankrupt.

But I have strayed from the book at hand. Newfield's chapters on SNCC and SDS are extremely valuable reading, particularly for those who politically matured in the 1930's and early 1940's and, thinking back to their own times, assume that youth organizations must be controlled by someone or organized by agents for one group or another. We must not project our past onto the present, for that is not wisdom but rigidity. Newfield points out that the existential New Left is basically different from what he terms the "Hereditary Left," which is made up of the actual or ideological sons and daughters of the Old Left. He is correct, for example, in assigning a group like the DuBois Clubs to this "Hereditary Left."

One of the peculiar things about the New Left—and I don't think Newfield develops this enough—is the degree to which this youth movement is genuinely without parents. It had a kind of virgin birth without even a virgin. The old Young People's Socialist League was the child of the Socialist Party. The Young Communist League (later American Youth for Democracy and then Labor Youth League) was the child of the Communist Party, and so on through all the youth groups. But SDS no sooner got going than it disowned its father, the League for Industrial Democracy, and broke from it. SNCC never really had parents. The most vital sections of the New Left are, in a sense, homeless.

And they will perish in time, for youth movements come with the wind and go with graduation. In 1960, the Student Peace Union was the organization (and it, too, had no parents). Now it is all but gone. SDS will go; SNCC may vanish. But I think Newfield is right in arguing that whatever the fate of any given organization, these young radicals, taken collectively, are "a prophetic minority."

Finally, I think Newfield is weakest in his furious attack on the Beat Generation, which he patronizes at best, and toward which he is obviously hostile. And I think he underestimates the degree to which the "drug revolution" is affecting students today. Newfield's book is a portrait or biography not of a whole generation but of a segment of a generation—the political activists. But, unlike other periods, one cannot simply divide youth today into the exciting and creative nonconformist minority and the conformist majority. There are two nonconformist groups today. One is Newfield's group, the political activists, the New Left. The other consists of the inheritors of the "Beat Generation," changed, altered, but still relentlessly pursuing its goal of building its own community within the framework of a disintegrating culture—or, if you like, creating its own society outside of society. In this, it differs basically from the New Left, which is committed to changing (not ignoring) the existing society, remaking it into a community. These two groups, so very different in so many ways, overlap. They often share the same heroes. And they generally share an interest in pot. (Question: Is this generation different because it uses pot, or does it use pot because it is different?)

Newfield's book, whatever its limits, is a treatment of the New Left that manages to be fair and yet also exciting, that reports and also probes and questions. I commend *A Prophetic Minority* to those of my generation if only so that they may have some idea of the gulf that separates us from the new radicalism. I would hope Newfield's book might also lead those of us in our thirties and forties and fifties to view the young radical with greater sympathy. It is wrong for the young radical to say no one over twenty-five can be trusted. Let us not be so foolish as to reply that no one under twenty-five is worth listening to.

As a kind of postscript to what I have written, I find, on reading it over, that Jack Newfield's book gets lost in my ruminations about the Old and the New Left. I do not apologize for this—if *A Prophetic Minority* set my mind wandering away from a chapter-by-chapter analysis into broader considerations, that is a tribute to the book. It is not only extremely well written, but helpfully provocative.

(1966)

CIA and US: The Face You See May Be Your Own

In all the excitement over subversion of the National Students Association by the Central Intelligence Agency, we are missing some important points. By blaming the CIA, we avoid a deeper examination of the level of national corruption, which led to that particular tie in the first place.

Let's begin by admitting that, if we insist on defending ourselves with nuclear weapons and on waging a cold war that has, as its central purpose, not the alleviation of those social conditions that might produce Communist victories, but rather the systematic suppression of any attempt—Communist or non-Communist—to achieve a social revolution, then we shall need a CIA. It will do some very nasty work, not different in kind from the nasty work done by the Soviet counterpart of the CIA. I feel no great pity for spies—they are self-chosen for work that is demeaning, risky, and, for the most part, boring. But neither do I feel any great sense of outrage or surprise that the United States and the Soviet Union (and Britain and Israel and France, etc.) do nasty things of this kind. (All of us owe a debt of gratitude to John Le Carré for *The Spy Who Came in from the Cold*. It was not only an excellent novel but, unlike most spy novels, it showed us that, when you play "cold war," "good guys" and "bad guys" become such distant and ultimate abstractions that they cease to exist as realities. Le Carré presented us with the painful truth that, at the operating level, there is no difference between their side and our side.)

One cannot, on the one hand, opt for "winning the cold war" and then draw back from what is involved. My own position, that of a pacifist who opposes both sides of the cold war, is such a privileged sanctuary that, within certain limits, I don't feel I have the right to question the tactics of one side or the other and have, instead, an obligation to question the basic premises from which both sides operate. However, in the present situation, I think the actions of the CIA require the thoughtful and systematic condemnation even of an irrelevant pacifist.

It is helpful, in approaching matters of this kind, to retain a sense of humor. Take the FBI and the Communist Party, for example. There is no governmental agency more sacred and holy to conservative Congressmen than the FBI, nor is there any enemy more deeply hated than the Communist Party. Is there not a wonderful sense of the absurd, therefore, when one realizes, that, without the FBI, the Communist Party would be bankrupt, and, without the Communist Party, the budget of the FBI would long ago have been slashed drastically? It has been estimated that perhaps a fifth of the CP membership are FBI agents. They would, one assumes, be the most active members—for the man who does the best job of recruiting and organizing is both least likely to be suspect as an agent and also in the best position to know the inner secrets of the Party. Thus, the CP finds itself heavily dependent on its FBI cadre for funds (dues, contributions) and organizational thrust. One can safely guess that, back in 1956, when the CP was on the verge of breaking up, the FBI contingent voted as a bloc with the Stalinists and kept the Party going. (I remember, at one point when the CP membership had dropped to a hard core of the faithful and FBI agents, that Hoover, frightened lest his budget be cut, went before Congress to argue that the CP was more dangerous than ever before, since, as it grew smaller, it grew more disciplined. Logically extended. this would mean that, when the CP shrank to one member, we would be on the verge of a revolution.) In any event, I find the situation funny—all those Southern Congressmen voting tax money for the support of the Communist Party. And, while I was at all times opposed to the persecution of the CP, I cannot be expected to feel great sympathy when an organization, itself guilty of covert actions, was corrupted by secret agents of the FBI.

There is also marvelous humor in the present revelation of the NSA-CIA link because, next to the FBI, the CIA is the conservative's favorite government agency. For years, the conservatives have been hammering at NSA as a Communist front and demanding its tax-exempt status be lifted, and, now, it turns out to have been a CIA front!

In examining the penetration of the NSA by the CIA, I will not waste sympathy on those student leaders who took the money. The current liberal line is that they were only students; they were tricked into signing binding oaths before they found out what they were up against; they faced legal prosecution if they broke that oath; and so on. I am sorry, but I remember NSA from my own campus days, and it was then, and has remained, essentially an organization for campus liberals who didn't have the courage of their convictions, for social misfits who couldn't make it into the best fraternities, and for student politicians. There were few exceptions. There were some very good men and women in NSA, but basically it was always something of a collection of finks. The CIA didn't corrupt them—it just bought goods that were already on the market. What, after all, am I supposed to feel toward the young men who accept special-for-me-only draft exemptions in exchange for playing games with the CIA? And, if I had any doubts whatever about the moral character—or lack of it—of most of the NSA leadership, those doubts were removed when twelve former presidents of NSA issued a joint public statement to the effect that the CIA had no impact on their policy decisions (*The New York Times,* February 26, 1967.) Leaving aside the interesting mechanics of who drafted the statement and tracked down twelve different individuals whose terms of office spanned more than a decade, I think it is obvious the CIA influenced and, to a great extent, determined the international policy of NSA. If the CIA had simply wanted to support NSA because it provided a healthy alternative to the world Communist student movement, it never needed, at any point, to make direct contact with the NSA leadership. All that was required was that CIA funds be pumped into foundations that would, in turn, provide grants to the NSA for its international program— no strings attached and no questions asked. That would have been a reasonable procedure, and there would have been no reason for anyone to be suspicious. Private foundations have given massive grants for everything from small liberal arts colleges to educational TV. No, the reason the CIA sent agents to talk to the NSA leadership is because they did want to determine policy and would not give the money unless they could. In this world, I am reminded, you don't get something for nothing.

I know how great the temptations were—draft exemptions, travel allowances to see the world, and, I assume, assurance of a secure and profitable future after their tour of duty with NSA was finished. But I cannot be asked in general to take students seriously and treat them as adults (which, incidentally, I think they are) and then be asked to make exceptions for NSA presidents. Students should be able to vote at eighteen, able to drink at eighteen, and mature enough to at least accept responsibility when they decide corruption is the swiftest road to the top. What hurts—and the reason my judgment is so harsh—is that these were not slum kids with broken homes and poverty and hunger driving them on toward an underground existence (those kids we send off to prison when they get caught). No, these were our "best." Give me the honest corruption of the slums every time.

The press of this country has played an extremely curious role in the whole affair—a role so curious it is not surprising that the press has chosen not to comment on that role. The CIA is very very big business. Wise and Ross, in *The Invisible Government,* gave us some idea just how big—and threw out a number of leads that might have been followed up. The *Times* did follow up—with a five-part series on the CIA, which ran last year and which, it is now obvious, was not a report but a cover-up. Is the public supposed to believe that the government can fund the major student organization in the country for fourteen years, can penetrate the trade union movement, can channel money through a range of foundations, and that it requires *Ramparts* magazine to break the story? That is a bit much!

Ramparts got the story by a very lucky accident. Without trained reporters or skilled sleuths, it managed to track the story down and crack it. (I have at least a vague idea how unskilled the reporters were because a friend of mine did some of the New York sleuthing—this was the first time in his life he had tried anything of the kind.) Are we truly to believe that, after all the hints about the CIA—from Wise and Ross, from the *Nation,* from Victor Reuther, and others—that it took *Ramparts* to locate a story? Where was *The New York Times? The Washington Post?* The *St. Louis Post-Dispatch* or the *Los Angeles Times?* Any of these papers has the staff and the skill required to crack the story. All of them knew it was there. Where was the late *Herald-Tribune* during all of those years? The press was implicated up to its neck and at the highest levels. For reasons, I assume, of national security, they chose silence. It is to the credit of the *Times* that, once the story broke they did follow it up—part of the way. But only a small part of the way. Everything we have been told thus far is only prelude to the kind of story the reporters would dig up if the publishers gave permission.

Let me say, in passing, that the recent statements by Meany and Lovestone reflect no credit on the labor movement. Their denial that the AFL-CIO has been closely tied, in its international work, to the CIA flies in the face of established facts. I would not term the two men liars, for I don't want to be sued for libel. But if they were not lying when they denied knowledge of links with the CIA, then they are the two most stupid men in a movement that has never been overly strong on brain power. Not only stupid, but, considering what it was they were standing in up to their necks, I would say their olfactory senses were also deficient.

I do not want to make the CIA the scapegoat nor do I want to term it as witless as it might seem. One student paper commented that, if the CIA had one clear head for every two black eyes it had acquired, it would be the brightest intelligence unit going. But in fairness to the CIA, they managed to carry off the penetration and subversion of the NSA over a fourteen-year period before a student blew the whistle. (Minor note on the niceties of international spy relations—the Soviets, whose own intelligence service must surely have had most or many of these facts for some time, refrained from exposing the NSA.) It was Senator Kennedy who pointed out that the decisions on this matter were approved at the highest levels from the time of Eisenhower through Johnson. Which means that Jack Kennedy also knew and approved. It would be much more comforting to me if I could feel the CIA had acted on its own, that the profound corruption involved was not known at the highest level of the government. But it is to Senator Kennedy's credit that he has forced us to face the extensive nature of the corruption involved, a corruption that includes himself and his late brother.

The liberals have been attacking the operations of the CIA on the grounds that it has been clumsy and inept and too often reactionary in its policy decisions (as in the Cuban invasion plot). But those are the wrong grounds on which to attack the CIA. They are also inaccurate grounds. It has not been as clumsy as liberals like to think nor is it always so reactionary. More than one former socialist or ADA member has chosen voluntarily to work with the CIA. There is no doubt that, within the CIA, there is, in addition to the East European refugee element, a "left wing." If *The New York Times* were to investigate the various extreme right-wing East European- and Cuban-refugee groups in this country, they would find them linked to the CIA. But, at the same time, the CIA financed the trips abroad of extreme left-wing student leaders. I know one former leader of the Student Peace Union, with a hard neo-Trotskyist anti-American and anti-Soviet line, who had no difficulty getting funds for trips abroad. The last conference this leader attended was, as I recall, in Rome. And, there, this radical anticapitalist student leader did an effective job for the CIA (wittingly or not) by organizing a bloc with the Chinese Communist faction to defeat every move by the Soviet faction.

There is an irony in this for me. For years, a favorite tactic of the Communist Party was to point to those of us who were not Communists but who held a radical position and charge us with being "agents of the state," with the sole purpose of "splitting the unity of the revolutionary movement." The last time I heard that charge was in Tokyo last year when I was attending a Japanese-American peace conference. One of the observers, a Canadian representing the Communist-oriented World Peace Council, was passing around the word to the Japanese and to observers from other countries that I was an agent for the State Department. I was both angry and amused—and, when I met with the World Peace Council people a couple of weeks later in Germany, I "filed an official complaint" against their Canadian friend. But now I must say I can't really blame the man. The CIA has not only undermined the credibility of NSA spokesmen abroad, but, paradoxically, it has also undermined the credibility of all of us on the left who have opposed U.S. policy for years, because it turns out that some of us were "agents of the state."

For me, the most shocking aspect of the information we now have on the CIA is the extent to which the CIA represents the corruption of American life. A little spying between enemies is a friendly and accepted thing. But the relationship of the CIA to the NSA (to pick out only one relationship among many) reveals to how profound an extent the American government has become the enemy of American values.

At the risk of being called a red-baiter for going back over old (but historically accurate) ground, let me compare the present situation to the rise of McCarthyism. I have always held that the Communist Party itself helped make McCarthyism possible. During the late 1930's and throughout the 1940's, the CP gained very real influence within this nation. It held key posts in publishing houses, school systems, trade unions, and the government.

Those posts were gained and that power acquired through hiding one's membership in the CP, moving up in the bureaucratic chain of command and winning power or influence through the sheer inertia of a seniority system. Various front committees were set up, enlisting, for the purpose of the letterhead, non-Communist public figures. The Communist Party did use deceit to win its moderate influence and power, and it justified that deceit by arguing that, if it were more honest, it could never have won such influence. The end justified the means.

The result, however, is that, when McCarthy emerged and made his insane accusations, they had a ring of truth. Since virtually all Communists denied ever having been Communists, the mere fact that a man insisted on his innocence might be seen as proof of his guilt. And those who might otherwise have defended the Communists in their time of troubles had been so burned and embittered at having earlier been used for political purposes with which they did not agree, and were so furious at having found their organizations subverted and their personal trust abused, that they became, too often, pathological in their anti-Communism. The secrecy of the Communists fed the paranoia of McCarthy, and, while I think that period was one of the most disgraceful in the history of our nation, the Communists must share in some part of the blame for the hysteria we term McCarthyism. Privately (of course not publicly), I think some CP leaders would now agree with me.

Yet we have done precisely this with the CIA. We have betrayed not only foreign trade-unions or foreign press-associations—which, God knows, would be evil in itself—but we have turned subversion upon ourselves, against our own citizens. I have no sympathy for the NSA leaders who sold out—but there were only a handful of those. What of the hundreds and thousands of students within NSA (or within any of the other organizations subverted by the CIA) who trusted their leadership and believed in the integrity of the policies their organizations adopted? A handful of the members of these groups will regret that no one offered them a slice of the CIA pie—but most of the members have been hurt in the terrible and dehumanizing way that we always hurt someone who trusted us and whom we then betray.

Even on a practical level, we are going to suffer. Every Peace Corps worker will now be suspect. Every dedicated archeologist working in the sands of time in Egypt or India will be looked upon as an agent. Every scholar will be doubted when he travels abroad. Every tourist will be seen as a spy. All of the positive work of American voluntary organizations working throughout the world will now be very much harder. What victories the CIA gained in the short run, it will lose in the long run, with interest.

But the price we will pay does not end there. Now that we know we have government that believes lying and deceit is not something for exceptional circumstances but simply standard operating procedure, it is a vast understatement to say our credibility has been weakened. Why, if the CIA could invade Cuba and could involve itself in the slaughter of between 300,000 and 500,000 Indonesian Communists and pro-Communists, should it not have arranged for the murder of Malcolm X? The French have been hostile to us in part because they think we plotted against de Gaulle several years ago. The French are probably right—but even if they are wrong, who would now believe any denial from the White House? There are those who believe John Kennedy's murder was the result of a plot in which the FBI and the CIA were involved. That is a fantastic, lunatic, paranoid charge. The trouble is it might also be true. And whether it is true or not true, many citizens will find it quite possible to believe that one part of the government plots the assassination of private citizens or even of public leaders; all that we have learned inclines us toward that kind of paranoid view. We have really corrupted something without which a democracy cannot endure very long— a sense of trust and good will that, to some extent, cuts across even class lines. The men who run the CIA are brilliant at tactics but very stupid in working out their long-range results.

But I return to an earlier point—I do not blame the CIA. I blame *us*—our society. We are lacking in moral fiber, as Goldwater used to tell us in 1964. That inner lack is not indicated by the amount of love-making going on among the kids, or by the fact they smoke pot, or by the fact homosexuals are more open now than they once were. The morality of a nation is not judged by how it makes love. Our corruption is shown by something quite different—our willingness to treat people as commodities that can be bought and sold. The CIA buys the NSA, and the liberals object because they feel it was either clumsily handled or unnecessary, while the conservatives object to the fact that any-one objects at all. It hasn't seemed to occur to many people that what the CIA did was morally wrong. And that those who knew about it and tolerated it or authorized it were also morally wrong.

When we talk about "morality" and the lack of it, about the "corruption of our youth," we like to take off after the queers and acid heads and pot heads and pornographers. It is painful to realize the corruption is not there at all—it was in Eisen-hower and Kennedy and Stevenson and *The New York Times.* They were willing to buy off the world if they could get away with it. The CIA isn't a monster of some kind—it is just a reflection of us. We will buy off a revolution, if we can, and, if we can't, then we'll get nasty and use napalm.

The CIA is being justified on the grounds that every method that will defeat Communism is valid. But why, may I ask, were we trying to stop Communism in the first place? Was it not be-cause Communism—particularly as we saw it under Stalin—used individual human beings as means and not as holy, unique, and absolute ends? What is the difference, really, between an American society run by the CIA and the Pentagon and one run by the Russians? (If I were given a choice, I'd opt for the former only because I am a poor student of language and don't think I could learn Russian.) It may be that, in some sense, the Russians or the Chinese are our enemies—in a very distant sense. But, in terms of immediate reality, it is *our* government that is subverting us. The "invasion of totalitarianism" is already well under way. Washington is the headquarters, and all of us are collaborators unless we begin to remind the government that there are some things decent and loyal Americans do not do. One of which is to work for or cooperate with or receive money from the CIA. We can take hope from one thing. While all men can be corrupted, they have also the power of their own salvation. The whore can stop whoring. The thief can reform. So long as a man is alive, he is never finally and truly lost. There is always the chance that he will find himself before his death and, thus, die as a man. A society such as ours is so terribly powerful that it can probably long survive its no less terrible corruption. But I frankly do not care whether such a society—corrupt and powerful—lives or dies. My loyalty is to the ideals of the past and the dreams of the future. I want us to be honest not because we would be more powerful (we would not) nor because we would endure longer, but because we would feel like men and women—like human beings—for however long such an experiment in decency might last.

(1967)

A.J.

Abraham Johannes Muste died Saturday, February 11, 1967. He was eighty-two years old. On Saturday morning, he felt pains in his side and back. A doctor could find nothing seriously wrong but advised him to go to the hospital for tests. He was taken by ambulance accompanied by Joyce Gilmore. He suffered a heart stoppage at 3:30 P.M. and lost consciousness. A. J. Muste died at about 6:30 P.M. His body was cremated on Monday, February 13. He is survived by three sisters, a brother, two of his three children, and eight grandchildren. His son, John Muste, is a professor of English at Ohio State University, and his daughter, Nancy Baker, lives in Thornwood, N.Y. Another daughter, Constance Hamilton, died early last year, and A.J.'s wife, Anna, died in 1954 at the age of sixty-seven.

I learned of A. J. Muste's death at 5:00 A.M. on Sunday morning, February 12. He died Saturday evening, but I had been at dinner with friends and could not be reached. The news of A.J.'s death came to me, as I had felt, for some months, that it would. I read it in *The New York Times* which I had brought home with me and was reading before going to sleep. I had no premonition of A.J.'s death, but I had felt there would be no lingering illness, no extended period of gradually weakening powers —just that one day he would be in his office, and, the next day, I should pick up the paper and read his obituary.

A. J. Muste was an old man when he died, though none of us were ever able to think of him as old. I will not say he died because he gave himself so freely for the causes in which he believed. He died because he was old, and, if anything, the heavy and relentless schedule he kept to the very end was exactly what had given him good health and abundant spirits. I did not weep when I read the obituary. I was stunned and half-unbelieving, and it was very late, and I slept. I dreamed of A.J. that night and the next—as if the unconscious mind was trying to come to terms with what I could not, consciously, accept. The only time I came close to breaking down was on Monday, February 13th, when I ran into Barbara Deming at the meeting that had been planned to launch the Spring Mobilization and that was turned into a memorial meeting. Barbara took my hand, and then, suddenly, we embraced, and I held her very close and realized the death was real, and all of us would have to go on now without A.J.

Tom Cornell said—and I agree—that "we are all sons of A.J." We were also his lieutenants. But we were not, in the sense the word is usually used, his disciples. We were coworkers and comrades as well as being his children. To the degree I am anything politically, it would be a "Musteite"—and yet, even as I would accept that title, I would point out that my disagreements with A.J. were public knowledge. With other leaders, it would have been impossible to disagree, in private or public, without being cast into outer darkness. A.J. taught me not only that I had the right to disagree with the leader—and he was our leader—but that he expected that disagreement of us.

I am glad now about a very small thing. Despite a certain political drift away from A.J. in the last year or so of his life, I am among the sixty or more people who can always have a special (and vain and human) pride that we were arrested with A. J. Muste on his last act of civil disobedience.

A.J. belonged to many people. He made friends across impossible ideological boundaries. He belonged to Presbyterians and Communists, to Catholics and Trotskyists, to Quakers and Anarchists. He belonged, in a certain way, to all of us who ever worked with him at one point or another in his life. But, in a special way, he belonged to young people. It was appropriate that, when WBAI arranged a spur-of-the-moment memorial broadcast the night after his death, those who could be reached and could make a midnight radio show were all under forty. Most of us grow impatient in talking with younger radicals. Sooner or later, we burst out with an imperious, irritated "When you have been in the movement as long as I have, you won't make such a silly statement." Never once, in the more than fifteen years that I knew A.J., did he ever take that tack with those of us who disagreed with him. He would listen to us, try to persuade us, and then, if we still disagreed, he accepted that we must find our own way and, perhaps, that way might prove to have greater merit than his own. In any event, every man had to follow where the light led him. Most of us talk *at* or *down* to young people or to political opponents. A.J. talked *with* every person he encountered. More important, he *listened*.

When A. J. Muste died, his name was not known to everyone in the peace and civil rights movement. He was not a man with a dramatic flair. His writing lacked fire, and his platform manner was just short of being a really good orator. And, I might add, A.J. was capable of balancing off his capacity for brilliant analysis with a sometimes baffling capacity to make tactical mistakes. I put these things down because, as a Musteite I want no legends or worship to blur the reality of this man and what he meant to us. He was human. He was fallible. Often his followers disagreed with him. And, often enough, the followers were right, and the leader was wrong. Why, then, was this man our leader, accepted by us all?

Perhaps it was because A.J. was a whole and natural man. He was the most "manly" man I have ever met in my life. Man enough to be gentle, to love poetry, to combine a rock-hard adherence to his political position with great compassion in the midst of conflict for his opponent. A.J. was a tough old bird— tough enough to love us all.

Perhaps it was because A.J. carried with him the peculiar mark of greatness—he had no time for petty gossip. He did have time for sunsets and a movie, for poetry and a dinner with friends, for following the baseball scores and for laughing. But he never, in the years I knew him, had time for bitter words about another person. The only other person I have known in my life who literally "had no time" for personal attacks on others is Norman Thomas. Norman is the liberal; A.J. was the eternal radical, the revolutionist, yet both men had this wonderful ability to discuss their opponents' political positions without discussing their opponents' personal faults. My anger over the war is such that I direct it to Johnson personally, in terms of his cowardice and dishonesty. A.J. was "foolish" enough to believe that, somewhere inside Lyndon Johnson (or Hitler, or Stalin, or Roosevelt, or Churchill), there is a human being crying to be let out. And, because he saw all men in this way, he also saw that of God within them. He treated his opponents with respect. When he lost his temper—and he did—his anger was not against the man himself but against the failing within that man, against the failure of that man to be his best.

Perhaps we accepted him as our leader because, foxy though he could be, and political though he often was, he was a man with an almost absolute integrity. We might disagree with his projects, but only little men distrusted his motives. Larger men, whether they were Quakers or Communists, would listen to A.J. because they knew they would not be tricked by him or used by him.

Perhaps we followed A.J. because of his extraordinary moral courage. He went when the spirit said go. He followed where the light led. He left his pulpit in World War I to go into the pacifist movement and then became involved in the labor movement. He finally became convinced of the utter failure of the Church, abandoned his Christianity and his pacifism, became a Marxist, and during the early 1930's—when he was no longer a young man— he became one of the most important of our American "revolutionists." In the late 1930's, he went to Norway to see Trotsky. He left the United States a dedicated Marxist and a follower of Trotsky. When he returned, now even less of a young man and with a wife and a family to support, he returned to Christianity and to pacifism and, making another complete shift in "life style," became a leader of the Fellowship of Reconciliation. Later in life, when other men retire to write their memoirs, A.J. moved to the left, toward revolutionary nonviolent direct action, and devoted himself to an effort to reunite an American Left that had been shattered by the divisions of World War I, with the voting of war credits by French and German Socialists and the Bolshevik Revolution in Russia.

A.J. believed in experimenting. Some of these experiments worked, and some didn't—but he never lacked the courage to make another effort. If one project bogged down, he would launch another. He was still launching projects when death intervened.

A.J. lived in extreme simplicity, not because he was an ascetic, but because there was always so little time, and so many things to do. In the midst of all of this, he remained human, with a gentleness and sense of humor I think was fully clear only to those of us who worked with him closely. A.J. was a paradox that probably none of us ever absorbed. He was both a Marxist and a Christian. His Christianity was so central to him that his life cannot be understood without realizing that he was, even at his most political moments, acting out his religious convictions. If I cut short any statements about his religious beliefs, it would be because A.J. didn't believe in talking about them. Religion was for him, as for Gandhi, something to be lived, not endlessly discussed. But let those who were moved by him examine what it was that moved A.J. himself. We would dishonor A.J. if we did not realize that his religious beliefs drove him to Marxism, to a profound hostility to capitalism, to a burning desire to transform the condition of man. I heard the last speech he ever made as the National Secretary of the Fellowship of Reconciliation. It was in Los Angeles, and he was retiring, and this was his final statement from that particular post. He used that occasion to excoriate the Church for failing to realize that, unless man was liberated economically, he could never be fully liberated spiritually—to make a moving appeal for a socialist society.

If we want to honor this old man, this proud but gentle fighter, who left us so suddenly on February 11, then let it not be with monuments but with the tribute of our lives. Let us be better people, gentler with opponents, and yet sharper in our own thinking. A. J. Muste never asked us to be like him. That would be an easy task. He asked of us something far harder. Quietly but insistently, he placed upon us the challenge to find the courage to be like ourselves, to follow the light wherever it might lead.

(1967)

Notes on Another Death—
and Our Shadowed Future

Medgar Evers. John F. Kennedy. Lee Harvey Oswald. Malcolm X. George Lincoln Rockwell. Martin Luther King. Robert F. Kennedy. Black, white; left, right. Politics by assassination.

It is impossible just now to arrange the events of the past week into order for some profound analysis. Too much is weighing on us. Too much is hurting us. If there were no riots this time, it was because we were, all of us, too exhausted from the assassination of Martin Luther King. Is there one among us who did not want to cry out, as we caught the first news of the attack on Kennedy, "Oh God, why don't they kill those who deserve it— why King, why Kennedy," or who did not want, in the baffled rage and confusion and sorrow of those moments, to scream "Kill the killers, murder the assassins!"

I realize, looking at the question I've just posed, that none of us can speak for others on this matter. We have each had our private thoughts this past week. These are, therefore, simply my own thoughts, notes to myself on a death.

. . . I did not support Robert F. Kennedy for President. I could not share the political enthusiasm for him of Jack Newfield and Mike Harrington and Mike Macdonald. But his death touched me more deeply than that of John F. Kennedy. Bobby may have been ruthless, but I cannot believe he was cold. He had those small shy gestures of his hands, those constricted and almost mechanical movements of his hands and arms when he spoke, and yet, to balance that, he had a smile that lighted his face, making him look younger than his years, and making it impossible to believe he was simply ruthless or simply ambitious. There was a radiance, a humanity, and a vitality to him that made the news of his death not only painful but almost literally impossible to accept.

. . . His death made me aware of how the Kennedy family has become for us all, whether or not we wish it, the "first family" of the land, giving us the pattern of a genuine contemporary aristocracy. At his death, the jets roared off from Paris and London and New York bearing the brightest members of this aristocracy to Los Angeles. Imagine, if you will, the murder of any other contemporary American political leader, and you will fail to conjure up the same image of a special class of people moving together to comfort one another. Robert Kennedy had close friends from a remarkable range of social groupings: rich, poor, white, black, politicians, artists, intellectuals. The late John F. Kennedy was not a secure aristocrat; there was in his Camelot something a bit brittle. But the very suffering and shock of the Kennedy family and friends following the murder of the President somehow deepened the group and, one felt, Robert Kennedy in particular. What had been a myth became a reality. There were many who argued that Robert Kennedy "was not the man his brother was." In fact I think Robert Kennedy was more impressive. The Kennedy family casts a long shadow over our future. As I looked at the front page of the June 7 *New York Post,* with its photo of Robert F. Kennedy, Jr., at the bier of his father, I felt I was looking at one of the earliest photos of our once and future President.

. . . I was unexpectedly sorry for Lyndon Johnson, a man whose impeachment I have urged and with whose political views I could not be in greater disagreement. Yet Johnson, despite his massive personal faults and political sins, is human, and there is something as terrible about the suspicions to which he has been subjected and against which he cannot defend himself as there is about the suffering to which the Kennedys have been subjected.

. . . America will not live down the events of the past five years for at least a generation to come. Even if we ourselves could forget the horror of these years, the world as a whole cannot. To them, the events here will appear as something like a blood purge of political opposition. The civilized world has not seen anything like the series of murders we have endured since Japanese extreme nationalists employed assassination as a political weapon in the years just before World War II.

. . . We have been lucky in our assassins. Blacks, not whites, cut down Malcolm X. No Jews have been involved, no deranged leftists. (Think what would have happened if Robert Kennedy had been killed by a hippie, or some ultramilitant Maoist student.)

. . . Now is the time for gun control. Everyone talks about this, but no one discusses it in practical terms. The National Rifle Association is well organized and well financed. They can pour letters into Washington. If every reader would write both senators and his congressman and demand (don't ask—demand) strong and very tight gun control laws, we would have a chance to get them now. Let the lobby of the American people be heard above the lobby of the NRA.

. . . One thinks of the Egyptians, whose first-born of every household had to be struck down before they would finally let the children of Israel go out of bondage—the gun that was used to murder Robert F. Kennedy was purchased at a sporting-goods store during the Watts riot by an old and fearful white man, who thought to protect himself and who, instead, started that particular gun on a journey toward an assassin's hand. We armed ourselves against the blacks, but the bullets struck Kennedy.

. . . There are those (including the President) who insist that we are not all sick, that the society as a whole is not deranged. But we are. We are sick, and we aren't going to get better by pretending we've only got a few crackpots loose. If Congress really wanted "law and order," it would long ago have passed a stiff gun-control law. If we were not sick as a society, a movie like *Scorpio Rising* (trash as art, sado-masochism as culture) would not be considered avant-garde. Leather wouldn't be in as high fashion. We would be less worried about words like "fuck" and more concerned with words like "kill." We would be deeply worried about the violence in our films, on our TV, in our daily papers, and even in the toys we buy our children. Politically, we wouldn't have let ourselves get boxed into a Johnson-Goldwater race in 1964, we wouldn't have a governor like Reagan, and we wouldn't have George Wallace as a serious minor-party candidate.

. . . As a native of Los Angeles, I am certain I speak for many—perhaps a majority—of the residents of that city, when I express my shame at the behavior of the Mayor of Los Angeles, Sam Yorty, in seeking publicity at the risk of making a fair trial impossible, and in seeking to invent a Communist plot out of the murder.

. . . The words "manly" and "unmanly" are often used loosely, but I felt, as I watched TV, that, while Yorty's appearances were a genuine example of an unmanly performance, the brief statement by Senator Eugene McCarthy was an equally genuine example of a manly reaction to a national tragedy. His face was not a mask; his words were not glib; his shock and grief were not feigned. The depth of the tragedy could be read in his face, as well as his own personal sense of shock.

. . . When I noted earlier that we are all sick, I meant all of us, not simply reactionaries or racists. I know myself how I have felt a morbid satisfaction that the President could not move safely through out streets, and that, if we could not keep him from sending men abroad, we had at least succeeded in making it impossible for him to travel freely at home. How much better if we had met Johnson's tours with black armbands and silence rather than with juvenile chants of "Hey, hey, LBJ, how many kids did you kill today?" And the students at Columbia, in most ways so correct and courageous, did not dignify their cause by adopting the chant "Up Against the Wall Motherfucker." It is time now for all of us on the left to recognize how close we are to losing what is left of our democracy, and to grasp how profound is the threat to the Republic. It is impossible to ask that politics be conducted without passion or that we approach our domestic and foreign policy without rage, but it is not impossible to remind the Left that, if we would in fact lead, rather than simply give vent to our own alienation, then we must prove ourselves not only more militant but also more compassionate and more responsible than our opposition. Anger is one thing, and hatred is another; rage is legitimate and necessary, but violence is destructive for all of us. The commandment against violence is as close to an absolute as we have, and we must not let ourselves be tricked into violence even by the violence of our opposition. Police violence does not justify mob violence. Our goal may well be the "destruction" of society as it now exists, but we also seek the creation of a new society. Nihilists are neither radical nor revolutionary. Even on those rare occasions when men may feel, with some reason, that violence is necessary, it remains an evil even if it becomes a necessary one. If we weep for the killing of Che, then let us also weep for the fact that he killed others.

. . . Finally, let us, for God's sake, be honest with ourselves. When politicians speak of the need for law and order in the wake of this assassination, it is clear they demand action against the blacks, the poor, the peace movement, the students, the hippies—in short, they are against flowers and beads as much as against guns and bombs. Would to God that this cry for law and order meant a demand that the state itself return to the rule of law, and that it meant a recognition that, without justice, there cannot be "order."

When President Johnson tells us that "we must not permit men that are filled with hatred and carelessness—and careless of innocent lives—to dominate our streets and fill our homes with fear," one must ask what threatens the man in the street more—random violence or the military draft? Are mothers more fearful that their sons will be knifed at school or killed in Vietnam?

I am raising what are, for me, fundamental questions, and they are directed not only to Johnson but to us all. Who can believe the CIA was not aware of plans to assassinate Diem, and, yet, who on the left protested against this exercise of murder? Who can believe the CIA was not implicated in the killing of Che, and, yet, who on the right protested that action? Did we think we could play this game abroad and not legitimize it here at home? When 500,000 Indonesians were slaughtered in the purge of Communists, did the President or the State Department express concern, dismay, and horror—or quiet satisfaction? How many of those who now oppose the war in Vietnam waited to cry out against it only when it becomes clear that it was not simply immoral and unjust but also unsuccessful? Our hearts must surely go out to the Kennedy family in this moment of their private grief—yet how many of us are aware of the numbers of Vietnamese families that have suffered losses as great and greater?

One has the feeling there may be little hope for us as a nation. We have not seen the last assassination—there will be more. But, if there is hope, it will lie in a courage we have rarely demonstrated—the courage to admit, as a people and a nation, that we have been wrong: the courage to realize that our violence at home is, in part, a reflection of our barbarism abroad. The courage to simply admit we have been wrong in Vietnam and to begin withdrawing our troops now. The courage to admit that we have imposed violence on the blacks of this land for hundreds of years and that we shall choose to pay higher taxes to reconstruct our society rather than pay higher taxes to police it. The "lawless rioting" of blacks is a result of our policy, and we cannot now say to the restless sea "be still." The "lawless rioting" of our students is a consequence of building a society in which they can find no place of human worth. Indeed, the healthiest aspect of our society is the alienation of our students, and we should welcome that and be grateful for it.

Law and order are reflections of justice and compassion. We must resolutely oppose, without exception, all violence. But we must, first of all, oppose the violence of the state, of the white majority. We must take the President at his word—and hold him to his word—when he says, "There is never—and I say never—any justification for the violence that tears at the fabric of our national life."

(1968)

Postscript: Repression and Revolution, or Agnew, Mitchell, and Nixon Set to Sea in a Sieve

The Left today calls for a revolution,
not seeing that in a true sense
the revolution has occurred, and
the revolutionary task is to organize
that revolution which is.

Repression and Revolution

There is not a single essay in this book I fully agree with, not one piece I did not wish I had time to comment on, and several pieces I had hoped to write and that I cannot write because the book must go to press and I must go on the road, organizing for the Anti-Draft Week of March, 1970, when, hopefully, there will be massive civil disobedience to the draft, and a serious beginning made at dismantling the war machine rather than merely protesting it. Thus, I have no time for third and fourth drafts or additional essays. The repression is here, and so is the revolution.

I write this not long after the Chicago trial came to an end, all seven defendants (plus Bobby Seale, whose case had been separated earlier) and two of the lawyers given jail terms for contempt, and five of the seven being found guilty of crossing a state line with the thought in their heads of starting a riot, and those five sentenced to five years in prison plus a fine.

This is scary, because I know these people. I remember disagreeing with Tom Hayden at a conference at Hudson Guild years ago when he was a moderate in SDS, one of its early founders. I met Abbie Hoffman at his home in Massachusetts, where I was the speaker of the evening for a small group, and Abbie was quiet, intense, and quite different from the theatrical force he later became. Jerry Rubin and I drove home from Sarah Lawrence in someone's car, hassling politics all the way and I found out he lived on Third Street, just behind my block. Bill Kunstler and I were on Long John Nebel's night show once with Dr. Fred Schwartz of the Anti-Communist Crusade. (I must report that Schwartz was attentive and polite.) Bobby Seale I never really met—he was asleep on the bed in the hotel room where I met with Cleaver in 1968 in an effort to work out some political problems. Dave Dellinger I've known and worked with for over ten years, and, if our disagreements have been sharp at times, our association has been close.

One begins to feel the lightning flashing in the sky and striking all around. These are men I know, and they are on their way to jail for crossing state lines with riotous *thoughts*! There is that haunting line from *The Three Penny Opera,* when Polly asks, "I wonder where we'll all be on Coronation Day?" It is a good question.

Items of interest taken from a quick span of time:

The New York Post, January 16, 1970, informs me that "Army Lieutenant William L. Calley, Jr., joined American Legion leaders in a party here (Florida) opening a campaign for $200,000 to bolster his defense against murder charges based on the alleged My Lai massacre." The Legion committee announced: "We feel Lieutenant Calley has been condemned and vilified for performance of his duties in combat."

The New York Times, Sunday, February 1, 1970, was filled with items. Supreme Court Justice William O. Douglas suggested that society needs radical restructuring, and this may require violent revolution. I quote: "The Powers-that-be faintly echo Adolf Hitler," who said in 1932, "The streets of our country are in turmoil. The universities are filled with students rebelling and rioting. . . . We need law and order." Douglas asks desperately, "Where is the force that will restrain the Pentagon?"

In the same issue, a report indicates that *Time, Life,* and *Newsweek* had files subpoenaed by the Department of Justice. In a column, Tom Wicker regretted the passage by Congress of measures that meant police can now enter our homes without warning, thus striking a heavy blow at the Bill of Rights.

And, also in that issue of the *Times,* three student militants in California were given prison terms of one to twenty-five *years* for taking part in campus disorders at San Fernando Valley State College in 1968.

The New York Times of February 9 informs us that the Mayor of Seattle, Wesley C. Uhlman, had turned down "a federal proposal" for a raid on Black Panther headquarters in Seattle. (Which provided, from an official source, proof of a Federal conspiracy against the Black Panthers, a conspiracy that accounted for the bloody December raids on Panthers in Chicago and Los Angeles.)

On February 11, *The New York Times* carried a story about the censoring of Judy Collins on the Dick Cavett show because of her critical comments about Judge Julius Hoffman. In earlier cases, Joan Baez was "blipped" when she tried to explain that her husband, Dave Harris, was in jail for resisting the draft, and the Smothers brothers had lost their weekly show altogether.

And, on February 20, the *New York Post* carried a story about the famous farewell address by the late President Eisenhower and how the Pentagon, upset at the stern warning on the dangers of a Military-Industrial Complex in that speech, had simply cut the offending paragraphs out and used the speech, without noting the abridgement, in large brown letters on a huge gold plaque in the "Eisenhower Corridor" of the Pentagon. (1984 comes to the Pentagon.)

These items are brief; they are few; they are a small handful from many possible items. The murder of the Panthers is more dramatic; the arrest and jailing of youth for refusing military service is more widespread. I have cited only a few items from a single month. The repression has begun. It has begun because the revolution is here.

After the Revolution

When I came to New York in 1956 to help edit *Liberation* magazine, I was a "third camp socialist," part of an extremely small grouping of radical pacifists grouped around either A. J. Muste or Max Shachtman. The theory of the third camp was, simply (much too simply), that neither Washington nor Moscow could fulfill the ethical and material needs of the people, that both great blocs tended to exploit economically, oppress psychologically, and threaten militarily those populations under their control. We hoped for a third grouping of nations that might, by seeking genuine social revolution and by abandoning the arms race, raise a flag to which the human race could repair. My own position, in 1956, was that of a lieutenant of Muste's and an ally of Shachtman's.

My anti-Communism was based both on personal experience with the Communists on campus (which is small potatoes to what they did in the civil-rights and trade-union movements) and on an understanding of events in the Soviet Union. Doubtless, I was too anti-Communist, but, in view of the events then occuring in the Soviet Union and in Eastern Europe, I am not sure if it was possible to be "too anti-Communist." While I worked for *Liberation* and in the years after that until the early 1960's, the following persons were part of the same very loose, general grouping: A. J. Muste, Norman Thomas, Bayard Rustin, Robert Pickus, Dave Dellinger, Robert Gilmore, Max Shachtman, Sid Lens, Roy Finch, Staughton Lynd, Michael Harrington, Paul Goodman, Dwight Macdonald, Irving Howe, James Farmer, Jim Peck, Allen Ginsberg.

I have not named a central committee of some kind, merely a kind of sociological-political grouping. Each of us in that grouping would have named a somewhat different list. I doubt if, in 1956, Sid Lens had heard of Allen Ginsberg or if Max Shachtman had heard of Robert Pickus. For that matter, most of those I've named had not heard of me in 1956. We were a grouping that shared a firm belief in democracy, in racial integration, in profound and radical social change. Our funds, such as they were, did not come from Moscow or the CIA. We were small, irrelevant, politically marginal. Dwight Macdonald had, a few years earlier, written a bitter attack on Henry Wallace and the Progressive Party, and we thought he was moving into the Establishment. Paul Goodman was a decent bisexual anarchist, certain to die in the integrity of anonymity. Norman Thomas was a toothless old warrior, a largely forgotten relic of the 1930's. A. J. Muste was active, but politically isolated, a foolish old man making, even late in life, foolish experiments in radicalism. Jim Farmer and Jim Peck were, for a while, both working for CORE.

One measures the depth of the events of the 1960's in part by the shifts that occured within this small grouping. Thomas became a leading platform speaker once more, in special demand on campuses. A.J. emerged as the central figure of a diverse coalition to end the Vietnam war. Dave Dellinger, an utter sectarian all his life and a dreadfully annoying political purist, got trapped leading the peace coalition after A.J.'s death, and, after a lifetime in the shadows of the most nit-picking sections of the pacifist movement, emerged in Chicago as a kind of New Left leader. Staughton Lynd abandoned his experiments in communal living to take an active part in the earliest days of the New Left; Paul Goodman became a culture hero to the young; Dwight Macdonald a leader of Resist, the antidraft organization.

Allen Ginsberg—whom none of us really knew back in those days—emerged as the major prophet of the period. (I remember that, in the late 1950's, I walked over from the *Liberation* office at 110 Christopher Street to where Allen and Peter lived on East Third Street in order to deliver his "contributor's copies" of an issue in which he had a poem. Normally, we mailed the contributors five free copies—*Liberation* never paid its writers—but in this case I wanted to deliver them in person, since Ginsberg was a folk hero of mine. He, Peter Orlovsky, and I did meet and have a discussion, which I was touched to find he remembered and referred to later.)

I'm not sure if Irving Howe knows yet where he fits; he is impatient with the New Left but has too much integrity to buy the Shachtmanite position that increasingly dominates what little is left of the old "social democrats." Nor do I think Harrington is sure where he belongs, wavering between decency and his post as Chairman of what is left of the Socialist Party. The others are a curious assortment, except for Finch who returned to an academic career. Rustin, who had been the "main man" for many young radicals, and who, in turn, had looked to A.J. as a father figure, broke with A.J. and took on the post of adviser to Johnson and Nixon.

Jim Farmer first condoned the firing of Jim Peck from his post at CORE, and then went on to take a job with the Nixon Administration. Peck continues to man a desk at the War Resisters League. Robert Pickus and Robert Gilmore, much as they irritate each other, retired together from the radical movement into the world of foundation money and the liberal wing of the Establishment. Max Shachtman, one-time Communist, a founder of the American Trotskyist movement, revolutionary Marxist, turned tail the moment the revolution showed on the horizon, and is now playing the role of a Jay Lovestone to Rustin, Gilmore, Pickus, and some of the others who have opted out of the movement.

I have gone into this detail because, under normal circumstances, this small a group would not have splintered so sharply in ten years' time. Only in a revolution does this rending of warm friendships and close alliances occur. Only in a revolution, also, do we find totally new characters walking on stage in mid-scene. Benjamin Spock was a Republican, William Sloane Coffin once worked for the CIA, and Marcus Raskin sat in on meetings of the Security Council under John Kennedy before the three of them (along with Michael Ferber and Mitchell Goodman) ended in the dock in Boston, charged with high crimes against the state.

I began this book treating the advent of industrial and technological innovations as an invasion, a cold intrustion of automated steel into the living flesh of human culture. That is clearly a metaphor. One may also view these innovations literally, as a revolution. The Left today calls for a revolution, not seeing that, in a true sense, the revolution has occurred, and the revolutionary's task is to organize that revolution which *is*. Revolutions are like earthquakes. They cannot be predicted. They cause a fundamental shift in the existing order. They are a sharp break with the past, and they cannot be successfully resisted (a point Berdyaev makes in his excellent *Origins of Russian Communism*).

A revolution is any basic and fundamental shift in the relationships men and women have to their institutions and to the means of production. The kind of spasm that shook the world in October, 1917, is not nearly as important as the events that led to that spasm, making it all but inevitable. When Marx wrote *The Communist Manifesto,* the revolution had already occurred and Marx was merely trying to organize it.

Into a feudal world, dominated by those who held land and constituted the aristocracy, had come the *bourgeoisie* with their hustle. The institution of monarchy, then everywhere triumphant, was doomed because it conflicted with this new power. Yet, even as the new class of merchants and industrialists took power, they had created a proletariat, a grouping of workers in the slums of the cities, who were shortly to begin a fundamental challenge to the structure of capitalism. Marx, with the insight of genius, looked at the scum of London's tenements and, even as that scum lay stinking in their gin and vomit, saw in them the power that would rock Europe. The Industrial Revolution had destroyed the foundations of the old order, though few saw this as clearly as Marx, with his concept of political parties and trade unions, helped create the institutions of the new society. "Revolution" turned out to be a process of organizing a society in which the revolution had already occurred.

Let us look at some of the facts of revolution around us today. First, we have youth. Until 1900 or so, we didn't have "youth." We had children, and we had adults, but we didn't have adolescents. Now we are stuck with them, and, worse yet, they are smarter than we are. I do not write this to curry favor with the little bastards—there is no virtue on their part in being smarter than us, and it is a development for which they can take no credit. Nonetheless, it remains a fact. A hundred years ago, a young man took up his father's trade, and he and his wife would settle in his father's village, and, in that village, where so little had changed for centuries, the oldest man was wisest, because he had the longest time to learn the customs of the village. Today we find that even "hard knowledge" about things like physics changes so swiftly that the older one is, the more likely one is to be foolish and flatly wrong.

Nearly twenty years ago, when I was arguing economics with my father, he made some remarks about the iron laws of supply and demand. I replied that Lord Keynes had questioned those laws and had suggested other dynamics. My father said that he didn't know who Keynes was, and he didn't care, because supply and demand was a "fact," and "basic things do not change." I did not argue further, because to encounter someone who didn't know who Keynes was meant that no real argument was possible.

Today, I am almost the age my father was when I disputed economics with him, and Milton Friedman is, I hear, the new guide to economics, and I don't even know how to handle statistics, let alone Friedman's monetary theories, and I see how easy it is to say to a younger person, "I don't care what you learned in school, some things never change, and I tell you . . ." The older we become, the further we are from the cutting edge of knowledge and, thus, the more foolish we are. This has never happened before in history. The speed with which knowledge changes is so great that, unless we work hard to keep up, we begin getting senile shortly after our twentieth birthday.

Second, we have a revolutionary combination of modern technology and profound human need. The most revolutionary magazine in the world is *Life*. Old copies of *Life* make their way slowly into remote villages in Latin America, Africa, Asia. A magazine with pictures showing a land where everyone is young, even the poor have cars, and food is a problem in reverse—people are worried about losing weight.

Do you know what causes riots in our own slums? The Panthers? The Weathermen? No. The agents of unrest are RCA, Zenith, Motorola, GE, and Sylvania. The kid in Harlem sits in a cold room, hungry, watching the screen show black kids, like himself, fighting cops. In Watts, Newark, or Philadelphia. Right there, in front of him, nineteen inches diagonally and maybe in living color. "If them, why not me?" And, so, a Harlem riot begins, as electronic sparks fly out from one city to another, catching on the sad tinder of a hopelessness so profound not even death is that fearful.

This, incidentally, is how riots spread from nation to nation, from Columbia University to Paris to Prague. Telstar. When the twentieth century began, the world was ruled by North Europeans who, by historic chance, had first hit upon the scientific method and had used it to extend their power over the world. The magic of our systems of transportation and communication and the power of our gunpowder—these seemed to insure our rule for centuries to come. However the very things which gave us dominion, insured our defeat.

The British, for example, needed civil servants in order to run India. But the Indians they so dutifully trained in England returned to India with their heads filled with the Magna Carta, the history of America's war of liberation and Declaration of Independence, and they became revolutionists—Gandhi is an outstanding example. Our communications meant the poorest village in Asia, which would, in other centuries, have starved quietly during famine, knew that parts of the world had food, medicine, clothing, fuel. We shifted Asians into the West as cheap labor, which is how Ho Chi Minh got to France during World War I and became a socialist, a founding member of the Communist International, and a Vietnamese patriot who would later humiliate the most powerful nation on the planet.

Even the Russian Revolution was brought about by young intellectuals who had studied in Berlin, Paris, London, and New York, and who returned to Petrograd and Moscow to find their talents in chemistry, physics, economics, and philosophy were not needed by a backward society. With no jobs open to absorb their energies and provide them a living, the Russian intellectual became a revolutionist, seeking to create a world in which he would be useful. It was this class—the "unused intellectuals" —more than the workers who destroyed the Czar.

Third, we have the problem of "black consciousness" in our own nation, a point I've tried to develop in the book, but certainly a profoundly revolutionary fact for American society. I state it, thus, briefly to emphasize its importance.

Fourth, and a subtle point, the role of American capitalism has been increasingly limited by revolution. I do not like the governments that run Russia and China and Algeria and Cuba. I do not like governments at all, if I am honest. But it is true that vast areas of the world have broken loose from Western control. This means that, while the United States may struggle with special desperation to put down resistance, it is no longer the sole power in the world and the very division of power between East and West gives a degree of power to smaller nations (the Middle East, Cuba, Vietnam) and even to groups within nations (as African independence had a direct impact on black Americans and as the "Third World" becomes a vital myth to mobilize the energies of the youth here).

Fifth, I discussed at length in the introduction the problem of technological shift in our society. I only point out here that those changes mean our relations to the means of production have changed and that the technological shifts create new institutions. (Cars create freeways, which destroy cities and create suburbs and smog. The old limits of a city are not meaningful—we need the cooperation of many cities or even of several states to resolve traffic problems, smog problems, water problems, and so forth.)

For all of the reasons given above, the revolution has happened. The society we are living in needs new institutions, and the cry of young radicals for revolution is paradoxically both valid and unnecessary. The revolution is over, the task is finding the "revolutionary institutions" that will save us.

Revolutionary Comments

Marx believed revolution could take place only in the most advanced industrial states, and Lenin defied his teachings and took power in Russia. Stalin codified Lenin's teachings and Mao defied those teachings and took power in China. Castro took power in Cuba in the face of organized opposition from the Cuban Communist Party, which thought of him as a romantic. The moral is that each revolution breaks the pattern of the revolution that came before it.

Revolutions can't be predicted. Lenin, surely a "master revolutionist," was teaching a class in Marxism to a handful of students in Switzerland and had written he did not expect to see the revolution in his lifetime, when it broke out in Russia and he hurried back to lead it. Even our own revolution, though it occurred a long time ago and was less a revolution than a break with a central power, is of interest simply because it was so unlikely. Language, law, religion, race—all served to tie us to England. Yet we broke with England—the *only* British colony to break *totally* until the rebellion of Ian Smith in Rhodesia.

Revolutions, while they cannot be predicted, have origins. In 1955, southern blacks revolted, nonviolently, against segregation. That revolt might have come in 1954 or 1957 or 1961, but it was (we see, looking back) inevitable. No one can understand the excitement of the events in Montgomery, Alabama, unless he was alive at the time or unless he has read widely in the literature of the period. I won't try to convey the drama of those events or the power they exercised over the emotions and intelligences of blacks and whites. It had been widely assumed integration would begin in New York—or Chicago or Seattle or Los Angeles —and work slowly south, reaching Montgomery around 1990. If ever. What caused it to begin in Montgomery?

The South had been industrializing during and after World War II, with the result that blacks were driven from farm lands being put under collectivized and mechanized farming and forced into the city. In some cases, the "city" was Harlem or Chicago's south side or Watts. But, in many cases, the "city" was Jackson or Atlanta or Houston or Miami—or Montgomery. Also, many blacks had been through the armed forces in World War II and the Korean War and were not prepared to come back home and scratch their heads. And a small, but essential, black middle class had been created and, in order to win its own place in society, had to provide leadership for all blacks. (If the whites had only had the sense to admit the black middle class to bars, schools, restaurants, and so on, the black "underclass" might have been silent much longer—but the foolishness of white racism meant blacks approached the struggle more or less united, regardless of class.)

There are ironies to the picture I've painted, including the irony that white southerners fought hard for the industry that helped destroy the southern way of life. My outline of the southern struggle is superficial; it misses entirely the moving, religious, impossible drama of those dangerous early days in the civil rights movement. My analysis does not explain the basis for that courage we saw, those few proud, human moments that illuminated a national history too often lacking in dignity or meaning. I have simply suggested that things have causes, even if we don't see those causes until after the event, or fully understand them even then.

There is always a great deal of talk about "revolutionary violence," and so, as a pacifist, I want to deal with revolution and violence. First, a revolutionary period is always violent, and there is no point wasting emotional energy deploring it. The violence is usually totally senseless, misdirected, tragic. It is possible I will be killed, for example, by an extremist of the Right, but it is also possible I might be killed by an extremely committed, courageous, decent, frightened young kid from the extreme Left, who views pacifists as the primary enemy of revolution. A Jewish merchant in Harlem, a man who has made a good living from selling poor people things they don't need, at prices higher than they would pay elsewhere in the city, may be cut down some night by a junkie who panics—not by some community "committee of justice," while, around the corner, an old Jewish doctor who undercharges his patients and overworks himself is knifed to death by some psychotic black militant who thinks the Jew is the enemy. There is no justice during a revolution. How do I find the justice involved in the death of kids from heroin? What is the sense of ghetto residents firing at fire trucks that have come to put out fires? All of this violence simply reflects a revolutionary period when old values and institutions have no power.

One must note—forcefully—in passing, that all the violence of black militants and white idiots, such as the Weathermen, does not begin to match the violence of the state. Each week, Nixon's policies mean a hundred American boys come home in aluminum boxes and thousands of Vietnamese die and are buried. If Abbie Hoffman crosses a state line with the *thought* of rioting, he will be sentenced to five years in prison, but, if the Chicago police actually *engage* in a riot, as charged by the Walker report, nothing will happen to them. Such is the nature of American justice.

Another example occurred just after November 15, 1969, when Dave Hilliard, a Black Panther leader on the West Coast, spoke to a crowd in San Francisco and said that, if Nixon stood in the way of justice, he would be killed. I didn't like Hilliard's statement (and neither did the crowd of young radicals who heard it), but it was *only a statement*. Yet, almost at once, Hilliard was arrested, while Nixon—who does issue death orders—remains secure as President, above all law, civil or moral, and, I assume, praying as Johnson must pray, that there is no divine punishment for evil.

In short, it is the lawlessness of the state itself that creates the greatest violence and that leads, because of its intense violence, to a breakdown of moral authority.

Revolutions are rarely particularly violent, though they are generally repressive toward the old order. Cuba under Castro is probably less violent than Cuba before Castro. Algeria, miserable as it may be under its present rule, is certainly less violent than during the long rebellion against France. And, while Nixon worries publicly about the "terror" the Communists might bring to Vietnam if they won, it must be said that it would take great technical skill on their part to kill as many Vietnamese as we have killed.

There are at least two prospects ahead of us. One is the creation of new institutions, new distributions of power, that would place us in a human relationship with the machinery of our times. The other prospect is the political reaction and physical repression Nixon has in mind.

Nixon, Agnew, and Mitchell are seeking to impose what must be termed a totalitarian regime. There can be no reasonable doubt about this. Agnew has attacked the press and TV, Mitchell ordered the Chicago trial and a general speedup in prosecutions of political opponents. Mitchell triggered the attack on the Panthers. It is also Mitchell who dredged into the cracker barrel for Haynsworth and then dredged deeper still for Carswell.

I deem it important not to exaggerate, to avoid paranoia where possible, and to understate a serious point rather than overstate it, in the hopes it will carry more weight with serious men. It is in that conservative mood that I say we have, in Richard Nixon, a man who lied his way into congress and then into the senate with false charges of Communism against his opponents; a man who sought (along with Dulles) to persuade Eisenhower to unleash our nuclear power in Vietnam in 1954 when the French were losing. Nixon is a consummate politician who has written off the black vote altogether and is striving instead to hold his southern base, hoping to destroy whatever chance Wallace might have in 1972. Nixon is a mechanical man, counting votes (effectively), and deciding to opt for a reactionary coalition that will build on Middle America's fear of the young, fear of change, fear of blacks, fear of hippies, homosexuals, Jews, and Communists. Nixon has always been a man who traded in fear, and he remains that today. His is an administration that carefully nurtures the worst in America.

Yet he will, I think, lose. He and Agnew and Mitchell have set to sea in a sieve and will sink. Hopefully, without a trace. One thinks of Kim Agnew wanting to protest the war and of Laird's son doing so. One thinks of the sons and daughters of the politicians jailed, caught smoking pot, refusing to be drafted.

Mitchell is a terrifying figure—a Stalinist Chief of the Secret Police puffing on a pipe—but he is out of his depth trying to deal with all of us. The repression today is much worse than in the McCarthy period, but that repression, back in the 1950's, came when the Left was weak, and reaction moved in to fill a vacuum. Today, the repression comes because there is a movement, genuine, deeply rooted, widespread, and very threatening. Our jailers in the early 1950's were smug. Today, they are frightened.

But there is always a chance the Left will make some or all of the following errors, permitting victory to go to these old men of the sea, sailing in their sieve.

First, partly by frustration, partly by lack of brains, partly by police agents in our midst, the revolution can be tricked into violence and provocative acts. Comrades, beware the police agent in our midst: He sounds more radical than any of us, and he will be released without bail after you have been jailed for a bomb plot.

Revolutionary theories of other lands do not fit us. If Mitchell had any business sense, he would give the Ozark mountains to the Weathermen, and other assorted violent revolutionists, and charge admission so that foreign guests could see "live American guerillas in their natural habitat." Neither in the city nor the countryside can guerrilla war be carried on. There is no ocean for us to swim in, if we seek to be violent fish.

Those are tactical points. More basically, we accomplish nothing if we chant, "Off the pigs," except to show what poorly trained Marxists we are. Cops are agents of the system, taking its pay to enforce its laws. Cops are not the system itself—just the agents. They are no different from the troops we've got in Vietnam, and, if we can learn to talk to our troops in Vietnam, why can't we learn to talk to our cops? The system is our target, not the cops.

But we also lose the battle morally if we permit ourselves to be brought to the level of treating any man as an object, seeing his uniform (or his color, or his religion) rather than seeing *him*. We understand that the black heroin addict who knifes an old lady to death to get a few bucks toward his fix is a poor bastard caught in a trap. Don't we realize the cop is caught in the same trap? The same society that puts a knife into an old lady puts the club up against your head.

Second, we have to stop seeing the "liberal spirit" as our main enemy. It is one thing to understand that "official liberalism" invaded Cuba, authorized the Green Berets, began the Vietnam intervention, and started the CIA. But many Americans are non-dogmatic, cheerful, and trusting and would work with radicals if we would stop biting them.

Third, the revolution may debate within itself, but it must not permit its own division. The political Right unites easily, because it has property and privilege and wants to defend them. The Right has little ideology, and it doesn't have much in the way of brains or courage. It simply has power. The Left has ideology, which more often serves to confuse us than send us forward into effective battle. The Communists are fond of saying that "Marxism-Leninism is the weapon of the working class," which may even be true, but it is certainly a weapon with which radicals have generally done more damage to themselves than to the Establishment.

Fourth, the revolution must be revolutionary. That is its most difficult task. It is easy to wear a guerrilla's beret, chant "Right On," and quote Mao. It is much harder to examine our own country, its needs, its people, and its special situation. Lenin examined Russia. Mao examined China. Castro examined Cuba. Why do our radicals examine Lenin, Mao, and Castro instead of America?

Fifth, either the revolution will have a program or it will fail totally. People cannot stand endless chaos. Chaos without meaning provides a kind of unbearable tension rather than liberation. If the farmer never knows whether he will be able to harvest his seeds, if the mother never knows when the milk will be in the store, and if none of us know when the subways will run, we will finally opt for concentration camps, secret police, troops, and Attorney General Mitchell. Revolutionists must offer a program that gets milk to babies, keeps the subways running, and allows the farmer to plant, tend, and harvest.

Sixth, the revolution must not have contempt for the people. We say we love the workers, but then we talk about "Middle Amerika." We love poor blacks and hate poor whites, though both groups are racist. If we do not understand that revolution seeks to liberate the whole people, then we will never win our revolution, will never organize our chaos, and should simply retire. If we insist on waging a revolution based on hatred and violence, we shall, in five or ten years, have a revolutionary leader who looks just like Agnew and a Chief of Secret Police who looks just like Mitchell.

When one has contempt for the people, one does not listen to them. When one does not listen to the people, they have contempt for the revolution.

And, so, the book ends—with this final observation: The task of the revolutionary is to know his period in history. The very technology that has destroyed the power of the old order has also made violence an impossibly dangerous method of changing society. One can applaud the courage of the National Liberation Front and the existential fury that brings men into the Black Panthers, but that courage must not be ours. Our task is to revolutionize society and to save it. If man can survive, it will be on the basis of deliberately breaking down the conscious barriers of race, class, nation—and, even, age.

If we see the threat violence poses to everyone, we shall not try using it to change society. It is not a question whether we are all saintly enough to abandon violence (we are not), but whether we are smart enough. I am not saintly, and neither are you. That is one reason why the surrender of violence is a revolutionary act —because we are being forced to stretch ourselves, to act beyond what we thought possible. History is brutal, catching us always before we are ready, forcing us into decisions we lack the courage to make.

It is a terrible time in which we live, the city streets haunted with violence, our ghettos swept with addiction, our friends in prison or on trial, unspeakable violence in Vietnam, profound wickedness in our government. And yet, when would it have been better to have lived?

Christopher Fry, in *A Sleep of Prisoners,* spoke for me when he wrote:

> Dark and cold we may be, but this
> Is no winter now. The frozen misery
> Of centuries breaks, cracks, begins to move;
> The thunder is the thunder of the floes,
> The thaw, the flood, the upstart spring.
> Thank God our time is now when wrong
> Comes up to face us everywhere,
> Never to leave us till we take
> The longest stride of soul men ever took.
> Affairs are now soul size.

Index

DATE DUE